Knowledge Region: Alps-Adriatic Challenges

Josef Langer
Nikša Alfirević
Goran Vlašić
(eds.)

Knowledge Region: Alps-Adriatic Challenges

Volume II – Actors and Cases

PETER LANG
Frankfurt am Main · Berlin · Bern · Bruxelles · New York · Oxford · Wien

Bibliographic Information published by the Deutsche Nationalbibliothek
The Deutsche Nationalbibliothek lists this publication in the Deutsche Nationalbibliografie; detailed bibliographic data is available in the internet at http://dnb.d-nb.de.

BM.W_F[a]

Printing of this book is financially supported by the Austrian Federal Ministry of Science and Research.

UNITY THROUGH KNOWLEDGE FUND

Editorial work on this book is financially supported by the Unity through Knowledge Fund from Zagreb, Croatia, through their financing of the project "Through the knowledge-based development of the Alps-Adriatic Region".

Cover Design:
Olaf Glöckler, Atelier Platen, Friedberg

ISBN 978-3-631-58557-3

Contents

Foreword

This is the second volume presenting the best peer-reviewed scientific and professional contributions and peer discussions from the *First International Symposium "Knowledge Region: The Alps-Adriatic Challenges"*, held from 1 - 3 June 2007 in Sibenik – Lusa (Croatia) and the *Second International Symposium "Knowledge Region: The Alps-Adriatic Challenges"*, held from 28 - 29 September 2007 in Klagenfurt (Austria). While the first volume analyses the general scientific approaches toward the conceptualisation of the idea of a *knowledge region,* this volume brings together diverse papers dealing with particular actors and cases in the Alps-Adriatic region.

Although rather diverse, the selected papers can be grouped into several streams, related to the authors' engagement in research, education and educational outcome. Besides the educational focus, the volume contains illustrative case studies of knowledge utilization in the corporate sector and case studies reaching out of the region.

We would like to extend our gratitude to many individuals and organisations that assisted us in organizing both symposia and in developing two edited volumes on the topic of *Knowledge Region*. We are especially indebted to Ms. Karen Meehan, who has served as the language advisor and editorial assistant for both volumes, as well as to our colleague Jurica Pavičić.

The *Austrian Federal Ministry of Science and Research* provided the necessary funds to print this book, while financial assistance for editorial work has been provided by the *Unity through Knowledge Fund* from Zagreb, Croatia, through their financing of the project *Through the knowledge-based development of the Alps-Adriatic Region.* We would also like to acknowledge the valuable cooperation with the *Croatian Life-long Learning Association (Hrvatsko andragosko drustvo)* from Zagreb, Croatia, which served as a Croatian partner, both for the first symposium in Sibenik (Lusa), and the second one in Klagenfurt, as well as with the *Institute for Innovation* from Zagreb, Croatia.

We hope that this volume will also serve as a contribution to the body of 'useful' knowledge and stimulate further discussion on the topic of regional knowledge-based development.

Klagenfurt – Zagreb – Split,
June 2009

INTRODUCTION

Josef Langer – Nikša Alfirević – Goran Vlašić

Knowledge and its Agents

The broad field of economics and business has been dealing with the idea of a *rational, information-processing and value-maximizing agent* since its inception. However, in order to differentiate between multiple stimuli received by individual agents, one needs to distinguish *data* (i.e. noticeable stimuli, providing the perception of different states of other agents and the environment) from *information,* which represents the extracted data, placed in a context, enabling an agent to alter his/her existing knowledge base (Boisot/Canals 2007). Access to reliable data, as well as the agents' competences to process such data and reach reasonable economic decisions, represent the fundamental tenets of the notion of the *Homo Oeconomicus,* who treats the information as a means of achieving his/her objectives. On the other hand, information itself can become an object of economic transactions, i.e. an economic good.

However, the very notion of *information* 'promises' much less than the concept of *knowledge,* which, in the positivist context, implies that an insight has been empirically tested and found to be true, while considering the objective limitations to such an assessment (cf. Searle 2003, p. 10). In this sense, the English language has an inherent limitation, referring to all forms of knowledge by using the same word, while the French term of *connaissance*, or the German notion of *Kenntnis* signalize that the agent may use such knowledge to perform a certain action, but without the institutional (scientific) assurance provided by the notions of *savoir,* or *Wissen* (cf. Foray 2004, p. 6).

This signals that *knowledge is a socially dependent category,* as demonstrated by the Marxist theory, seeing the information/knowledge asymmetry as a form of domination[1], or by the feminist approaches, which perceive the female experiences and knowledge as disqualified by the masculine-influenced law[2], society and, ultimately, social theory itself. Sociology, therefore, acknowledges the dependence of knowledge on the patterns of agents' social embeddedness and cognitive limitations, which may arise from the influence of power and institutions (cf. Boisot/Canals 2007, p. 23). The issue of *dominance* arises in this context, as the position of power may affect the assessment of knowledge, as it has, historically, been the case with the knowledge of the colonizers *versus* the knowledge of indigenous people (see, for example, the writings of James M.

---

1 Marx, Karl (1970), *Capital: A Critique of Political Economy,* Lawrence & Wishart, London; as cited by Boisot/Canals 2007, p. 21.

2 Smart, Carol (1989), *Feminism and the Power of Law*, Routledge, London; as cited by Held 2002, p. 162.

Blaut on indigenous technical knowledge, as described by Wisner 2006). Even those opposing dominance and calling for radical social change have not been able to escape the temptation of proclaiming their own exclusivity over the scientific truth and, thus, robbing the other agents of social legitimacy (Tormey/Townshend 2006, p. 5). The discourse on knowledge has been ultimately questioned by the post-modernists, especially J. F. Lyotard, whose fundamental book (*La Condition postmoderne: rapport sur le savoir*) is concerned with the issue of *legitimation of knowledge,* which is interpreted as entirely relative: Even 'institutionalized' knowledge is nothing more than a narrative (Lyotard 1984), which makes it impossible to differentiate scientific (or any other) 'truth' from a wealth of other (dis)information. Why should, then, anyone bother to invest resources in obtaining knowledge, or even information, if its inherent feature is the absence of the opportunities for verification? This could contradict the very concepts of *knowledge economy/society/region,* etc., which have been discussed in this book, as well as in its accompanying volume[3]. The issue at stake here is not related to the epistemological issues, but rather to the *practical relevance of knowledge.*

Building a Better Mousetrap: On Practical Knowledge and Its Value

According to Giddens[4], knowledge of social situations and relationships enables different actors to achieve their objectives, with social practices based on the enactment of the shared knowledge base simultaneously reinforcing the existing social relationships and structures. Knowledge is, therefore, not only socially embedded (as already indicated), but it also recursively interacts with the same social fabric that defines it (cf. Layder, op. cit.), which makes the unbiased assessment of the practical value of knowledge extremely difficult, if not impossible. However, if the discourse of 'practicality' is limited to the economic perspective, i.e. to the market valuation of knowledge, the task is immensely simplified. Such a simplified concept seems to be a predominant concept within the political class, both in the EU, as well as globally. For instance, the EU programmes on *'information society development'* (eEurope 2002, eEurope 2005, iEurope 2010, etc.)[5] reduce the subject to the efficient usage of Information & Communication

---

[3] Langer/Pavičić/Alfirević (eds.) (2009), *Knowledge Region: Alps-Adriatic Challenges, Volume I – General Perspective,* Peter Lang, Frankfurt/Wien/New York.

[4] Giddens, Anthony (1976), *New Rules of Sociological Method,* Hutchinson, London; as cit. by Layder 2006, pp. 165 - 166.

[5] See, for example: Commission Communication of 13 March 2001 on eEurope 2002: Impact and Priorities – A communication to the Spring European Council in Stockholm, 23 - 24 March 2001, COM(2001) 140 final, Bruxelles; Communication of 28 May 2002 from the Commission to the Council, the European Parliament, the Economic and Social Committee and the Committee of the Regions – The eEurope 2005 action plan: An information society

Technologies (ICTs) by social actors. The actual information society-related policies do not even have to be dependent on their social context, but rather designed in a generic manner, i.e. according to the 'one-size-fits-all' approach. Namely, they are to provide incentives/subsidies for connecting to the Internet, especially by means of high-speed linkages ('broadband'), acquiring relevant ICT skills, creating public sector services to be accessed via electronic channels, etc. The logic of such a socio-economic intervention could be explained by the following figure.

Figure 1 The logic of socio-economic intervention, based on the 'information society' concept

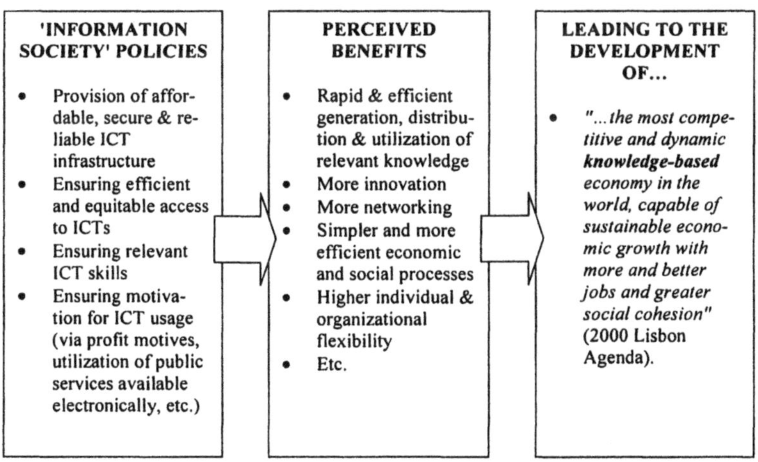

The attractiveness (if not the lure) of such an attempt to evoke and sustain socio-economic change lies in the simplification, as well as in the commercial promise of the new technologies, adequately illustrated by one of the fashionable three-letter and four-letter acronyms – the ICT4D (Information & Communication Technology for Development)[6]. The drive toward the practical, 'hands-on' ap-

for everyone, COM(2002) 263 final, Bruxelles; Communication from the Commission of 1 June 2005 to the Council, the European Parliament, the European Economic and Social Committee and the Committee of the Regions – "i2010 – A European Information Society for growth and employment", COM (2005) 229 final, Bruxelles. Official EU documents on the theme of information society are available from the Internet, at [http://europa.eu.int/information_society] retrieved in December 2008.

6 Many abbreviations/acronyms wishing to project the 'contemporary' image often (mis)use the fact that commonly used English words, such as 'to' and 'for', are pronounced similarly to the numbers two (2) and four (4).

proach, promising rapid results, seems to lead toward a superficial understanding of the issue. As observed by Heeks (2006): *"There has been a bias to action, not a bias to knowledge. We are changing the world without interpreting or understanding it"*. While the novelty of the field and the motivation to facilitate social change may be the most significant reasons for such an approach, one should not neglect the hidden agenda of the world's ICT corporations to enlarge their markets into the realm of 'emerging'[7] information economies and societies (cf. Miranda et al. 2007)[8].

Therefore, the promise of practical usefulness should not be viewed as the only valid paradigm for the analysis of knowledge-based processes in society and the economy, as it may sometimes seem. Epistemological theory and practical methodologies should meet and reinforce each other in a virtuous circle, which has also been the guiding idea of the twin-volume *Knowledge Region* book project. This volume hopes to bring together 'practical' and 'useful' approaches and illustrate them by providing the relevant images from within the Alps-Adriatic region and also from beyond its borders. It builds upon and complements the theoretical viewpoints toward knowledge-based development. On the other hand, theories 'merely' explaining new, knowledge-based realities, without the capacity to assist socio-economic development and other relevant forms of change[9], only reinforce the image of the academic community as a socially irrelevant ivory tower. This, much needed balance between 'theory' and 'practice' is, naturally, the principle, which has been described by the adage, usually attributed to the theorist of change, Kurt Lewin, maintaining that *nothing is more practical than a good theory.* Since the 'reality' of knowledge reflects who we are and how we think of ourselves, 'good' theories provide us with a new and improved perception of the desired objectives, as well as the means to reach them (cf. Kof-

---

7 Although such a term may seem inappropriate, it is, actually, the standard terminology of the business community, denoting the less developed, but promising markets (especially financial ones).

8 Authors illustrate their point by quoting the UN Secretary General speech, held at the December 2003 UN-sponsored *World Summit on Information Society* meeting in Geneva, Switzerland: *"The future of the IT industry lays not so much in the developed world, where markets are saturated, as in reaching the billions of people in the developing world who remain untouched by the information revolution"* (op. cit., p. 16).

9 Paraphrasing the famous sentence by Karl Marx, in his 1845 *Theses on Feuerbach.* However, the knowledge society could (should?) disprove the conflict-based theory of social change by facilitating the transition from technology to wisdom (see, for example: Tchurovsky, D., *Netocracy – Transition from Money-driven to Knowledge-based Society,* [http://www.netocracy.org.uk/index.htm] retrieved in December 2008. For readers interested in an overview of social change theories, see Langer/Alfirević/Pavičić (2005, pp. 8 - 14).

man/Senge 2001, pp. 4 - 5[10]). They provide us with a way of building a better mousetrap, in the hope of the power of ideas that may be attracted in the process.

A Reflection on the Power of (Applied) Ideas

The power of knowledge lies in its uncommon economic characteristics (cf. Foray 2004, pp. 15 - 18), as it is (at least, to some extent) *nonexcludable,* i.e. it is notoriously difficult, if not impossible, to stop it from 'leaking' into the environment. On the other hand, the needs of efficient industrial production require human resources to specialize, with the effect of *dispersing* the knowledge and making its availability questionable. Namely, if not *encoded into an explicit form*[11], knowledge tends to disappear, as the natural process of forgetting takes place. These characteristics of an economic good are associated with the (more or less) negative assessments, while the economic power of knowledge is usually found either in *durability* (in the context of the unusual manner in which it is being depreciated), or *nonrivalry.* The fact is that knowledge can become outdated, i.e. completely unusable as an economic good. However, until such a moment, its inherent value does not need to be written off, although it is being used in the value-producing economic processes. Knowledge of a specific material, production process, managerial technology, etc. is worth more as its usage increases. Propagation of knowledge helps those acquiring it to work more efficiently, which produces *positive effects for the entire society.* This is the reason why knowledge is, sometimes, quoted as (potentially) the only public good not subject to the *'tragedy of the commons'* [12].

The 'common' public goods, belonging to the wider community, usually become depleted, as its members do not have enough incentive to provide an appropriate compensation, which is usually referred to in terms of *externalities.* They are produced in a process, which resembles the domino effect, i.e. the be-

---

10 Kofman, Fred/Peter Senge (2001), *Communities of Commitment: The Heart of Learning Organizations,* Spring 2001, [http://www.axialent.com/uploaded/papers_articles/documentos/Communties%20of%20Commitment.%20The%20Heart%20of%20Learning%20Organizations.pdf] retrieved in December 2008.

11 Cf. discussions on explicit vs. tacit knowledge in contributions by Vittorio OLGIATI, Thomas DÖRING and Birgit AIGNER, as well as Tomaž ČATER in the first volume of *Knowledge Region.*

12 The 'tragedy of the commons' has been discussed in a variety of economic disciplines, especially in public economics and development. However, this is also the issue of systemic thinking, as the usage of the public good can be analysed as a continuous process of overusage and underinvestment, while one can also look at the motivation of actors to continue such a behaviour. For further discussion, cf. Hardin/Garett (1968), 'The Tragedy of the Commons', *Science,* 162, pp. 1243 - 1248, as reproduced on the following Web page: [http://dieoff.org/page95.htm] retrieved in January 2009.

haviour of a system ruled by the positive feedback link. According to Peter Senge, the well known theorist of organizational learning, this is a common systemic error: Once actors form the expectation that the public good will be exploited, their behaviour starts to reflect such a conviction, leading to a 'vicious circle' (cf. ten Have et al. 2003, pp. 77 - 78). On the other hand, knowledge is *not depleted* as its usage increases and intensifies: Its value is, rather, enhanced, as subsequent research and/or practical application make the original knowledge more useful to society, which brings about the notion of *positive externalities*. In addition, the *nonrivalry* of the knowledge resource signifies that many actors can concurrently utilize it in a non-competitive manner. This is illustrated by Charles Leadbeater[13], who uses the metaphor of a chocolate cake (as a private good, which is appropriated by actor(s) eating the cake), versus the chocolate cake recipe, which can be used by multiple actors concurrently, without any value depletion in the process (Hartley 2004, pp. 128 - 129).

The *cumulative effects* of knowledge usage (cf. Foray, op. cit.) are related to the fact that both fundamental research, as well as applied innovation usually do not emerge from thin air, but rather emanate from the existing body of knowledge. In this context, the idea of *"standing on the shoulders of giants"* (Merton 1965) usually signifies the connection between the previous and current generation(s) of scientists: Today's scholars are continuing traditions by critically using and contributing to a centuries-old body of knowledge. In the academic community, research is presented to the wider public free of charge, in order to contribute to society by advancing the knowledge, while merit is acknowledged by means of citing and peer review. The *hacker community,* consisting of ICT enthusiasts, contributing to the early development of the 'high tech', reflects the values deeply embedded into the academic world by the often used description of the *information wanting to be free*[14]. Such a notion is, in many instances, interpreted along the lines of the own 'inner life' of knowledge, reflected by the culture of free sharing. However, this opens the issue of *compensating innovators and other producers of knowledge* for their hard work and ensuring that *the re-*

---

13 Leadbeater, Charles (1997), *Living on Thin Air: The New Economy*, Routledge, London; as cit. by Hartley 2004.

14 In line with a quote from the Bible (*"You shall know the truth and the truth shall make you free"*, John 8:32, as quoted by Roger Clarke), members of the hacker community use the phrase *"information wants to be free"*, starting with the viewpoint that costs of copying and distributing information are becoming insignificant. On the other hand, the value of information is indisputably high, which is reflected by the entire sentence, taken from the speech by Stewart Brand (to whom the quote has been attributed) to the 1984 Hackers' Conference. Namely, on that occassion, Brand also mentioned that the *information wants to be expensive,* on the grounds of its value, which creates an inherent conflict between these two aspects of knowledge. (Clark 2000, *Information Wants To Be Free* ... [http://www.rogerclarke.com/II/IWtbF.html] retrieved in January 2009.)

sources are committed to this purpose in the future, which will not be the case, if the resulting knowledge is to be unconditionally released to the public domain (cf. Foray 2004, pp. 113 - 119). According to some authors (Kaser 2000[15]), the idea of free information may be compelling[16], but unrealistic, as costs of producing information need to be covered, if such an intellectual enterprise is to continue.

Therefore, there is knowledge belonging to private parties, to be used as a source of appropriating economic returns, as well as knowledge belonging to the public, to be used as a means of achieving public benefit. In contemporary societies, the mix of interests in producing and appropriating knowledge is reflected by the varied sources of funding for research and development, coming both from the public, as well as the private sector (Scotchmer 2004, pp. 228 - 235). This fact is reflected by contemporary legislature, which recognizes knowledge as a form of intellectual property (ibid., pp. 65 - 95) but, on many occasions, to little avail to many innovators and authors, whose works are easily copied, once transferred into a digital form. On the other hand, free sharing and open collaboration, based on digital communication and communities, have led to the development of innovation as successful as the *open-source* operating system *Linux* and other pieces of software, used to run most of the information services on the Internet, such as the *Apache* software for providing World Wide Web services (Raymond 2001). So, it seems that multiple models of knowledge production, distribution and usage are able to coexist in the developed economies/societies, which needs to be addressed by analysing the 'soft' side of knowledge.

Beyond the Economic Value: Multiple 'Soft' Appearances of Knowledge

A comprehensive volume on the (re)definition of contemporary capitalism along the lines of knowledge and culture (Thrift 2005) reaffirms the idea of capitalism as a path-dependent, contingent and performative project (ibid., pp. 2 - 3), resonating Schumpeter's idea of *creative destruction* as the fundamental driver of socio-economic development. Creative 'reshuffling' of the existing order can be, ultimately, attributed exclusively to the development of new knowledge, i.e. *in-*

---

[15] Kaser, R. T. (2000), 'If Information Wants to Be Free . . . Then Who's Going to Pay for It?', *D-Lib Magazine,* Vol. 6/No. 5/May 2000, [http://dlib.org/dlib/may00/kaser/05kaser.html] retrieved in January 2009.

[16] However, the meaning of the term 'free' needs to be discussed, as Richard Stallman, one of the 'gurus' of the open-source software developers once remarked that: "I believe that all generally useful information should be free. By 'free' I am not referring to price, but rather to the freedom to copy the information and to adapt it to one's own uses ... When information is generally useful, redistributing it makes humanity wealthier no matter who is distributing and no matter who is receiving" (ibid.). Here, freedom is not the freedom of getting something of value (i.e. information) free of charge, but rather is freedom as the expression of one's right not to surrender control of his/her own life to an external entity.

novation, which makes it possible to leap forward as described by the model of *punctuated equilibrium*[17]. However, the very assumptions of the nature of knowledge and the manner in which it is created reflect both the reality of capitalism, as well as its future tendencies. The changing context of humanities, especially of philosophy and sociology, transforms the epistemological presumptions stemming from modernity, related to the belief of the rational comprehension of the material world. The 'postmodern' account of society, economy and their actors can serve as a corrective of the previous discourse, although it produces its own myths on partiality and ephemerality of knowledge (cf. Thrift, op. cit., pp. 24 - 29). This is reflected in the *Zeitgeist* by the mounting quantity of practically oriented literature on managing change and surviving in a complex, non-linear world, which sees *collective and experiential learning,* including its *embodiment* as a *human,* or even *organizational capability,* as the relevant answer (ibid., pp. 32 - 33). Nevertheless, editors of this volume do not wish to offer such a 'totalizing' framework, or even a view toward the usability (and, hence, value) of knowledge, both in general, as well as in the context of the Alps-Adriatic region.

Nevertheless, the 'practical' orientation of this volume will be maintained by bringing together a variety of contributions, diverse in all their aspects, except for the orientation toward the notion of *knowledge* as a means of socio-economic change/development in various contexts. With respect to the postmodern discourse, the targeted (and/or realized) changes will not be referred to as *progress,* but rather presented as fragmented pieces of evidence for the usability of knowledge in our 'messy' world. The reality of 'soft' capitalism (Thrift, op. cit.), praised by the 'cool' bestsellers, such as *Funky Business* (Nordström/Ridderstråle 2002), will be rather addressed by giving special attention to the *practices related to development of social actors' knowledge and motivation in all relevant sectors.* Those include the places and arrangements of work life, traditional education at all levels, as well as civil society.

Renata RELJA and Darko RENDULIĆ address knowledge work in contemporary society and identify its underlying determinants. Those include several issues, which will be further explored throughout this volume. One of the areas that should be analysed more closely is, without any doubt, the field of education. As knowledge-society can not be developed without individual interactions, the value of social contacts and inter-cultural competences gained in the process of student exchange are becoming one of the major 'obsessions' of education professionals. This process might be also somewhat venerated, up to the point that its facilitation becomes a cornerstone of the Bologna-style higher education re-

---

[17] *Punctuated equilibrium* explains social and economic change/development in terms of 'quantum leaps' from one to another stable state (configuration), with the transitions taking place between the longer periods of stability due to innovation. For additional discussion in the context of change management theory, see Langer/Alfirević/Pavičić (2005, pp. 51 - 52).

form. Jurica ŠIMURINA, Jurica PAVIČIĆ and Morana FUDURIĆ discuss the case of the student exchange programme at the Faculty of Economics and Business at the University of Zagreb, Croatia and identify the practical success factors and consequences of such an educational practice.

In order to reach out toward the more fundamental levels of educational work, the volume continues with a paper discussing the interplay of managerial practices and marketing orientation of elementary schools in Croatia, contributed by Vladimir GNJIDIĆ, Nino GABELICA and Miše KUTLEŠA.

Two specific marketing practices from the profit sector are analysed in the next two contributions in this section. In the paper authored by Martina SOPTA and Bojan MAKAR, outsourcing of a core knowledge-based activity, such as marketing, as well as its fundamental components, are analysed using a sample of Croatian enterprises. However limited, analysis of the present situation should be considered just one of the first steps, taken in the direction of defining key knowledge-based services, to be offered by the Alps-Adriatic providers to the wider business community. The second paper, contributed by Nenad BRKIĆ and Almir SALIHOVIĆ, looks at the issue of service quality of a rather unusual subject – the central banks, measured by their online activities.

The last contribution here turns to specific technologies, such as pen-based computing, which can assist educators in achieving the previously stated objectives. In his contribution, Zdeslav HREPIĆ analyses the influence of this specific technology on student preferences and satisfaction.

Along the lines of the practical usability of knowledge and adapting to environmental change, the ultimate objective of the contemporary education system can be interpreted in terms of flexibility and resourcefulness, which is discussed by Gunhild SAGMEISTER, in her contribution on flexibility of recent graduates' work in innovative working situations.

Two case studies from the Alps-Adriatic region are, in a certain sense, based on the notion of contributing to the community to which a person 'originally' belongs. Such a contribution, going beyond the individualism sparked by the development of modernity, can be viewed in terms of either institution-building, or the activism performed within the civil society. In a very general framework, all such activities can be considered as drawing on the shared knowledge of multiple social actors, in order to ensure a better quality of life, both for the direct recipients of assistance, as well as for the community as a whole. In this context, Gabriella RIGONI analyses development and functioning of a specific institution – ERDISU, which ensures the equal access to higher education in the regions of Trieste and Udine. On the other hand, Gordana FORČIĆ and Bojana ĆULUM discuss voluntary work in the Primorsko-Goranska County in Croatia, demonstrating that positive 'outliers' may be used as a benchmarks in the development of nonprofit sector. This issue can be treated as a matter of motivation, but it also represents a vehicle for the voluntary exchange of knowledge and contribution to the wider community.

The growing pace of knowledge generation requires companies to adopt the 'learn or perish' approach. Three short illustrations of the value of knowledge in particular enterprises active within the entire Alps-Adriatic region (*Moving Board, Kapsch* and *Tondach*), contributed by Vanja SERTIĆ and Morana FUDURIĆ, Josef ELTANTAWI and Manfred RUPRECHTER, can serve as a starting point for such a discussion.

Knowledge enables social actors to reach out of the region and engage in productive co-operation, as well as to look out for the examples of knowledge-based development, which should serve as benchmarks – to be used in the Alps-Adriatic, in an adapted form, customized to the requirement of the local context. Networking among the universities on the very edge of the Alps-Adriatic region, both in the framework of cross-border co-operation and searching for the 'fit' with the common European blueprint of the Bologna-Process, are discussed by Gerhard STROHMEIER in a paper on relationships between the Austrian and Hungarian institutions of higher education. The same issue, in the somewhat narrower regional milieu of western Hungary, is addressed by János RECHNITZER and Melinda SMAHÓ. The volume is concluded by a case study located, by geographical standards, the farthest from the Alps-Adriatic, as it looks into the challenges to integration of the aspiring knowledge region of Øresund, which lies between Denmark and Sweden. By exploring national regional policies and the cross-border institution-building processes, Magnus GRUBBE implicitly opens up new questions related to the state of the (dis)integrated European Union and its proclaimed policies of knowledge-based development. However, the future of the EU, even in its narrow segment of fostering the role of knowledge in spatially defined regions, represents the issue to be addressed in the not so distant future.

References

Boisot, Max H./Augusti Canals (2007), 'Data, Information, and Knowledge: Have We Got It Right?', in Max H. Boisot/Ian C. MacMillan/ Kyeong Seok Han (eds.), *Explorations in Information Space: Knowledge, Agents, and Organization,* Oxford University Press, Oxford, pp. 15 - 47.

Foray, Dominique (2004), *The Economics of Knowledge,* MIT Press, Cambridge/MA.

Hartley, John (2004), *Communication, Cultural and Media Studies: The Key Concepts* (Third edition), Routledge, London.

Heeks, Richard (2006), 'Theorizing ICT4D Research', *Information Technologies and International Development,* Vol. 3/No. 3, pp. 1 - 4.

Held, Virginia (2002), 'Feminism and Political Theory', in Robert M. Simon (ed.), *The Blackwell Guide to Social and Political Philosophy,* Blackwell Publishers, Oxford, pp. 154 - 176.

Langer, Josef/Nikša Alfirević/Jurica Pavičić (2005), *Organizational Change in Transition Societies,* Ashgate, Aldershot.
Layder, Derek (2006), *Understanding Social Theory* (Second edition), SAGE Publications, London.
Lyotard, Jean Francois (1984), *The Postmodern Condition: A Report on Knowledge,* University of Minnesota Press, Minneapolis.
Merton, Robert K. (1965), *On the Shoulders of Giants,* The University of Chicago Press, Chicago.
Miranda, Alvaro de/Dirk-Jan Peet/Karel F.Mulder/Paul Arthur Berkman/Thomas F. Ruddy/ Werner Pillmann/Marcus A. Ynalvez/Wiebe E. Bijker (2007), 'ICT for Development: Illusions, Promises, Challenges, and Realizations', in Wesley Shrum/Keith R. Benson/Wiebe E. Bijker/Klaus Brunnstein (eds.), *Past, Present and Future of Research in the Information Society,* Springer Science+Business Media, New York, pp. 13 - 32.
Nordström, Kjell/Jonas Ridderstråle (2002), *Funky Business: Talent Makes Capital Dance* (Second edition), Financial Times Prentice Hall, Edinburgh Gate.
Raymond, Eric S. (2001), *The Cathedral and the Bazaar: Musings on Linux and Open Source by an Accidental Revolutionary,* O'Reilly Media, Sebastopol/CA.
Scotchmer, Suzanne (2004), *Innovation and Incentives,* MIT Press, Cambridge/MA.
Searle, John R. (2003), 'Contemporary Philosophy in the United States', in Nicholas Bunnin/Eric P. Tsui-James (eds.), *The Blackwell Companion to Philosophy* (Second edition), Blackwell Publishing, Oxford, pp. 1 - 22.
ten Have, Steven/Wouter ten Have/Frans Stevens/Marcel van der Elst/Fiona Pol-Coyne (2003), *Key management models: The management tools and practices that will improve your business,* Financial Times Prentice Hall, Edinburgh Gate.
Thrift, Nigel (2005), *Knowing Capitalism,* SAGE Publications, London.
Tormey, Simon/Jules Townshend (2006), *Key Thinkers from Critical Theory to Post-Marxism,* SAGE Publications, London.
Wisner, Ben (2006), 'James M. "Jim" Blaut', in David Simon (ed.), *Fifty Key Thinkers on Development,* Routledge, Abingdon, pp. 40 - 44.

KNOWLEDGE, INFORMATION AND AGENTS

Renata Relja – Darko Rendulić

Work in the Era of Knowledge-based Development – Conceptual Foundations and Analysis of Social Determinants in the Alps-Adriatic Context

Work in Knowledge-based Societies: Conceptual Foundations

Information-, post-industrial, service-, knowledge-, intellectual- and informatics'-society are the words by which the transformation of the industrial societies in the second half of the Twentieth century is commonly explained. Despite the words used, a common characteristic of the created changes is reflected in the transformation of society into a form in which technology takes a key role. Thus, the post-industrial society represents a new form of the social and technology organisation and a new way of life while emphasized principles cause movements within crucial concepts such as time, space, market, strategic resources, importance of work, organization structure etc. (Bell 2001, pp. 41 - 44; Kostyukhin 2005). Modern networked society represents the most important structural consequence of the influence of information technology. The largest influence of the network is evident directly in the changes of the basic forms of work. The network has enabled large number of employees to work at home and consequently life is increasingly reduced to "my job, computer and me"[1]. The result of the changes indicated is reflected in the changed structure of jobs. In that manner more than half of the employees in the most highly developed countries are directly engaged in jobs that may be characterized as information activities (Garača 2004, pp. 6 - 7).

At the same time, speaking of the new forms of work, their newly created forms endanger the usual understanding of the community, as well as the feeling of security or comfort. In this way career, work, job and increasing consumption become mutually very dependant meanings (Leicht 2001, pp. 421 - 422). In this context, post-industrial technologies also redefine the meanings of the nature of work, which leaves the unskilled and/or the undereducated without the demand for work. Knowledge and technology become key factors that define criteria for elite positions, while the system of education decides on who is selected for a particular role (Bell 2001, pp. 72 - 73). Thus, the process of technological transformation of the entire society is expanded exponentially, due to the possibility of interfacing technology areas by using a common digital language. Therefore, ac-

[1] UCLA Center for Communication Policy: The UCLA Internet Report: *Surveying the Digital Future*, [http://www.ccp.ucla.edu] retrieved on 3.11. 2006.

cording to Castells (2000, p. 64), the nucleus of contemporary transformation is found in the technology of processing and transferring information.

On the other hand, globalisation processes, which use infrastructure shaped by new information technologies, are necessarily connected with the improvement of information technology (Castells 2000, p. 125). Giddens defines globalisation as a complex group of processes that enforces social relationships worldwide. It connects distant places in such a way that local events are influenced by the distant ones (Giddens 2003, pp. 6 - 19). A large number of authors are mainly occupied by the advantages and disadvantages of the globalisation process and its evaluation from different perspectives (Brown 2008, pp. 42 - 53). Therefore, defining the process of globalisation depends on the research aspect, i.e. whether it is an economic, social, cultural, communication, environmental or a managerial one. Recent research focuses on implications of mentioned socio-historical changes as well as their influence on the social sciences (Gille/Riain 2002, p. 271). Globalisation is *"certainly the most used, mistreated and the least defined, (...) most incredible and politically most efficient word of the recent and coming years"* (Beck 2001, p. 46) . The same author also warns about the necessity of investigating various dimensions of globalisation such as its communication-technical, ecological, economic, work-organizational, cultural and civic-social dimension (Beck 2001, pp. 104 - 112). From that perspective, the goods, the capital, the knowledge and the communication break territorial boundaries so that transactional networks, social movements and informal relationships spread over whole range of human activities. Global trade, financial and manufacturing systems bind the lives of homes, communities and nations worldwide, making territorial and political borders irrelevant (Galić 2000, p. 26).

Globalisation directly influences the need of spreading communication and requires coordination at various locations. Implicitly, the flexibility of information technology (IT) enables quick and necessary adaptation to such drastic changes. Certain working communities can act as unique entities with the help of communication networks and IT, enabling the collaboration of a large number of people despite their geographical distance. Therefore, within an information society, there exist information technologies which offer potential to transform the way of work. From the sociological aspect, in such a changed configuration of work and life, the *groups*, not individuals become the basic working unit (Moore et al. 2001; Yager et al. 2002). Most of the contemporary social changes are determined by globalisation processes in which, by eliminating territorial borders and differences, a network of various global social relations and communication is formed (Galić 2000, p. 21). Contrary to deterministic cultural approaches, networks leave free space for human activity, offering a sort of third way (Powell/Smith-Doerr 1994, p. 365).

Technological and managers' transformation of work and work relationships represents the mainframe by which globalisation and informatization influence society as a whole. In that way the theories of post industrialism and "informationalism" themselves consider the creation of the new social structure as the most persuasive proof. It is primarily characterised by the change from goods to services, the rise of managing and specialized jobs, decrease of agricultural and production jobs and primarily information content of the work in the most highly developed economies. In this information era we are witnessing significant changes in the field of work and employment. New structures and professions are appearing and social forms are being changed as a direct consequence of the development of technology and globalisation that inflicts upon manpower. At the core of the social structure is the process of work while technological and managerial transformation of the work and working relationships in networked companies is a basic lever by which informatics pattern and the process of globalisation influence society as a whole (Castells 2000, p. 232). Lyotard finds in information technology the main production factor that analogically responds to the engagement of the post-modern, particularly in the field of communication and information storage. Economic activity concentrates on information technologies, which change the patterns of work and its relationships. Lyotard (2005, pp. 1 - 7), thus, speculates about the society of the future as being based on production and the exchange of knowledge.

Within contemporary analysis of the work processes, the emphasis is placed on "informationalism", instead of post-industrialism, as the era after industrialism. Contemporary societies are information societies due to the fact that they organise their production system by increasing productivity based on knowledge, spreading information technologies and fulfilling other preconditions (adapting human resources and communication infrastructure) (Castells 2000, p. 235). At the same time, some authors suggest that the unemployment might be also a consequence of information technologies. However, new technology neither generates, nor eliminates employment, but influences the change of the nature of work and the organisation of production enabling restructuring and organisation of the company in a new way.

Trends initiated by competition and led by technology are in the background of the contemporary transformation of work relationships, therefore, the fastest growing categories of work are temporary and short-term work, flexible work and instability of employment (Castells 2000, p. 29; Carnoy/Castells 2001, p. 12; Šporer 2004, p. 14). Within these mentioned changes, knowledge positions itself as a new element in production, and information technology is, due to those circumstances, forced to adapt and change the predominant content of work (Exton/Totterdill 2008).

One general feature of the rise of capitalism is also reflected in influence on the specialized tasks within the jobs, as well as the general division of labour among the employees in the society. This influences the establishment of the model of mandatory schooling in general and specialization of training for each particular employee, which results in the system of rewarding that takes the form of certificates and acknowledgements confirming knowledge for various types of jobs. Weber himself pointed this out as a form of "rationalisation" of education and training. In this context, it is illustrative that the British departments of education and schooling were merged and renamed into the department of education and skills in the Fifties (Edgell 2006, pp. 13 - 17).

At the same time, as the answer to rising needs, educational institutions are enlarging the number of programmes offered at all levels. Continuous learning, as well as *training programmes,* is becoming part of the strategy of business units as well as of educating institutions. Relations between the sphere of business and universities have never been closer and more tightly bound, making obvious that knowledge and skills have become key factors of successful economic growth (Šporer 2004; Baily 2008). Within those recently generated circumstances, the central position of knowledge in the new economy underlines the role and importance of schools as new productive forces (Carnoy/Castells 2001, p. 12; Willinsky 2005). In new business organisations, beside interests for improving processes of gaining knowledge, it has been attempted to reduce the discrepancy between the younger and older employees by creating the model of mentoring as an elements of lifelong learning. Therefore, in the contemporary workplace, managers need to provide training, support and the creation of new opportunities. A high level of skills, communication, social skills, ability to solve problems as well as informatics skills with their basis in the education system create the precondition for survival on the labour market (Šporer 2004, p. 130).

Listed trends resulting from the integration of education and work, as well as the need for continuous learning at all social levels are the reflection of the wider strategy upon which, according to UNESCO, the knowledge society stands (UNESCO 2005, pp. 191 - 194):

- Invest more in quality education for all to ensure equal opportunity
- Increase places of community access to information and communication technologies
- Widen the contents available for universal access to knowledge
- Develop collaboratories: towards better scientific knowledge sharing
- Share environmental knowledge for sustainable development
- Making linguistic diversity a priority; the challenges of multilingualism
- Move towards knowledge certification on the internet: quality labels
- Intensify the creation of partnerships for digital solidarity

- Increase women's contribution to knowledge societies
- Measure knowledge: towards knowledge society indicators

It is obvious that knowledge appears as a new axis around which innovations and progress cross so that the key factor for the state becomes the equipment of the university and the capability to research in science as well as technology progress (Bell 2001). Out of that comes the conclusion that "knowledge-based society is a system where knowledge capital and innovation starts to play a dominant role in the national economy" (Šporer 2004, pp. 131 - 132).

New Patterns in Knowledge-based Work

Globalisation has, besides having other effects, eroded the monopoly over *scientific knowledge.* The power that comes from the knowledge in the global economy takes away control from the state because innovations are globalised, too. Thus the discourse of knowledge is removed from state control particularly due to the increased information availability caused by the expansion of technology and communication (Carnoy/Castells 2001, pp. 10 - 11). Modern technology makes changes in the content of work in a way that employees create and generate knowledge themselves and jobs become places of continuous learning. The influence of the informatics' revolution is manifest in increased need for new labour, particularly those who execute jobs requiring a high level of knowledge. At the same time the need for performing traditional tasks is becoming secondary.

Managing knowledge and flexible work are two key subjects of the discussion within modern socio-economic literature. The general attitude is that long-term competitiveness is possible only by enlarging knowledge and the offer of flexible work. The definition of *knowledge work* is based on cognition skills, planning, solving problems and taking decisions which are realised by *knowledge workers* who have a high level of education, experience and status within the organisation (Pérez Pérez et al. 2002, p. 272). Nowadays, in the companies of the informatics society, the work is done through projects but, most importantly, within the dimensions of continuous learning and the process of gaining new ideas (Malone/Lauchbacher 1998, pp. 146 - 147).

It is obvious that technology development generates specific forms of the organisation of work and work experience. Productive, flexible, skilled and educated workers contribute to the competitiveness of the company. *Teleworking,* i.e. the remote performance of individual jobs emerges as an alternative form of organization, which involves the use of Information and Communications Technologies (ICT), in order to provide workers with the remote access to operations. Improved quality and cost reduction enable the generation of so-called mobile tele-employees today, who work anywhere and anytime (Zakaria et al. 2004, p. 25).

Table 1 Proportion of enterprises that have remote employed persons who connect to IT systems from home, 2006 (% of enterprises)

	Total (10 or more persons employed)	Small (10 to 49 persons employed)	Medium (50 to 249 persons employed)	Large (250 or more persons employed)
EU-27	17	13	30	55
Euro area	15	11	30	57
Belgium	27	21	50	71
Bulgaria	9	9	10	17
Czech Republic	19	15	31	48
Denmark	53	46	81	95
Germany	21	15	39	65
Estonia	22	18	34	53
Ireland	25	20	38	59
Greece	16	14	25	52
Spain	8	5	17	40
France	:	:	:	:
Italy	3	2	7	23
Cyprus	14	10	28	62
Latvia	7	5	12	27
Lithuania	12	11	13	30
Luxembourg	19	16	25	66
Hungary	10	8	16	36
Malta	:	:	:	:
Netherlands	35	29	56	85
Austria	20	16	37	64
Poland	4	3	8	15
Portugal	9	7	21	49
Romania	7	6	9	20
Slovenia	26	23	32	65
Slovakia	13	12	17	34
Finland	32	24	56	77
Sweden	39	34	59	84
United Kingdom	32	26	49	79
Iceland	47	42	67	66
Norway	49	44	78	94

Note: (*) Enterprises with 10 or more full-time persons employed; enterprises that have their main activity in NACE Sections D, F, G, I and K or NACE Groups 55.1, 55.2, 92.1 and 92.2.

Source: Eurostat (isoc_ci_tw_e)

Almost all companies within the EU use the telework, although there are significant discrepancies within the countries. Thus, Denmark reaches the highest percentage of tele-workers while Poland has the lowest.

The emphasized mobility of work postulates three interdependent aspects of working mobility:

- *space mobility* – concerning the geographical mobility of workers,
- *operational mobility* – concerning flexible acting as independent part of work,
- *interactive mobility* – related to intensive fluid interaction with a wide range of people.

Solutions for mobile work not only improve planning and efficiency but also provide other advantages such as an increased level of security and better balance of tasks for mobile employees (Brodt/Verbung 2007, pp. 53 - 64). The environment of virtual work intermediated by informational and communication technology initiates the interdependence of the team members, promotes equality in participation, decreases organisational hierarchy and increases participation of the members in virtual meetings. In that way, they could very soon transform from entity into structure and likely become an integral common component of the global work environment. Perceiving them in this way will increase the trust of the organisation concerning their success, the number of allocated resources will increase, as well as positive influence within the knowledge environment they share, intermediated by information and communication technology (Zakaria et al. 2004, pp. 23 - 25).

Finally, in the context of the emphasized debate about the interrelation of the dimensions of knowledge and work, Pérez Pérez et al. (2002, p. 274) summarize the main results of recent research in the field of *knowledge management* and point out the following as most important: *knowledge creation* – for that segment companies require and understand qualified experts but need a stimulating system which urges involvement of specialists to permanently improve and generate ideas too; *knowledge acquisition* – process of internalisation of external knowledge which is optimal when it includes a larger number of employees; *knowledge retention* – minimising losses of company knowledge that helps to reduce the fluctuation rate of employees with valuable knowledge; *knowledge distribution* – required regarding practice of mobilizing and sharing of knowledge.

Analysis of Social Determinants of Work in the Knowledge-based Society

Education

Effects of education on the economy are not absolute, nor are they unchangeable. They vary from state to state in different times and scope, depending on the importance paid to various aspects of education. The differences exist despite the fact that national systems of education develop similar teaching curriculums independently of the specifics of their own economic system (Rubinson/Browne 1994, pp. 594 - 596). This is particularly obvious within the Bologna Process, the goal of which is to promote the unique European area of higher education with the intention of creating a common labour market (Relja/Dragun 2005, pp. 23 - 24; Dragun/Relja 2006, pp. 63 - 64). In the context of the debate about the position and role of knowledge and the direct connection of the society of knowledge and the society of information with the world of work, the European Union (EU) goals of providing regional help have been designed, primarily aimed at the support and promotion of contents that lead towards the realisation of a higher level of education and employment (Boehm et al. 2006, p. 65).

The goals stipulated by the EU itself are summarized in further subparagraphs (*Commission of the European Communities*, 2008):

- The EU set itself the overall ambition of achieving five benchmarks by 2010 - those related to literacy, reduction of early school-leaving, upper secondary attainment, maths, science and technology graduates and participation in adult learning. Only the benchmark on mathematics, science and technology graduates is likely to be exceeded. Indeed, low performance in reading literacy, which was benchmarked to decline by 20 percent by 2010, has actually increased by more than 10 percent between 2000 and 2006 and has reached 24.1 percent.
- Education and training in the EU is improving slowly, but steadily. However, there are significant divergences between the member states.
- All countries have relative strengths and weaknesses in the five benchmark areas. Finland, Denmark, Sweden, the United Kingdom, Ireland, Poland, Slovenia, Norway and Iceland exceed the composite objective of the five benchmarks set for 2010 and are progressing in yearly averages; while France, the Netherlands, Belgium, have an average performance below the composite objective and have not made progress.
- Participation in lifelong learning is becoming a reality in Sweden, the United Kingdom, Denmark, Norway and Iceland, countries that have developed comprehensive and coherent lifelong learning strategies. Slovenia, Finland, Austria, Belgium and Spain are following closely behind.

The number of pupils and students in any particular country represents an important potential for creating a society of knowledge.

Some 98.3 million pupils and students within the EU-27 were included in the system of education in 2005, taking the total almost 2.5 million higher than in 2000. The largest proportion of pupils and students in the EU-27 was in the UK, where 16.7 million pupils and students were included in the system of education – this number was 2.2 million higher than the student population in Germany.

The results of analysis regarding the wider region, which encompasses most of the Alps-Adriatic countries, are indicative, and show how much the countries considered are behind in the key dimensions that define the knowledge-based society of the western economy.

Table 2 Pupils and students (excluding pre-primary education)

	Total (ISCED 1-6) (1000)		Primary level of education (ISCED 1)		Lower secondary level of education (ISCED 2)		Upper and post-secondary non-tertiary education (ISCED 3-4)		Tertiary education (ISCED 5-6)	
	2000	2005	2000	2005	2000	2005	2000	2005	2000	2005
EU-27	95840	98318	32,5	29,3	23,7	23,8	27,2	27,9	16,6	18,8
Euro area	56682	57785	31,4	30,4	27,4	26,8	23,2	23,4	17,8	19,3
Belgium	2235	2380	34,6	31,0	16,7	18,1	32,8	34,5	15,9	16,4
Bulgaria	1357	1226	29,0	23,7	27,0	25,9	24,7	31,0	19,3	19,4
Czech Republic	1906	1912	33,8	26,3	27,5	25,9	25,3	30,2	13,3	17,6
Denmark	1003	1144	38,3	36,2	20,6	20,5	22,2	23,0	18,9	20,3
Germany	14549	14467	25,1	22,9	38,2	37,7	22.D	23,3	14,1	15,7
Estonia	303	289	40,7	29,6	20,2	22,0	21,3	24,9	17,7	23,5
Ireland	990	1037	45,4	43,8	18,8	16,9	19,6	21,3	16,2	18,0
Greece	1883	2053	34,3	31,7	19,5	16,5	23,9	20,4	22,4	31,5
Spain	7769	7537	32,7	34,8	26,4	26,3	17,4	:	23,5	24,0
France	11934	12315	32,6	32,6	27,7	27,2	22,2	22,3	16,9	17,8
Italy	9049	9409	31,3	29,7	20,0	19,5	29,1	29,5	19,6	21,4
Cyprus	138	147	46,3	41,8	23,7	22,2	:	:	7,5	13,7
Latvia	499	491	27,1	17,2	33,1	33,0	21,6	23,2	18,3	26,6
Lithuania	767	805	28,5	19,6	42,1	40,2	13,5	15,9	15,9	24,3
Luxembourg	69	73	47,2	48,1	23,1	24,5	26,1	27,4	3,5	:
Hungary	1906	1976	26,3	11,8	26,6	14,9	31,0	31,3	16,1	22,1
Malta	78	80	44,2	37,1	37,2	35,3	10,5	15,7	8,1	11,8
Netherlands	3171	3289	40,3	38,9	23,8	24,0	20,5	20,0	15,4	17,2
Austria	1459	1462	26,9	24,8	26,1	27,3	29,1	31,2	17,9	16,7
Poland	9074	8887	43,7	30,6	6,8	18,7	32,1	26,8	17,4	23,8
Portugal	2032	1913	40,2	40,4	20,9	19,9	:	19,8	18,4	19,9
Romania	3962	3847	30,0	25,2	33,0	26,7	25,5	28,9	11,4	19,2
Slovenia	389	409	22,3	22,8	26,0	20,3	30,1	29,5	21,5	27,4
Slovakia	1123	1101	27,6	22,0	36,4	32,7	23,9	28,8	12,1	16,5
Finland	1152	1240	33,7	30,8	17,2	16,2	25,7	28,3	23,4	24,7
Sweden	2089	2114	37,1	34,0	17,0	19,8	28,3	26,0	16,6	20,2
United Kingdom	14955	16714	31,0	27,7	15,3	14,0	:	:	13,5	13,7
Croatia	:	736	:	26,7	:	28,3	:	:	:	18,3
FYR of Macedonia	386	374	32,8	29,4	33,6	31,7	24,0	25,7	9,6	13,2
Turkey	13169	16021	75,3	65,9	:	:	:	:	7,7	13,1
Iceland	73	83	42,6	37,1	16,0	16,5	28,3	28,1	13,2	18,3
Liechtenstein	5	6	46,6	37,1	34,8	26,7	:	27,4	10,8	8,7
Norway	989	1052	42,4	40,8	16,0	17,7	22,3	21,2	19,3	20,3
Switzerland	:	1334	:	39,3	:	22,3	:	22,7	:	15,0
Japan	20583	19218	36,6	37,6	20,7	19,2	22.D	21,0	19,3	21,0
United States	62323	66597	40,1	36,7	19,8	19,8	19,0	17,6	21,2	25,9

Source: Eurostat (tpsOO051 and educ_end1tl)
This table includes the total number of persons who are enrolled in the regular education system in each country. It covers all levels of education from primary education to postgraduate studies. It corresponds to the target population for education policy.

Isolation and the independent nature of centrally planned economy that characterised this region, along with globalisation processes which have avoided it, institutional structures that have not been able to keep up with the western market as well as lower technology sophistication are all recognized as core factors of created inferiority. Šporer concludes that a wider sample of the countries of Central and Eastern Europe, including the relevant countries in the Alps-Adriatic region are also *"(...) faced with the legacies of their isolation from globalising trends of the world economy"* (Šporer 2004, pp. 133 - 134).

Šporer points to the educational structure as the most important indicator of the knowledge-based society, concluding that only an educated population with a high level of capabilities can be innovative and answer future economic challenges. The calculation is simple; a higher number of students enrolled provides a higher chance for society based on knowledge in the future. The analysis from 2001/2002 shows that within the range of countries which also includes the Alps-Adriatic region, the participation in higher education ranges from 2.45 percent, related to the total population in Croatia, up to 4.49 percent (in Estonia – as new member of the EU). In EU countries that range goes from 2.25 percent (in Greece) to 7.067 percent (in Finland) while the number of students included in higher education is equal in both groups of countries: 3.47 percent in Middle and Eastern Europe and 3.92 percent in the EU. Similar percentages are found when considering the average participation of GDP spent on public education within the countries of Middle and Eastern Europe, which equals 5.15 percent. This is close to the EU countries (5.45%). Comparing indicators related to education, it is evident that countries of Middle and Eastern Europe, including the countries from the wider region, do not fall significantly behind the EU countries although the indicators do not say much about the quality of the system of education (Šporer 2004, pp. 139 - 140).

Employment and Unemployment Regarding the Level of Education

The European Commission requires as a goal the consideration of the *Lisbon Strategy* and focuses on growth and the creation of better jobs. In order to achieve those goals the need for mobilisation of all resources is emphasized – national and of the community as well as the promotion of partnership among the members, social actors, civil society and all interested participants. It is pointed out that the wealth of European citizens significantly depends on the efficacy of the adaptation to rapid socio-economic changes, which are now reflected in new economic activities and jobs (*European Commission*, 2006). Employment is one of the key indicators of the dynamics and direct changes within the economy. At the time of the analysis by Šporer, Ireland had the most impressive economic development with the highest rate of creating new jobs and the lowest level of unemployed in the EU (Šporer 2004, pp. 137 - 138). Hungary and Slovenia came closest to that average, while e.g. Croatia had negative or slow growth of employment and high unemployment.

Table 3 Total employment rate, by highest level of education, 2006.

	Pre-primary, primary and secondary education - ISCED levels 0-2	Upper secondary and post-secondary non-tertiary education - ISCED levels 3 - 4	Tertiary education ISCED levels 5 - 6
EU-27	47,9	69,3	83,1
Belgium	40,1	65,1	82,4
Bulgaria	28,9	68,1	82,1
Czech Republic	23,2	71,9	83,9
Denmark	61,1	80,2	87,1
Germany	44,3	71,7	84,7
Estonia	32,2	72,8	86,9
Ireland	49,6	74	85,6
Greece	51,9	60,5	82,2
Spain	56,9	67,7	81,3
France	47,2	68,4	77,6
Italy	46,4	67,9	78,2
Cyprus	53,3	72,4	85,6
Latvia	35,6	72,7	86,9
Lithuania	24,5	68	87,8
Luxembourg	48,1	68,1	84,3
Hungary	27,6	65,1	81,2
Malta	46,2	73,2	83,3
Netherlands	58,4	76,7	86,2
Austria	49,6	74,8	85,5
Poland	23,3	58,3	81,7
Portugal	65,9	64,5	84,5
Romania	39,6	64,9	86,1
Slovenia	41,9	69,7	87,8
Slovakia	14,5	67,5	83,9
Finland	46	72,9	85
Sweden	53,3	79,2	86,2
United Kingdom	60,5	76,8	87,3
Norway	46,7	78	88,6

Source: Eurostat (tsdec430)

Data indicative for our analysis are related to variables that indicate relations among education, kinds of jobs and total employment. The data related to the part of those employed in EU-27 within the population who were aged between 15 and 64 years in 2006 accounted for 64.4 percent. The percentage is still far from the goals stipulated for 2010. The targeted 70 percent of employed was reached only in Denmark, The Netherlands, Austria, Sweden and UK. Significant discrepancy exists within the part of employed regarding the level of education. Therefore those educated to tertiary level participate with 83.1 percent, which is remarkably higher than 47.9 percent for those with a lower educational level (primary or lower secondary education) (Eurostat Yearbook 2008, p. 248). The average percentage of unemployment in the EU-27 for those who have the lowest secondary education was 10.1 percent in 2006, which is more than double compared to the percentage of unemployed with tertiary education (4.1%). This discrepancy in relation to unemployment was highest in Slovakia (44% compared to 2.7%) (Eurostat Yearbook 2008, p. 259).

Figure 1 Unemployment rates (among persons aged 25 - 59 years) by level of educational attainment, 2006.

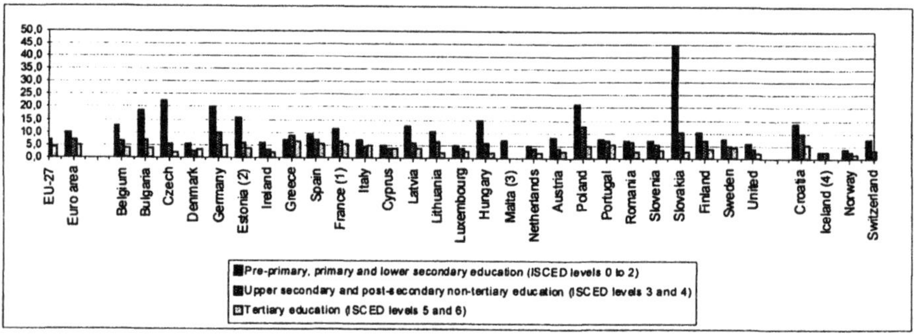

(1) Provisional.

(2) Pre-primary, primary and lower secondary, 2004; tertiary education, 2005.

(3) Upper secondary and post secondary non-tertiary education, and tertiary education, not available.

(4) Tertiary education, not available.

Source: Eurostat (tps00066)

Thus, the level of education is one of the key discrimination factors and it was noted that unemployment decreases as education increases, which is indicative for almost all member countries.

Development of Information and Communication Technology

Speaking of indicators of information and communication technology development, each of the EU countries has more telephone lines per capita than the countries in the wider region.

Figure 2 Internet access of households (% of all households)

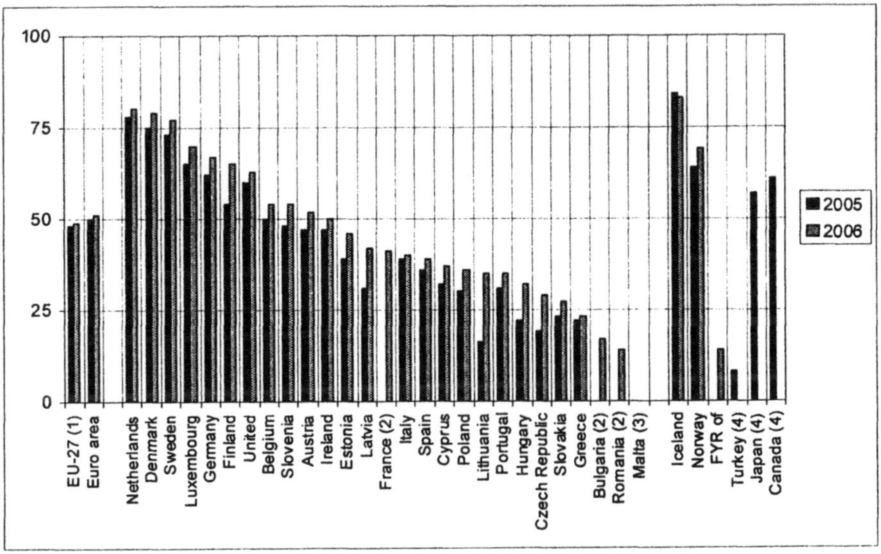

(1) EU-25 for 2005.

(2) Not available for 2005.

(3) Not available.

(4) Not available for 2006.

Source: Eurostat (tsiir031)

However, in the last two decades information and communication technologies (ICT) have become more available for the wider population. Thus, in 2006, almost half (49%) of all households in the EU-27 had Internet access (Eurostat Yearbook 2006, p. 483). The percentage of the population connected by traditional telephone lines varies from 89.13 percent (Denmark) to 41.2 percent (Ireland), while the average in the EU equals 56.31 percent. On the other hand, the percentage of the population with Internet access within the region is significantly lower. Croatia is one of the regional leaders (39.2%).

However, the EU itself invests a relatively small amount in ICT, if the investments are shown as a part of GDP. Investments in IT in the EU-27 amount to 2.7 percent of GDP compared to 3.4 percent in Japan or 3.3 percent in the USA (Eurostat Yearbook 2008, p. 484), countries that represent the main global competition to EU countries. It is closely related to the trends of development of new forms of work and their efficiency.

Figure 3 Information technology expenditure, 2006 (% of GDP)

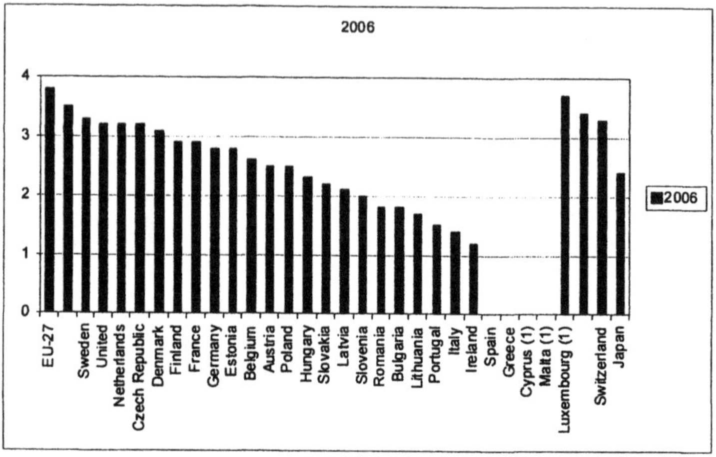

(1) Not available.

Source: Eurostat (tsiir071), European Information Technology Observatory (EITO)

Annual data on expenditure for IT hardware, equipment, software and other services as a percentage of GDP.

Conclusion

The main changes of the basic forms of work in the contemporary information and knowledge-based society are the result of numerous socio-economic factors. They occur as the subsequence of various socio-economic and historical aspects, predispositions and circumstances that significantly influence the creation of dominant individual characteristics of the particular society, making it impossible to simply state the coming of the post-modern era regardless of the waves of globalisation which contain the seed of technological acceleration and information revolution, the changes are differently reflected in many fields of social life. The analysis of socio-economic indicators related to the countries of the EU and the wider region indicates certain similarities and differences as consequences of the specific circumstances of development.

Knowledge and innovation become crucial for modelling jobs and new forms of work in contemporary society. The results of secondary analysis show that new forms of work in the EU area have their basis in educational standards and the strategy of the particular country regarding investments into science and new technologies. Depending on these indicators it is possible to conclude that countries, which usually invest more into science and education, are able to reduce unemployment by developing new forms of jobs that are now based on knowledge and technology. If knowledge presents one of the crucial constitutive characteristics of contemporary society, then production, reproduction, distribution and realisation of knowledge cannot be in the sphere of politics. Therefore the accent in the future will be how to monitor and control the knowledge that should lead towards the development of a knowledge policy resulting in the rapid growth of new knowledge in society as well as the influence on its development (Stehr 2001, p. 92).

References

Baily, C. (2008), 'Reverse intergenerational learning: a missed opportunity?' *AI & Society.* 23/1, pp. 111 - 115.

Beck, Ulrich (2001), *Što je globalizacija? Zablude globalizma-odgovori na globalizaciju,* Vizura, Zagreb.

Beck, Ulrich (2004), *Moć protiv moći u doba globalizacije,* Školska knjiga, Zagreb.

Bell, Daniel (2001), *The Future of Technology,* Pelanduk Publications, Subang Jaya.

Boehm, W./O. Lahodynsky/H. Biščević (2006), *EU for you! Kako funkcionira Europska unija.* Zagreb, Ministarstvo vanjskih poslova i europskih integracija RH i Ministarstvo znanosti, obrazovanja i športa RH.

Brodt, T. L./R. M. Verbung (2007), 'Managing mobile work-insights from European practice.' *New Technology, Work and Employ*ment, 22/1, pp. 53 - 64.

Brown, G. W. (2008), 'Globalization is What We make of it: Contemporary Globalization Theory and the Future Construction of Global Interconection', *Political Studies Review.* 6/1, pp. 42 - 53.

Carnoy, M./M. Castells (2001), 'Globalization, the knowledge society, and the Network State: Poulantzas at the millennium), *Global Networks: A Journal of Transnational Affairs.* 1/1, pp. 1 - 18.

Castells, M. (2000), *Uspon umreženog društva,* Golden Marketing, Zagreb.

Castells, M. (2002), *Moć identiteta*, Golden Marketing, Zagreb.

Commission of the European Communities (2008), *Commission staff working document. Progress towards the Lisbon objectives in education and training. Indicators and benchmarks.*

Dragun, A./R. Relja (2006), 'Akademska mobilnost studenata: Stavovi studenata Ekonomskog fakulteta u Splitu', *Revija za sociologiju,* 37/1 - 2, pp. 63 - 76.

Edgell, S. (2006), *The Sociology of Work. Continuity and Change in Paid and Unpaid Work,* Sage Publications, London.

Ennals, R./L. Stratton/N. Moujahid/S. Kovela, S. (2008), 'Global information technology and global citizenship education', *AI & Society,* 23/1, pp. 61 - 68.

European Commission (2006), *Employment in Europe,* Brussels.

Europe in Figures (2008), Eurostat Yearbook 2008, Brussels.

Exton, R./P. Totterdill (2008), 'Workplace innovation: bringing knowledge and pratice', *AI & Society,* 23/1, pp. 3 - 15.

Galić, B. (2000), 'Paradoksi globalizacije i multipolarni svijet', in Ivan Cifrić (ed.), *Znanost i društvene promjene,* Zagreb, HSD, FFZG Zavod za sociologiju, pp. 21 - 35.

Garača, Ž. (2004), *Poslovna informatika,* Split, Ekonomski fakultet.

Giddens, A. (2003), *How Globalization is Reshaping Our Lives. Ran a Way Word,* Routledge, New York.

Gille, Z./Ó. S. Riain (2002), 'Global Ethnography', *Annual Review of Sociology*, 28, pp. 271 - 275.

Grint, K (1933), *The Sociology of Work: An Introduction*, Polity Press, Cambridge.

Kostyukhin, A. A. (2005), 'How Information Revolution Influences Development Prospects of Modern Society', *Military Thought*, 14/3, pp. 207 - 211.

Leicht, K. T. (2001), 'The Future of Work', in Y. W. Bradshaw/J. F. Healey/R. Smith (eds.), *Sociology for a New Century*, Sage Publications, Boston, pp. 421 - 422.

Lyotard, J. (2005), *Postmoderno stanje*, Ibis grafika, Zagreb.

Malone, T. W./R. J. Laubacher (1998), 'The Dawn of the E-lance Economy', *Harward Business Review*, September - October, 76/5, pp. 144 - 152.

Malone, T. (2004), *The Future of Work: How the New Order of Business Will Shape your Organization, Your Management Style, and Your Life*, Harvard Business School Press, Boston/MA.

Moore, J. E./S. E. Yager./M. Summer/G. B. Crow (2001), 'Facilitating career changes into IT', *Communications of the ACM*, 44/7, pp. 70 - 73.

Pérez Pérez, M./A. Martínez Sanchez/M. P. De Luis Carnicer/M. J. Vela Jiménez (2002), 'Knowledge tasks and teleworking: A taxonomy model of feasibility adoption', *Journal of Knowledge Management*, 6/3, pp. 272 - 284.

Powell, W. W./L. Smith-Doerr (1994), 'Networks and Economic Life', in N. J. Smelser/R. Swedberg (eds.), *The Handbook of Economic Sociology*, Princeton University Press, New Jersey, pp. 368 - 402.

Relja, R./A. Dragun (2005), 'Želje i razlozi studenata za uključenjem u programe akademske mobilnosti', in N. Šćukanec (ed.), *Stipendije.info:uloga stipendija u povećanju akadamske mobilnosti*, Studentski informacijski centar u Zagrebu, Zagreb, pp. 23 - 30.

Rubinson, R./I. Browne (1994), 'Education and the Economy', in N. J. Smelser/R. Swedberg (eds.), *The Handbook of Economic Sociology*, Princeton University Press, New Jersey, pp. 581 - 599.

Scholte, J. A. (2000), *Globalization. A Critical Introduction*, Palgrave, New York.

Stehr, N. (2001), 'A world made of knowledge', *Society*, November/December, pp. 89 - 92.

Šporer, Ž. (2004), 'Knowledge-based Economy and Social Capital in Central and Eastern European Countries', in J. Švarc/J. Lažnjak/Ž. Šporer/D. Polšek (eds.), *Transition Countries in Knowledge Society. Socioeconomic analysis*, Institut društvenih znanosti Ivo Pilar, Zagreb, pp. 129 - 166.

The World Bank (2002), *Building Knowledge Economies: Opportunities and Challenges for EU Accession Countries*, Final report of the Knowledge Economy Forum, Paris. Feb. 19 - 22, 2002, The WB and the World Bank Institute, mimeo.

UNESCO (2005), *Towards Knowledge Societies*, UNESCO World Report, UNESCO, Paris.

Willinsky, J. (2005), 'Just say know? Schooling the knowledge society', *Educational Theory* 55/1, pp. 97 - 111.

Yager, S. E./J. F. Schrage/R. L. Berry (2002), 'Preparing end user support specialists', *Journal of Education for Business*, 78/2, pp. 92 - 96.

Zakaria, N. (2000), 'The Effects of Cross-cultural Training in the Process of Acculturation of the Global Workforce', *International Journal of Manpower*, 21/6, pp. 492 - 510.

Internet sources:

[http://www.efzg.hr]

[http://www.europa.eu.int]

Jurica Šimurina – Jurica Pavičić – Morana Fudurić

Economics and Business International Programme (EBIP) – The Exchange of Knowledge and Experience[1]

Introduction

The exchange of knowledge and experience and the means of delivery have become buzz words in the academic community. Almost every school is aiming at offering as much as possible to current and prospective students, thus giving them a specific incentive to go to a particular school. The more dynamic and innovative the exchange is, the bigger the chances of a student choosing that very institution and, more importantly, recommending it later on. The major influencing factor on the Croatian higher education system, as well as on the education systems of the neighbouring countries is the European Union and its regulations (i.e. the Bologna Process). The basic concepts of the process, among other things, also include the notion of greater student mobility within the Union. In order to ensure the former, faculties across Croatia were forced to adapt their programmes and courses to the stated EU requirements (ECTS points, lecture and seminar hours, course syllabus, number of students per group etc.) (Barić 2001) But all the efforts concerning student mobility have a major pitfall – aside from being seen as a great opportunity, they also represent a threat: The discrepancy between the number of incoming and of outgoing students can, other than financially, harm the faculty image. In this context, marketing represents one of the most important tools a faculty can use, although many public faculties (along with most non profit organizations in Croatia) abhor the usage of any marketing activities (Pavičić 2003). Note here that the emphasis is on *marketing*, not *advertising* activities. Gibbs and Knapp (2002) suggest four key areas where marketing can help in shaping the future provision of education, namely the complexity of the offering, the complicated social role of educational institutions, the increasing importance of financial performance and an approach to the market that sees students as informed customers.

The faculty therefore has a lot of room for improvement especially in the area of the product or offering (aside from knowledge, the faculty has to work on the quality of all other "supporting" services that add value to the core product and influence the student's or customer's decision making process) and in the area of market approach (developing new programmes and courses that best

---

[1] This contribution was presented as an invited lecture to the *Second International Symposium "Knowledge Region: The Alps-Adriatic Challenges"*, held on 28 - 29 September 2007, in Klagenfurt (Austria).

serve students' needs and wants). This is where strategic plans and partnerships come into the picture. Aside from partnerships among universities, which will be discussed later in the paper, faculties should also consider strategic marketing partnerships with publishers, global corporations etc. (Gibbs/Knapp 2002; Bok 2003). In the US alone there are over 4000 corporate universities, far more than in Europe, and none in Croatia and neighbouring countries.

The aim of the EBIP (Economics and Business International Programme) programme therefore, is to elevate the education and exchange process to a higher level, offering not only to students, but also to the faculty members, an opportunity to gain knowledge through international contacts and experience. This article, thus, explains the basic concepts of the EBIP, its advantages, disadvantages and implementation issues, followed by authors' recommendations for future growth and development.

The Basic Concepts of the EBIP

EBIP is the international programme at the Faculty of Economics and Business, University of Zagreb. The programme offers a variety of courses in all areas of business and economics, but does not have a separate diploma or a full 4-year programme. The reason why there is no full 4-year programme lies in the fact that the faculty offers a number of majors in many different categories of economics and business, and simply does not have the capacity to perform a full 4-year EBIP programme for all majors. However, an improvement is on the horizon. Recently, the Faculty Council accepted a new regular programme for business and economic studies. The major change is that there are only two courses of study, economics and business, in a regular 4-year programme. This way, the EBIP was altered as well. The EBIP will become a separate study programme with a complete 4-year programme in business studies. Subjects covered by economics will be available as electives; however, there will be no separate programme for economics, at least not for now. By doing this, the Faculty of Economics and Business will become the first school in Croatia to have a separate 4-year programme with a separate degree in the English language.

The programme itself was initiated in 1998, and was not exclusively designed for foreign students, but was open to all students wishing to study in English language. This principle is kept up to this date. In order to become more appealing to foreign and domestic students, the School plans to increase the number of elective courses, and the number of visiting lecturers from other universities, primarily from Europe and the US, but from other parts of the world as well.

Exchange Categories

If one would look at the programme from an organizational point of view, there are three major exchange categories that emerge, and need to be successfully co-ordinated to ensure the functioning of the entire programme. These are: faculty exchange, student exchange, and institutional arrangements.

By faculty exchange we mean the exchange of knowledge and experience among faculty members. Here is what the process looks like: Mr. Martin Medeiros is a professor at the Institute of European Studies, UC Berkeley, USA. The Institute has an arrangement with the Faculty of Economics and Business, Zagreb, Croatia, so Professor Medeiros comes to Zagreb to teach a group of 50 students Microeconomics for one semester. He lives at the Faculty premises, and is paid a monthly fee for his work. During his stay in Zagreb, aside from his work with students, he exchanges experience in communication with the faculty members. After final grades are out, he goes back to the US. Based on this short example, one can conclude what are the main areas of interest in this exchange category: teaching methodology, departments and courses and their comparison, funding, and, finally, organizational structure.

The second category has to do with the exchange of students among schools. Croatian students can choose a semester or two for study abroad, as can foreign students. As for the student structure at the EBIP (Figure 1), there is still a majority of Croatian (domestic) students, who prefer to study in English for a number of reasons: it is an element of comparative advantage; visiting lecturers tend to have a different approach to lecturing, and finally, the size of classes, which are limited to 50 students.

Figure 1 EBIP student structure per academic year

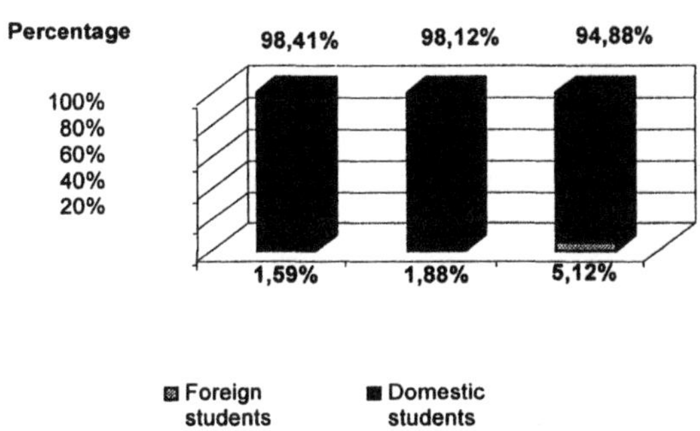

Source: Faculty of Economics and Business, EBIP statistics

Figure 1 shows a clear increase in the *relative* number of foreign students enrolled in the EBIP, especially in the 2006/2007 academic year (5.12%), compared to the previous year (1.88%). This is definitely a good sign for the school and can lead to new arrangements with other schools across, mostly, Europe and the US. If we look at the foreign student structure (Figure 2), some conclusions can be drawn concerning the citizenship of the students attending the programme.

Figure 2 Foreign student structure by country

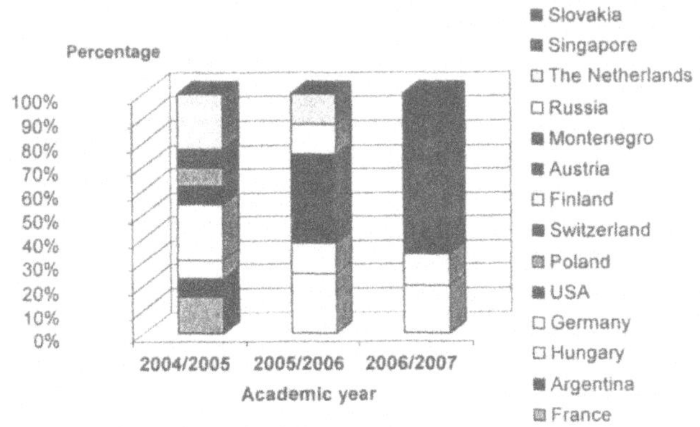

Source: Faculty of Economics and Business, EBIP statistics

Figure 2 shows that students from Austria, Germany, Hungary, Slovakia and Montenegro constantly come to study to Croatia. The reason behind this is quite simple: Croatia and Germany have a very good relationship with Croatia, and, in addition, there are a lot of Croats studying in these two countries. In addition, Hungary and Austria share a lot of history with Croatia (all three countries formed a part of the Habsburg Monarchy). Montenegro, aside from the similarities in the language, also took part in Croatia's history: both countries were part of Yugoslavia. Slovakia might be the only country that is a bit harder to explain: the authors assume it is due to language and culture similarities between the two countries, and Slovakia was also a part of the Habsburg Monarchy.

The explanation for other countries of origin brings us to the final exchange category: institutional arrangements. Perhaps the simplest way to account for other countries presented in Figure 2 is to provide a list of schools with bilateral agreements:

1. Wirtschaftsuniversitaet, Vienna, Austria
2. Fraunhofer Institute for Systems and Innovation Research ISI, Karlsruhe
3. Fachhochschule, Vorarlberg, Austria
4. School of Economics and Business, Sarajevo, BiH
5. Jyvaskyla Polytechnic, Finland

6. Economic Faculty, University "Sv. Kliment Ohridski", Bitola, FYR Macedonia
7. Leeds Metropolitan University, UK
8. Institute of European Studies, UC Berkeley, USA
9. Ekonomski fakultet, Maribor, Slovenia

All the faculty websites (as compared to the Faculty of Economics and Business Zagreb website) provide similar information to prospective (foreign) students, with Leeds Metropolitan University, Economic Faculty Maribor and Wirtschaftsuniversitaet in Vienna that stand out in terms of providing timely, clear, accurate and well structured information on: pre-arrival, scholarships and fees, application procedure, courses and programmes, accommodation, health insurance, partner universities, directions to the university, and finally, useful information on the city the faculty is located in and the surrounding area. The previously mentioned faculties, universities and schools also have a significant number of partner faculties (Maribor over 80, Leeds Metropolitan over 200) and very well developed exchange systems (undergraduate and postgraduate level, teacher and student exchange, summer schools etc.) that can serve as a useful benchmark. But before engaging in the process of finding the best practices, the Faculty has to be able to determine the main issues and problems the programme is facing or might face in the near future.

Advantages, Disadvantages and Implementation Issues

In order to provide a clear overview, advantages, disadvantages and implementation issues have been compiled in Table 1.

Table 1 Advantages, disadvantages and implementation issues of the EBIP programme

Advantages	Multi-level exchange Development of the schooling system Growing number of courses offered
Disadvantages	Decreasing number of students Decreasing number of foreign lecturers Neglecting the programme: • Insufficient co-operation among universities • Insufficient promotion of the programme • Poor operational support at the faculty level
Implementation issues	No separate diploma for students (before 2008/2009) No full 4-year programme (before 2008/2009) Accommodation for foreign students Low rights of foreign lecturers

The multi-level exchange was explained when describing the three exchange categories. The development of the system enables the programme to grow and become more important, if not *the* most important "product" offered by the School. In addition, combined with a growing number of courses offered, it has a positive effect on the School image.

Neglect of the programme, visible through insufficient co-operation among universities and insufficient promotion has led to a decreasing number of students and visiting lecturers. This does not come as a surprise, since there is little or no attention, time and other resources devoted to inter-faculty correspondence and co-operation. This is the main reason for the decreasing number of students, and, especially, foreign lecturers which are greatly appreciated. If you do not water the plant, it will not grow, and that is the case with EBIP.

Therefore, most of the issues mentioned in Table 1 have everything to do with faculty capacity, especially the previously addressed issue of the full 4-year programme, and foreign student accommodation. The Ministry of Science, Education and Sport, however, provides a place in student dormitories for international exchange students who come to study in Zagreb within an official exchange programme (CEEPUS network or bilateral agreements between University of Zagreb and a university abroad). All other international students need to find housing by themselves.

For the location of student dormitories, students are encouraged to visit a student centre web site: www.sczg.hr/lokacije.html. As for those unable to obtain accommodation in a student dormitory, there are two youth hostels in Zagreb: Omladinski Youth Hostel and Ravnice Youth Hostel. Alternatively, students can rent their own apartment, which does not come cheap.

Every student of the University of Zagreb is given an identification card (x-card or "iksica"). The card enables you to have subsidized meals in student restaurants (there is one at the School) and buy local public transportation tickets with a student discount. International students who have the right to "iksica" are CEEPUS exchange students and students coming to Zagreb within a bilateral exchange at the university level. International students, who come to study in Zagreb as "free movers" (on an individual basis, no exchange agreement at the university level) or within exchange programmes at faculty level, are not eligible for "iksica". This is the way the School tends to compensate for not providing on-campus accommodation, common to other European countries and Schools, but this unfortunate situation will change as new campuses are being built across the country. However, the construction of campuses is a long term project which will take several years to complete. The separate diploma issue can and will easily be fixed, but the issue of the inferior rights of foreign lecturers will require more work. Basically, because of the current system, foreign lecturers do not have the right to formally enter grades, which means the student is left without reference as to who the lecturer was (it might as well be Al Ries or Phillip Kotler, the student has no evidence to confirm that they took their courses). Nevertheless, all these issues can be fixed, and turned into advantages. Surely, the overall changes in the Croatian education system are a big help.

Conclusion

The international study programme (EBIP), available at the Faculty of Economics and Business, University of Zagreb, is one of a kind at the University. Only the Medical School at the University of Zagreb had a comparative programme of study. However, as of school year 2008/2009, our School is introducing a full four year programme in Business Administration.

The difficulties associated with the introduction of a programme in English language range from practical and administrative to overall acceptance by the faculty members. At the beginning of the programme, there was stiff opposition, however, this problem was alleviated in subsequent years, and the programme became widely accepted. Today, the programme is well established, with more and more foreign students applying for the programme. It is expected in the near future, with the new four year programme, that more foreign student will apply and complete the programme. Also, the programme is essential for student and faculty exchange programmes outlined within the Bologna Process. Thus, the programme will be a flagship programme that will foster exchange, quality and the European future of Croatia.

References

Barić, V. (2001), 'Financiranje obrazovanja u Hrvatskoj u politici strukturnog prilagođavanja i približavanja europskim obrazovnim standardima', *Ekonomija*, Vol. 8/No. 1, pp. 409 - 434.

Bok, D. (2003), *Universities in the marketplace: The Commercialization of Higher Education*, Princeton University Press, Princeton/USA.

Gibbs, P./M. Knapp (2002), *Marketing Higher and Further Education (Creating Success)*, Stylus Publishing Inc., Sterling/USA.

Pavičić, Jurica (2003), *Strategija marketinga neprofitnih organizacija*, Masmedia, Zagreb.

Internet sources:

Ekonomski fakultet Maribor, Slovenia [http://www.uni-mb.si/podrocje.aspx?id=0&langID=1033] retrieved on 10.06.2008.

Ekonomski fakultet Zagreb, Croatia [http://www.efzg.hr] retrieved on 10.06.2008.

Institute of European Studies UC Berkeley, USA [http://ies.berkeley.edu/visitingscholars/] retrieved on 13.06.2008.

Jyvaskyla Polytechnic, Finland [http://195.148.135.6/internet/jamk.nsf] retrieved on 10.06. 2008.

Leeds Metropolitan University, UK [http://www.lmu.ac.uk/] retrieved on 12.06.2008.

School of Economics and Business Sarajevo, BiH [http://www.efsa.unsa.ba] retrieved on 10. 06.2008.
Studentski centar Zagreb website [http://www.sczg.hr/lokacije.html] retrieved on 05.04.2008.
Wirtschaftsuniversitaet Vienna, Austria [http://www.wu-wien.ac.at/portal/english/units/] retrieved on 02.06.2008.

Vladimir Gnjidić – Nino Gabelica – Miše Kutleša

Educational Management and Marketing Orientation of Croatian Elementary Schools – Results of Preliminary Empirical Research

Management of Educational Institutions

Management as a normative activity involves work and operations that are goal-directed, as it strives to ensure organizational performance and desired outcomes. It includes planning and problem solving, working with human and material resources, and directing operations within the context of internal influences, environmental demands, and normative role requirements (Immegart 1994).

Although the school principal role was always recognized as complex, it has either not always been defined in terms of *educational management,* or has been overly influenced by the management concepts 'borrowed' from the industrial (for-profit) environment (Bell 1991). Several researchers have written about the discontinuous and demanding nature of principal's work (see Bridges 1982 for a somewhat older review of classical theoretical studies and Hallinger/Heck 1996 for a similar overview of empirical studies related to the effectiveness of the principal's role) and/or of those belonging to the educational administration in general (Macpherson 1984). Principals have felt a need for professional development to help them perform their onerous and ambiguous role successfully (Johnson 1994). On the other hand, however specific the arena in which management processes are being applied, the universal theoretical approach to management states that five 'generic' functions (i.e. planning, organizing, human resource management, leadership and controlling) are always being carried out by administrators/managers (Buble 2006), although the context and the actual managerial roles may be changing. Of those functions, three (planning, organizing and controlling) may be considered as those related to "hard" organizational factors, while human resource management and leadership are "soft", i.e. people-related.

For instance, in the educational setting, literature has documented the changed role of school principals, which is reflected by increasing pressures related to high stakes testing and accountability, the increased role of management, altered relationships with community, dilemmas related to school choice, etc. (Whitaker 2003). Despite their sometimes positive impact, these role changes have led to an increase in overall workloads and have contributed to increased stress for principals, pressures to be more accountable for student achievement, particularly student test scores, etc. (ibid.). These may even lead to so-called 'principal burnout' (Whitaker 1996).

Several school characteristics positively impact student learning and promote effective education as a value, with one of those being leadership by the school principal, being dedicated to obtaining quality performance from teachers and students alike (Weller/Hartley 1994). Leadership is a discretionary activity involving strategic choice or decision-making directed toward improvement, development, change and making a difference. Leadership is important in developing effective, innovative schools and in facilitating quality teaching and learning (Dinham et al. 2004). The importance of the principal's role as the instructional leader and the direct relationship on changing instructional practice to improve student performance has been researched extensively (Quinn 2002).

For some, the principal is considered to be the single most important factor related a school's success or failure (Calabrese/Zepeda 1999). Other authors would rather not overgeneralize the impact of the principal in relation to indicators, such as student achievement in defining school success. Most, however, agree that principals need to be effective leaders (ibid.), with the emphasis being placed on democratic leadership. In the school environment, this implies both being active toward staff and other stakeholders, as well as influencing the school's development agenda Johansson 2004). Rather than being "strong" and decisive, effective school leadership is intensely interpersonal, involving working with individuals and teams to transform educational processes (Dinham et al. 2004).

On the basis of Jantzi and Leithwood's work (as cited by Quinn 2002), there are six dimensions critical in the practice of leadership including:

(1) identifying and articulating a vision;
(2) fostering the acceptance of group goals;
(3) providing individualized support;
(4) intellectual stimulation;
(5) providing an appropriate model; and
(6) high performance expectations.

Principals must also deal with competing expectations and with the dilemmas inherent in simultaneously administering, supervising instruction, being accessible, delegating, accepting responsibility, etc. (Johnson 1994). A recent body of evidence has underscored role changes in regard to the functions of the principal related not only to leading school staff, but also managing relationships with the external stakeholders, such as parents and community (Whitaker 2003).

Marketing Orientation of Educational Institutions: Theoretical Determinants

The research on school marketing has been receiving increasing attention in recent years as more and more researchers have illuminated marketing mechanisms within educational institutions, including schools, colleges and universities (Oplatka/Hemsley-Brown 2007). In that sense, the introduction of educational markets into compulsory education in many Western countries throughout the

1980s and 1990s has led to more competitive environments for schools (Oplatka/Hemsley-Brown 2004). Schools, such as many other non-profit organizations, therefore need to become more business-like and responsible for their own financing. In this context, schools need "a new breed of senior manager – one who is looking outwards to seek opportunities to enhance his or her school, to gain the competitive edge and to invest money from the school budget to generate income" (Bennet/Gabriel 1999). In order to achieve these goals, school principals should accept implementation of the marketing concept, aside their managerial orientation, as implementation of the marketing concept enhances the competitive strength of a non-profit organization (Pavičić et al. 2000).

One immediate issue is the fact that the "senior manager" (i.e. school principal) should be able to understand the benefits for the school's overall results coming from implementation of the marketing concept. However, there are instances where school staff has a negative perception of what school marketing is, with this implicit negative meaning relating to their narrow definition and understanding of marketing. Frequently, marketing is perceived as a synonym for "selling", with an emphasis on advertising, promotional activities, public relations, glossy messages, poaching and persuasion (Oplatka/Hemsley-Brown 2004). Hence, the perception of the marketing concept greatly relies on the managerial capabilities and characteristics of the senior management.

An individual head's overall managerial orientation influences his or her perception and behaviour in a variety of fields and can be described as falling into one of four possible categories, as outlined by Bennet and Gabriel (1999):

1. Autocratic (task-centred)
2. Consultative
3. Democratic (people-centred), or
4. Innovative.

While autocrats focus on task leadership, taking the initiative in developing activities, defining problems and suggesting solutions, democrats conversely focus on social-emotional leadership (ibid.).

The establishment of educational markets urged schools to incorporate various forms of marketing perspective into their strategy in order to successfully recruit students in the new competitive environment (Oplatka/Hemsley-Brown 2004), the structure of which is directly related to the interference developing among the individual subjects who might be considered as competitors in realizing a comparable mission (Pavičić et al. 2000). Although education is usually being conceptualized as a non-profit activity, marketing in education can be defined in a similar way to the for-profit marketing. For instance, Kotler and Fox (1995, p. 6) defined educational marketing in terms of "the analysis, planning, implementation and control of carefully formulated programmes designed to bring about voluntary exchanges of values with a target market to achieve organizational objectives".

The traditional orientation starts from the assumption that a non-profit organization should be oriented toward the realization of the social benefits, i.e. toward the fulfilment of its own mission, which would mean that the interests of external stakeholders are not (so) important. Nevertheless, such an approach would be contradictory, when applied in practice, both regarding the management of non-profit organizations, as well as regarding the irrationalities in their financing, which would certainly bring about problems in managing relationships with benefactors and beneficiaries (Pavičić et al. 2000). This applies to schools, as well: The survival of many schools is dependent on their capacity to maintain or increase the school's "market share" of pupils, results and resources and, in general, on the success of school's marketing (Oplatka/Hemsley-Brown 2004). Of all the marketing activities, a significant role is attributed to the relationship marketing approach in devising and implementing marketing plans/strategies in schools (ibid.).

It is widely held that a relationship marketing approach begins with a commitment to *marketing orientation (MO)* and to developing a customer-driven organizational culture, which focuses on the quality of the service. Research into market orientation has been extensive in all kinds of different environments throughout the 1990s and 2000s (Pulendran et al. 2002). The past studies can be divided into two streams: (a) those examining the relationship between market orientation and business performance (which generally link the market-oriented behaviour with better performance) and (b) those trying to identify the characteristics of the market oriented firms/organizations (ibid.).

There is also a difference in the usage of terms *marketing orientation* and *market orientation*, with the term *marketing orientation* initially referring to the implementation of the marketing concept, being focused on consumer needs. *Market orientation*, on the other hand, is the more recently utilized term for instituting the marketing concept. A market-oriented approach is more likely to be accepted by non-marketing departments (Lafferty/Hult 1999).

In the marketing area, market orientation is becoming one of the most important factors for explaining organizational performance (O'Cass/Viet Ngo 2006). However, there are alternative theoretical standpoints related to the nature of market orientation, arguing either that the market orientation is a set of behavioural activities (e.g. Kohli/Jaworski 1990), or that it is an aspect of an organization's culture (e.g. Narver/Slater 1990). In general, the term market orientation implies an expanded focus, paying balanced attention to both customers and competitors by some researchers, or "just" being customer oriented (according to other authors).

As Kohli and Jaworski (1990, p. 13) defined, *"a market orientation appears to provide a unifying focus for the efforts and projects of individuals and departments within the organization, thereby leading to superior performance"*. In practice, market orientation influences the behaviour of staff, as it provides a better environment for information gathering and analysing, as well as responding effectively to the findings emerging from such information (Hunt/Morgan, as cited by O'Cass/Viet Ngo 2006). When applied to the field of education, schools adopting the marketing orientation concept should be more responsive to needs of children, their parents and the community in general. The focus points in these schools are parents and children, and their need satisfaction is of high priority and importance (Oplatka/Hemsley-Brown 2004).

Market orientation can be, thus, described as philosophy of the organization and/or its basic value and, therefore, more a cultural rather than a behavioural phenomenon (Pulendran et al. 2002), regardless of the specific characteristics of the culture (Lafferty/Hult 1999). It is believed to directly affect the organizational performance both in for-profit and non-profit settings (as discussed by Caruana et al. 1998, for the case of universities). Many empirical studies have tried to establish the relationship between the degree of marketing orientation adoption and performance (e.g. Narver/Slater 1989). They have produced significant empirical evidence that such a relationship actually exists (Avlontis/Gounaris 1999).

Deshpande and Webster (as cited by O'Cass/Viet Ngo 2006) argue that market orientation, in the form of customer orientation, is considered as an aspect of organizational culture that is created and maintained to provide individual norms for behaviour within organizations. Therefore, the degree of marketing orientation could be used to explain the propensity to innovate, as the term "customer orientation", according to Deshpande, describes a specific set of beliefs that puts the customers' interests first (Avlontis/Gounaris 1999). Nevertheless, marketing orientation as an element of the school culture extends beyond customer orientation (Oplatka/Hemsley-Brown 2007).

On the basis of the work by Narver and Slater (as cited by Oplatka /Hemsley-Brown 2007), three related components of marketing orientation can be suggested for schools in order to help educational administrators, managers and teachers to understand the school and its environment, and may also provide them with norms for behaviour (ibid.):

(1) Customer orientation,
(2) Competitor orientation *and*
(3) Inter-functional coordination.

While the first two elements of the marketing orientation put an emphasis on collecting and processing information related to customer preferences and competitor capabilities, the third element is related to dissemination of the obtained marketing insights within the entire organization, in order to achieve the organizational objectives (ibid.).

Empirical Research of a Relationship Among the Managerial Functions and Marketing Orientation in Croatian Elementary Schools

The quality of management functions, performed by the school principal, can be described as the 'internal' determinant of the school effectiveness, while the effectiveness of its relationships with the environment are primarily determined by the school's marketing & public relations efforts which are, in practice, also relying on the qualities of the school principal. Therefore, a comprehensive research project, dealing with the analysis of the Croatian elementary school managers' competencies was carried out in 2006. It had multiple components, including: (a) assessment of principals' managerial skills/capabilities, (b) analysis of marketing practices adopted by elementary school principals (including specific fields, such as market research, public relations, marketing orientation of the Croatian elementary schools, etc.) and (c) performance analysis. As only partial research results of the project have been published[1], this paper will try to report on the managerial practices in Croatian elementary schools, as well as establish the existence of potential relationships among these practices and the marketing orientation of the school.

Namely, as the preliminary results of this research project suggest, some performance indicators are even being *negatively* correlated with some components of the marketing orientation construct[2]. The authors therefore wanted to take a 'second look' at the data and identify the potential sources of inadequate management/marketing practices. The notion of a *"virtuous/vicious circle"* comes into mind as a possible explanation for the situation in Croatian elementary schools (as a part of the non-profit sector in the country): The lack of knowledge/skills in a specific area might be reflected by a similar situation in a related area (and *vice versa*). Such a standpoint justifies the analysis of interdependencies between management and marketing practices, in order to establish whether an example of such a "vicious" circle has been in play here.

The convenience sample of 210 elementary school principals, attending the annual principals' conference in 2006, was used as a dataset for the project. Such

---

[1] Cf.: Alfirević/Pavičić/Kutleša (2008), 'Organizacijske performanse i orijentacija hrvatskih osnovnih škola prema temeljnim ciljnim skupinama' (Organizational performance and orientation of Croatian elementary schools toward target groups), *Ekonomska istraživanja*, Vol. 21/No. 3, pp. 88 - 99. Some preliminary results have also been reported by the same authors at the professional conference Decentralization of Croatian educational system, organized by Faculty of Economics Split and the County Office of the state administration, held in Split, in April 2007.

[2] As reported in the previously mentioned study.

an approach has its obvious limitations, related to the possible biases, as the sampling procedure was rather simplified and the resulting sample provided only indicative (instead of representative) results. However, as the project was only intended to provide the first empirical directives in the further research of management and marketing in Croatian elementary schools, the methodological limitations can be considered satisfactory. Out of 210 distributed questionnaires, 204 were returned, which have been coded and entered into the SPSS software package.

Two separate constructs – *realization of selected management functions in elementary schools* and their *marketing orientation (MO)* were measured simultaneously. Marketing orientation of Croatian elementary schools was measured by a well-described and often used instrument, initially developed by Hooley, Saunders and Piercy (1998), which has also been previously applied to the Croatian context (see Renko/Pavičić/Alfirević 2001, for the case of Croatian public libraries). The instrument measures five dimensions (assessment of user satisfaction, orientation toward competition, long-term orientation of the organization, effectiveness of internal organization and user-centered organizational culture). The assessment of each dimension is based on several indicators, subjectively measured by respondents on Likert scales with five levels of (dis)agreement. The final degree of MO is calculated as a sum of the mean values for five dimensions of the MO construct. Final results of MO scores, for each of the five components, as well as for the entire MO construct, are presented in Table 1. Taking into account that the obtained value of 65.1 indicates a moderate degree of overall MO, these findings are rather satisfactory.

Table 1 MO construct scores in Croatian elementary schools

MO dimension	Theoretical minimum and maximum values of the scale	Average value (assessment of the individual MO dimension)	Standard deviation
1. Assessment of user satisfaction	5 - 25	10.4	3.02
2. Orientation toward competition	4 - 20	13.96	2.82
3. Long-term orientation of the organization	3 - 15	10.99	1.84
4. Effectiveness of internal organization (from the users' perspective)	4 - 20	15.19	2.19
5. User-centered organizational culture	4 - 20	14.56	2.82
6. Value of the overall MO measure		**65,1**	

On the other hand, *managerial practices* applicable for the practice of elementary school principals have been identified on account of several preliminary in-depth interviews with the practicing principals of Croatian schools. Those have been further refined on the basis of the previously described secondary sources and used to design a separate section of the research instrument, containing several most relevant items for measuring each of the five managerial functions (i.e. planning, organizing, human resource management, leadership and controlling). Unfortunately, the obtained results related to the realization of the two "soft" managerial functions have demonstrated that the initial selection of items for assessment of human resource management and leadership were inadequate. Although this will be accounted for in the course of future research, the currently available empirical results are, thus, restricted to the measurement of "hard" managerial functions.

The *planning function* of school principals has been conceptualized according to the development of plans related to different relevant stakeholders, with the resulting section of the questionnaire containing seven items. Realization of *organizing (as a function of management)* has been conceptualized in a particularly simplified manner, as suggested by several practicing elementary school principals during the in-depth interviews. Although this may be limiting for further analysis, a single item with a simplified description, related to scheduling and coordination of individual activities performed within the school, was used for this purpose. Assessment of the *controlling function* of school principals included checks on the realization of previously scheduled activities and their effectiveness, as well as controlling of financial and other relevant resources, resulting in four items used in the final research instrument. Tables 2 - 4 demonstrate the values of these indicators.

Table 2 Realization of the planning function in Croatian elementary schools

		Frequency	Percent	Valid Percent	Cumulative Percent
Number of relevant items	0	1	0,5	0,5	0,5
	1	1	0,5	0,5	1,0
	2	7	3,4	3,4	4,4
	3	19	9,3	9,3	13,7
	4	13	6,4	6,4	20,1
	5	36	17,6	17,6	37,7
	6	71	34,8	34,8	72,5
	7	56	27,5	27,5	**100,0**
	Total	**204**	**100,0**	**100,0**	

The obtained results can be interpreted as *relatively encouraging*, as both planning (cf. Table 2) and controlling (cf. Table 4) seem to be realized by performing multiple relevant activities, while majority of the responding principals (88.7%)

also practice organizing by employing, at least, fundamental principles of scheduling and coordinating activities of individual employees.

Table 3 Realization of the organizing function in Croatian elementary schools

		Frequency	Percent	Valid Percent	Cumulative Percent
Number of relevant items	0	23	11,3	11,3	11,3
	1	181	88,7	88,7	100,0
	Total	204	100,0	100,0	

Although the major "hard" managerial responsibilities/functions seem to be performed by addressing a highly appropriate scope of relevant activities, a problem may be identified in the *association of managers with the realization of operative activities*. Namely, managers are, in general, supposed to create the adequate organizational climate and provide both resources and support to the staff performing operative work. This is accomplished by performing the managerial functions in an appropriate manner and methodical development of organizational resources/capabilities, instead of "jumping into" the operative work and continuously "fixing" the organizational weaknesses (cf. Buble 2006). Such a short-term orientation does not seem to be a novelty for the Croatian non-profit sector as a whole, as demonstrated by results of another empirical project (Alfirević/Gabelica 2007).

Table 4 Realization of the controlling function in Croatian elementary schools

		Frequency	Percent	Valid Percent	Cumulative Percent
Number of relevant items	0	8	3,9	3,9	3,9
	1	11	5,4	5,4	9,3
	2	33	16,2	16,2	25,5
	3	57	27,9	27,9	53,4
	4	95	46,6	46,6	100,0
	Total	204	100,0	100,0	

Accounting for a high possibility of such a "fire-fighting" orientation among the managers of elementary schools (as such a result has already been obtained by a previous study), four typical short-term activities, oriented toward "fixing" the current problems, have been included in the questionnaire. Those items have also been developed on the basis of the previous in-depth interviews, which have suggested that most common are different forms of required routine reporting toward external stakeholders (two items) and performance of operative activities that can not be delegated, either due to the deficient human resource capabilities (one item), or due to the inadequate scheduling, time management, or another inadequate managerial practice (one item). Table 5 illustrates the obtained results, with an alarming 31.4 percent of elementary school principals performing three and 6.9 percent performing all four groups of "fire-fighting" activities.

Table 5 "Fire-fighting" managerial activities in Croatian elementary schools

		Frequency	Percent	Valid Percent	Cumulative Percent
	0	12	5,9	5,9	5,9
	1	67	32,8	32,8	38,7
	2	47	23,0	23,0	61,8
	3	64	31,4	31,4	93,1
	4	14	6,9	6,9	100,0
	Total	204	100,0	100,0	

Correlation analysis, presented by Table 6, has been performed by applying the traditional Pearson correlation coefficient. It reveals several groups of highly significant clusters of relationships (mostly at the 0.01 level), but *with mixed overall findings*. Realization of each of the three "hard" managerial functions (planning, organizing, controlling) is related to the other two, but *there is also a significant association of moderate strength among all these functions and operative/"fire fighting" activities of elementary school principals*, which suggests that there is, at best, an unsystematic and somewhat mixed practice of educational management. In addition, *most components of the marketing orientation (MO) construct are interrelated*, as demonstrated by the significant correlation of individual MO components, although with the strength of association ranging from low to moderate. This might imply that the *marketing practices, introduced/implemented by the school principals, are coherent to a certain extent*, as opposed to their realization of the three management functions analysed in this paper.

Table 6 Bivariate correlations of measures related to realization of management practices and individual components of the MO construct

		Realization of planning	Realization of organi-zing	Realization of controlling	Operative, "fire-fighting" activities	MO COMPONENT: Assessment of user satisfaction	MO COMPONENT: Orientation toward competition	MO COM-PONENT: Long-term orientation of the organization	MO COMPONENT: Effectiveness of internal organization	MO COM-PONENT: User-centered organizational culture
Realization of planning	Pearson Correlation	1								
	Significance									
Realization of organizing	Pearson Correlation	,397(**)	1							
	Significance	0								
Realization of controlling	Pearson Correlation	,414(**)	,296(**)	1						
	Significance	0	0							
Operative, "fire fighting" activities	Pearson Correlation	,438(**)	,262(**)	,318(**)	1					
	Significance	0	0	0						
MO COMPONENT : Assessment of user satisfaction	Pearson Correlation	-,190(**)	-0,002	-0,088	-0,051	1				
	Significance	0,008	0,983	0,225	0,485					
MO COMPONENT : Orientation toward competition	Pearson Correlation	0,021	0,058	0,053	0,055	-,341(**)	1			
	Significance	0,771	0,427	0,467	0,452	0				
MO COMPONENT : Long-term orientation	Pearson Correlation	0,069	0,023	0,05	0,096	-,160(*)	,446(**)	1		
	Significance	0,329	0,75	0,481	0,174	0,027	0			
MO COMPONENT : Effectiveness of internal organization	Pearson Correlation	0,023	-0,01	-0,064	0	-,346(**)	,285(**)	,330(**)	1	
	Significance	0,746	0,882	0,362	0,995	0	0	0		
MO COMPONENT : User-centered organizational culture	Pearson Correlation	-0,021	0,037	0,057	,176(*)	-,232(**)	,410(**)	,380(**)	,485(**)	1
	Significance	0,772	0,613	0,428	0,014	0,002	0	0	0	

Notes: ** Correlation is significant at the 0.01 level (2-tailed). * Correlation is significant at the 0.05 level (2-tailed).

The most helpful result can be attributed to the *almost nonexistent correlations among planning/organizing/controlling with most of the MO components*, which suggests that *the marketing and management practices are not being linked in the exercise of school principal duties*. A potential implication for management/marketing practice emerges from this finding, as there seems to be an opportunity for transfer of a somewhat "better" practice from the marketing to the management field. Unfortunately, there are some downsides to the marketing implementation in the primary schools, as well.

Namely, the MO component related to the assessment of user satisfaction is *significantly, but negatively correlated with all the other MO components, as well as with the planning function.* This might lead to the conclusion that the *methods/activities related to assessing and managing pupils' and parents' satisfaction are discouraging rational managerial planning, as well as being misaligned with the other components of the marketing practice/orientation.*

Concluding Remarks

Although the presented research findings are of indicative value, they demonstrate a relatively low level of management development in the Croatian primary school (sub)sector, which requires extensive development of principals' managerial skills. Marketing practices seem to be better developed and mutually coherent, except for the methods/activities in the field of assessing and managing users' satisfaction, which even negatively influence the other aspects of the marketing orientation. Another practical implication of this work is, therefore, related to the attention that has to be paid to the professional development of principals in this area, as well.

Furthermore transfers of somewhat "better" practices from one field to another seem to be lacking within the institution of primary education itself, which also indicates the need for principals' professional development in the areas of performance management and (maybe even) benchmarking.

References

Alfirević, N./N. Gabelica (2007), 'Management practices in Croatian non-profit organizations: Results of the empirical research', *Management – Journal of Contemporary Management Issues*, Vol. 12/No. 1, pp. 25 - 44.

Avlontis, G. J./S.P. Gounaris (1999), 'Marketing orientation and its determinants: an empirical analysis', *European Journal of Marketing*, Vol. 33/No.11/12, pp. 1003 - 1037.

Bell, L. (1991), 'Educational management: An agenda for the 1990s', *Educational Management, Administration & Leadership*, Vol. 19/No. 3, pp. 136 - 140.

Bennet, L./H. Gabriel (1999), 'Headteacher characteristics, management style and attitudes towards the acceptance of commercial sponsorship by state-funded schools', *Marketing Intelligence & Planning*, 17/1, pp. 41 - 52.

Bridges, E. M. (1982), 'Research on the school administrator: The state of the art, 1967 - 1980', *Educational Administration Quarterly*, Vol. 18/No. 3, pp. 12 - 33.

Buble, M. (2006), *Osnove menadžmenta* (Fundamentals of management), Sinergija, Zagreb.

Calabrese, R.L./S. J. Zepeda (1999), 'Decision-making assessment: improving principal performance', *International Journal of Educational Management*, 13/1, pp. 6 - 13.

Caruana, A./B. Ramaseshan/M. T. Ewing (1998), 'Do universities that are more market orientated perform better?', *International Journal of Public Sector Management*, Vol. 11 No. 1, pp. 55 - 70.

Dinham, S. (2005), 'Principal leadership for outstanding educational outcomes', *Journal of Educational Administration*, Vol. 43/No. 4, pp. 338 - 356.

Hallinger, P./R. H. Heck (1996), 'Reassessing the principal's role in school effectiveness: A review of empirical research, 1980 – 1995', *Educational Administration Quarterly*, Vol. 32/No. 1, pp. 5 - 44.

Hooley, G. J./J. A. Saunders/N. F. Piercy (1998), *Marketing strategy & competitive positioning*, Prentice Hall Europe, London.

Immegart, G. L. (1994), 'The School Head, Director, or Principal and School Asessment', *International Journal of Educational Management*, Vol. 8/No. 1, pp. 25 - 34.

Kohli, A.K./B. J. Jaworski (1990), 'Market Orientation: The Concept, Research Propositions, and Managerial Implications', *Journal of Marketing*, Vol. 54/No. 2, pp. 1 - 18.

Johansson, O. (2004), 'Introduction: Democracy and leadership or training for democratic leadership', *Journal of Educational Administration*, Vol. 42/No. 6, pp. 620 - 624.

Johnson, N. (1994), 'Education reforms and professional development of principals: implications for universities', *Journal of Educational Administration*, Vol. 32/No. 2, pp. 5 - 20.

Kotler, P./K. F. A. Fox (1995), *Strategic marketing for educational institutions*, Prentice Hall, New Jersey.

Lafferty, B. A./G. T. Hult (2001), 'A synthesis of contemporary market orientation perspectives', *European Journal of Marketing*, Vol. 35/No.1/2, pp. 91 - 109.

Macpherson, R. J. S. (1984), 'On being and becoming an educational administrator: Some methodological issues', *Educational Administration Quarterly*, Vol. 20/No. 4, pp. 58 - 75.

Narver, J.C./S. F. Slater (1990), 'The effect of a market orientation on business profitability', *Journal of Marketing*, Vol. 54/No. 4, pp. 20 - 35.

O'Cass, A./L. Viet Ngo (2007), 'Market orientation versus innovative culture: two routes to superior brand performance', *European Journal of Marketing*, Vol. 41/No.7/8, pp. 868 - 887.

Oplatka, I./J. Hemsley-Brown (2007), 'The incorporation of market orientation in the school culture: An essential aspect of school marketing', *International Journal of Educational Management*, Vol. 21/No. 4, pp.292 - 305.

Oplatka, I./J. Hemsley-Brown (2004), 'The research on school marketing: Current issues and future directions', *Journal of Educational Administration*, Vol. 42/No. 3, pp.375 - 400.

Pavičić, J./N. Renko/N. Alfirević (2001), 'Role of Marketing orientation and competitive analysis in improving competitiveness of the non-profit sector: Theoretical background and empirical evidence from the Croatian Public Libraries', *Proceedings of the 4th International Conference "Enterprise in Transition"*, 24 - 26. May 2001, Split-Hvar, published by the Faculty of Economics Split and World Bank, pp. 115 - 116 (extended abstract); pp. 422 - 437 (CD-ROM).

Pulendran, S./R. Speed/R. E. Widing II (2003), 'Marketing planning, market orientation and business performance', *European Journal of Marketing*, Vol. 37/No.3/4, pp. 476 - 497.

Quinn, D. M. (2002), 'The impact of principal leadership behaviours on instructional practice and student engagement', *Journal of Educational Administration*, Vol. 40/No. 5, pp. 447 - 467.

Whitaker, K. S. (1996), 'Exploring causes of principal burnout', *Journal of Educational Administration*, Vol. 34/No. 1, pp. 60 - 71.

Whitaker, K. S. (2003), 'Principal role changes and influence on principal recruitment and selection: An international perspective', *Journal of Educational Administration*, Vol. 41/No. 1, pp. 37 - 54.

Weller, L. D. Jr/S. H. Hartley (1994), 'Total Quality Management and school restructuring: Georgia's approach to educational reform', *Quality Assurance in Education*, Vol. 2/No. 2, pp. 18 - 25.

Martina Sopta – Bojan Makar

Knowledge-based Services – The Case of Outsourcing Marketing in Croatian Companies

Introduction

Along with the processes of globalization and joining the EU, Croatian businesses are increasingly exposed both to national and international competition, which requires them to focus on fundamental business activities, i.e. those parts of their business in which they possess the required core competences (Prahalad/Hamel 1990). One of the methods to concentrate on core business is to separate less important activities by using the knowledge-based services of specialized external providers, i.e. by using '*outsourcing*'[1]. In this manner, a temporary organisational structure is created, which enables all participants in the outsourcing process to obtain the best possible implementation, even of non-core processes and 'perfect' final products.

There are two methods of realising competitive advantages by applying outsourcing, i.e. by focusing on core activities or functions, which they perform on a 'world class' performance level, or by externalizing activities which are not considered strategically important, or which cannot be performed at a required level due to the lack of special skills and competences. In order to explore the role of *knowledge-based services* and *outsourcing* as a manner of their provision, this paper analyses practices, opportunities and (dis)advantages related to the outsourcing of marketing in Croatian companies. Data for the empirical study has been collected by a standardised questionnaire on a sample of 100 Croatian businesses and statistically analyzed.

The Outsourcing Concept

Outsourcing has become one of the fundamental approaches to organisational restructuring, which reshapes the traditional borders of the organisation. The term *outsourcing* could be defined in terms of using external resources, i.e. implementing services from outside providers. This implies the separation of core from non-core activities, which should provide a higher quality of core activities, as well as a more professional, faster and cheaper implementation of outsourced activities. Belak et al. (1999) define *outsourcing* as the externalisation of activities from the leading company, along with assets and employees, by forming new, smaller companies which are bound by agreements to the leading company. The alterna-

---

[1] See also: The Outsourcing Institute [http://www.outsourcing.com].

tive approach to externalisation is the allocation to the already existing external providers of knowledge-based services, which are allocated to a network of virtual companies (ibid.). Outsourcing can also be defined as a management strategy of contracting out secondary and auxiliary activities to those providers specialised for the specific area(s). (Šestić 2001) The *Outsourcing Institute* (1999) defines outsourcing in terms of the strategic usage of external resources for functions which have, traditionally, been carried out by own resources[2]. Gravier (1999, p. 3) defines outsourcing as transferring internal repetitive activities and the decision-making authority of an organisation to an external supplier, as determined by mutual agreement.

However, Peter Bendor Samuel (1999) warns that, when an organisation cedes the right of implementing a business process to an external supplier, special attention should be paid to the balance between the flexibility of the contract and its desirable long-term nature. What defines outsourcing and makes it such a challenging and 'painful' process is the assignment of property rights (Gravier 1999, p. 3), as it implies that a company 'leases' one or more of its business processes to the external supplier (Boone/Koortz 1997). However, outsourcing is also a venue for lowering costs (Citra 2002), as well as for introducing innovation by exploiting the knowledge, experience and creativity of new suppliers, which has not been used before (Engelke 1996).

However, it can be concluded that different authors disagree over the term of *outsourcing*, although the different theoretical concepts can be 'boiled down' to the idea of a contractual relationship between the company and one (or several) external partners, serving as external providers of business services. This is, in fact, the decision on performing certain activities independently or sourcing them from the market (Makar 2006, p. 10). Factors influencing such a decision include the number and competence(s) of external partners, technological improvement and competition. Since those factors are subject to continuous change, management has to dynamically adapt to the changing situation.

Implementation of Marketing Outsourcing in Croatian Companies: Results of the Empirical Research

Introduction to the Empirical Research Project

The degree of implementation of outsourcing in the marketing domain primarily depends on the organisational structure and the position of the marketing department within the company. The organizational structuring/positioning of the marketing department depends on many factors, including the size of the organisation, size and complexity of the target market, type of product and technological

2 [www.outsourcing.com] retrieved on 27.09.2005.

processes, etc. However, a crucial influence on the role and status of the marketing department depends on the general acceptance of the marketing concept and the sensitivity toward the needs of consumers (Previšić/Ozretić Došen 2004). Beside the decision whether marketing activities are performed within the organization at all, another decision is related to the structuring of a separate organizational unit, or performance within another department. This may indicate that the level of implementation of marketing outsourcing is increased as marketing is removed from the central management function of a company, which has been one of the topics of the empirical research.

In addition, the empirical research had to determine whether new market/business trends affect the practice of using the knowledge-based services by means of *outsourcing*. The research has been conducted in the context of well-known marketing activities, including pricing, determination of distribution channels, promotion and other forms marketing communication (personal selling, public relations, publicity, etc.). Hypotheses tested by the empirical project are as follows:

H1 Croatian companies extensively use the existing knowledge-based services by utilizing outsourcing to a great extent.
H2 Outsourcing enables their users to reduce business costs.
H3 In case of marketing outsourcing, large companies are the prime users of external providers' services.

Sample of the Empirical Research

The convenience sample for this research project has been constructed from the secondary data collected by the Institute for Business Research in Zagreb. It consists of one hundred Croatian companies, of which 40 percent are of small size, 30 percent mid-sized and 39 percent belong to the large enterprises (cf. Figure 1). Although the Croatian legislation *(Croatian Accounting Law, N.N. No.90/92 from 30.12.1992., section VII, article 16/2)* uses multiple criteria (value of assets in the balance sheet, income in the last period covered and annual average of employees) to classify companies according to their size, only the last criterion has been used for the purpose of research design simplicity. Namely, it was difficult to choose companies which were ready to provide information and simultaneously belong to the categories defined by the mentioned accounting law. The sample has also been controlled for equal regional representation and ownership structure.

Figure 1 Ownership structure of the surveyed companies

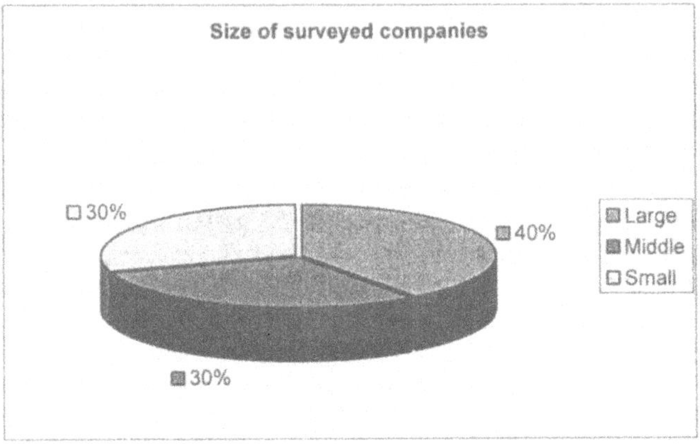

Source: Empirical research results

Methodology of the Empirical Research

The primary data has been collected via a questionnaire, which is considered to be a simple and cost-effective research instrument, although it may not lead to the desired response rate (Zelenika 1998). It consisted of three groups of variables, related to general data, outsourcing practices and specific marketing activities being outsourced. The data have been analysed according to marketing research procedures, in order to obtain both scientific insights and practical implications for marketing practice (Marušić/Vranešević 2001). Along with size, other general 'business demographics' variables added to the empirical project included ownership and business activities. Ownership of the responding companies has been classified as private (from the beginning), companies in the process of being privatised, companies where the transformation has been completed, mixed companies and public companies or rather companies owned by the state. Table 1 and Figure 2 present data on the ownership structure of surveyed companies, which is dependent of company size, with most small and mid-sized companies (SMEs) being owned by private entrepreneurs (83.33% middle companies, or rather 97.5% small companies). There is still mixed ownership in the large enterprise sector, with 10 percent of large companies still owned by the state, and a large number of large companies managed by the City of Zagreb. However, privatisation processes are also in progress in this company group, and therefore in 46.67 percent of large companies the privatisation has been completed.

Table 1 Ownership structure of all surveyed companies

According to the ownership structure the company is:	Large	Middle	Small	Total
Private from the beginning	26.67%	83.33%	97.50%	72.00%
Privatisation in progress	3.33%	3.33%	0%	2.00%
Privatisation completed	46.67%	10.00%	0%	17.00%
Mixed ownership	13.33%	0%	2.50%	5.00%
Public/state ownership	10.00%	3.33%	0%	4.00%
Total	100%	100%	100%	100%

Source: Empirical research results

Figure 2 Ownership structure of interviewed companies

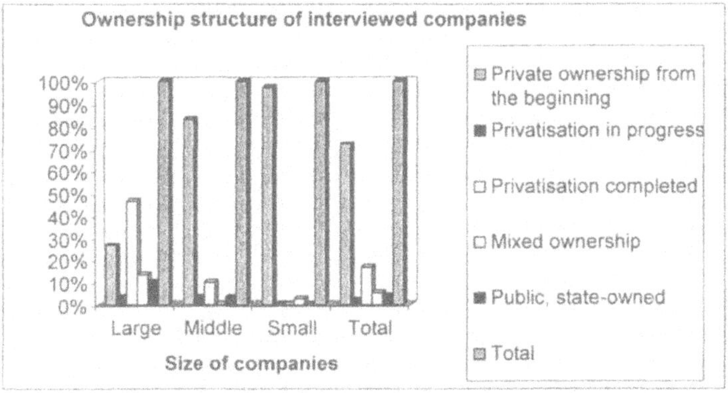

Source: Empirical research results

The business activities of the company, i.e. the business sector to which the responding company belongs, have also been recorded. The generic sector scheme used by the research included: agriculture, manufacturing industries, construction, transport and communication, wholesale and retail sales, tourism and catering, finance and other business services. Results are presented in Table 2 and Figure 3, and demonstrate wholesale and retail sales (29.9%) as a predominant business activity. Another 23.36 percent belong to the manufacturing sector, 6.54 percent to the tourism/catering sector and only 1.87 percent to agriculture.

Table 2 Business activities of the surveyed companies

Major sector to which the company belongs	Large	Middle	Small	Total
Agriculture	2.94%	0%	2.33%	1.87%
Manufacturing industry	41.18%	10%	18.60%	23.36%
Construction	0%	20%	6.98%	8.41%
Transport and communication	2.94%	10%	2.33%	4.67%
Wholesale and retail sales	26.47%	40%	25.58%	29.91%
Tourism and catering	2.94%	3.33%	11.63%	6.54%
Financial and other business services	11.76%	3.33%	6.98%	7.48%
Other	11.76%	13.33%	25.58%	17.76%

Source: Empirical research results

Figure 3 Business activities of the surveyed companies

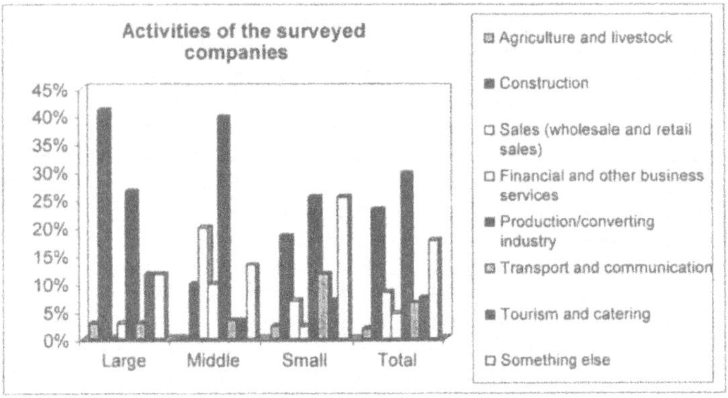

Source: Empirical research results

The research results demonstrate that **Croatian companies use outsourcing services to a significant extent,** with only 16 percent who have not used external provision of business services. The amount of outsourcing usage in large and mid-sized companies is approximately equal (mid-sized companies 76.67% and large companies 83.33%). Small companies use outsourcing even more extensively (90%), which can be explained by a relatively low level of organizational development, which motivates them to search assistance from external providers of knowledge and service by means of outsourcing. This is especially true for the case of accounting and local services which are of great importance to small companies.

Figure 4 Degree of using outsourcing services

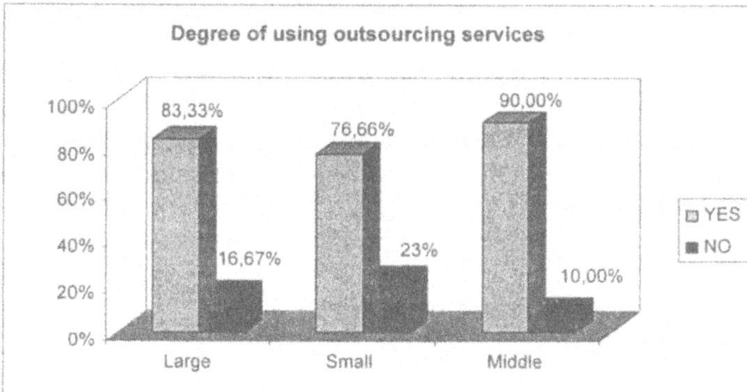

Source: Empirical research results

Most frequently outsourced activities (Table 3) include accounting, issues related to implementation and management of information technology, research and development, some segments, or even the entire production/manufacturing segment of the company. Beside such major functions, Croatian companies routinely outsource less important, but still indispensable activities, such as maintenance, cleaning, canteens, etc.

Perceived benefits of outsourcing include the **reduction of business costs**, but **only in large and mid-sized companies,** which report cost reduction of up to twenty percent due to outsourcing (Table 4 and Figure 5). On the other hand, only 1.27 percent of small enterprises perceive reduction of costs as a viable strategic advantage of outsourcing. This might imply that small companies view knowledge-based business services, such as outsourcing, more as a necessity than a potential source of competitive advantage, as opposed to mid-sized and large enterprises.

Table 3 Most frequently outsourced activities

Outsourced activities (multiple answers were allowed):	Large	Middle	Small	Total
Accounting	2.22%	15.55%	41.43%	23.13%
Information Technology	22.22%	24.44%	20%	21.88%
Marketing	37.78%	17.77%	14.23%	21.88%
Research and development	6.67%	6.66%	4.23%	5.63%
A segment of production/manufacturing	17.78%	24.44%	11.43%	16.88%
Entire production/manufacturing	2.22%	0%	0%	0.63%
Other	11.11%	11.11%	8.57%	10.00%

Source: Empirical research results

Small companies see the advantages of outsourcing in obtaining higher quality (26.58%), shortening cycle time (17.72%) and opportunities for entering new markets (16.46%), which might be of special importance for small businesses, as they need to develop new options for growth. However, mid-sized companies also emphasize higher quality (27.12%), lower costs (22.03%) and lower capital investments (20.34%) as potential outcomes of outsourcing. Perceptions of large enterprises related to outsourcing benefits do not differ much, although they seem to emphasize higher quality (32.1%), which is also evident, as large enterprises need to actively and successfully compete on the international market.

Table 4 Perceived advantages of outsourcing

The most important perceived advantages of outsourcing is/are (multiple answers were allowed):	Large	Middle	Small	Total
Lower costs	20.31%	22.03%	1.27%	22.28%
Higher quality	32.81%	27.12%	26.58%	28.71%
Faster development of new products and services	7.81%	5.08%	11.39%	8.42%
Faster cycle time	20.31%	15.25%	17.72%	17.82%
Access to new markets	9.38%	8.47%	16.46%	11.88%
Lower capital investments	7.81%	20.34%	3.89%	9.90%
Something else	1.56%	1.69%	0%	0.99%

Source: Empirical research results

Regarding the outsourcing of marketing, it could be expected that the large companies use services of marketing agencies more often. Of all the respondents, regardless of the company size, 55.9 percent outsource marketing, with 77.8 percent of large companies using the marketing-related knowledge-based services. In comparison, 58.3 percent of mid-sized companies externalize marketing activities, while less than a half of small enterprise (44.7%) use marketing outsourcing.

Figure 5 Perception of outsourcing advantages

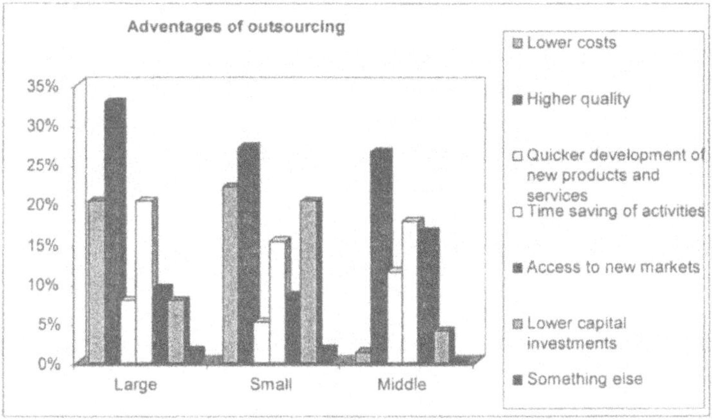

Source: Empirical research results

Figure 6 presents the structure of marketing service providers and confirms the 'rule of the thumb', implying that promotional activities are the most significant knowledge-based service in marketing, with more than 51.1 percent of respondents outsourcing this activity. The other significant marketing activity outsourced just slightly less than promotion is marketing research.

Figure 6 External providers of marketing services

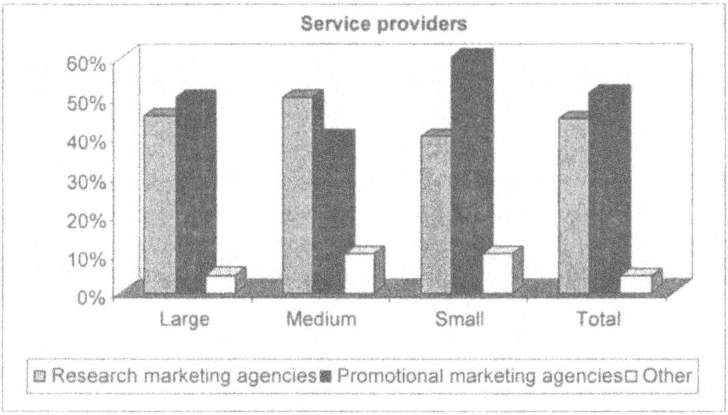

Source: Empirical research results

The distribution of marketing outsourcing according to company size provides similar results (cf. Table 6 and Figure 7). Large companies use marketing for market research (26.5%), advertising (26.5%), public relations (23.5%), sales promotion (11.8%) and publicity (2.9%).

Considering that all these activities belong to the *marketing communication* field, it 'stands out' as the most significant business services provided by the external marketing partners. A similar situation is found in clusters of mid-sized and small companies. However, small enterprises also use outsourcing for distribution-related decisions (5.9%), which is also logical, due to their natural tendency to rapidly expand their business.

Table 6 Outsourced marketing activities

The marketing purposes of using *outsourcing*:	Large	Middle	Small	Total
Market research	26.5%	29.4%	23.5%	25.9%
Pricing	8.8%	0%	8.8%	7.1%
Distribution channels decisions	0%	0%	5.9%	2.4%
Advertising	26.5%	23.5%	23.5%	24.7%
Personal sales	0%	0%	0%	0%
Sales promotion	11.8%	23.5%	20.7%	17.6%
Public relations (P.R.)	23.5%	11.8%	8.8%	15.2%
Publicity	2.9%	11.8%	8.8%	7.1%

Source: Empirical research results

It should be also noted that there is a general tendency of large companies to employ different and specialised external service providers, which is true for 92.3 percent of respondents. Such a situation may be the result of the large companies' efforts to become as competitive as possible on the (international/globalized) market. On the other hand, larger enterprises possess enough resources to outsource marketing, if it is not one of their core business activities.

This might lead to the conclusion that the degree of outsourcing of marketing activities primarily depends on the organisational structure. By using more providers of individual marketing services, large providers can obtain a better deal in knowledge transfer through more creative solutions. Simultaneously, small companies are mostly linked to a single provider, usually offering unintegrated services, often due to budget restrictions of small companies, which still need to externalize promotion and fundamental market research.

Figure 7 Outsourced marketing according to responding company size

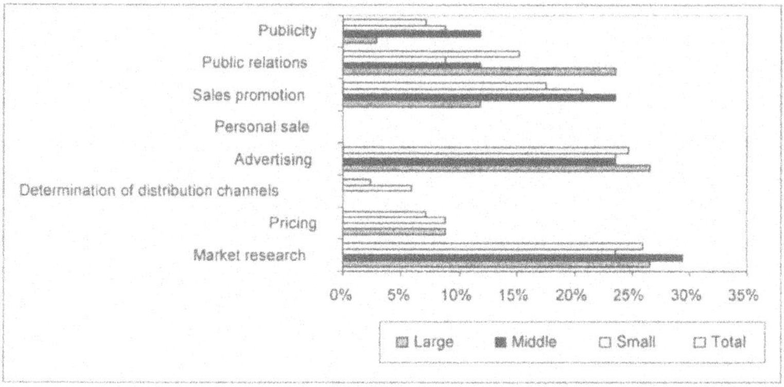

Source: Empirical research results

Figure 11 confirms the previous findings, as 92.3 percent large companies use multiple providers of external marketing services, while the same amounts for mid-sized companies equal 62.5 percent, i.e. 50 percent for small companies.

Figure 8 Number of providers in marketing outsourcing

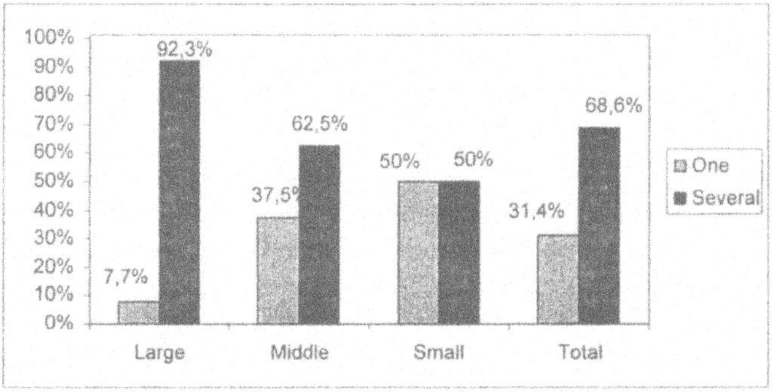

Source: Empirical research results

Conclusion

Outsourcing is a result of globalisation of the market, which requires contemporary organizations to focus on their basic competences. It enables rationalisation of the business processes but also serves as a source of innovation, including development of new technological solutions, enhancement of production, acquisition of specific skills and knowledge, avoidance of unnecessary investment and adoption of new strategies. Therefore, companies have to strategically select among the activities in which the best results (in comparison to the competitors) can be achieved and to focus their potentials on performing these activities. The same applies to marketing, which should be outsourced, if an enterprise is not able to perform marketing activities at the desired level of excellence. This paper analysed the situation related to marketing outsourcing in Croatia, with the following general findings:

- **Hypothesis H1 is accepted, as outsourcing is used extensively in Croatian companies,** which also opens opportunities for specialized companies to serve as providers of more or less specialized business services, either in Croatia, or in the entire region. Namely, 84 percent of the surveyed companies use *outsourcing* services, which applies especially to small enterprises. This can be explained by the fact that small enterprises have not yet reached the level of organizational development, which would make it possible to carry out different functions internally.
- **Hypothesis H2 is also accepted**, as most of the respondents **perceive** that *outsourcing* reduces the costs, with the estimation for large and middle companies of approximately twenty percent. However, this perception has not been verified by empirical analysis, as it would need to be measured by means of financial reports during the period of at least several years before and after the introduction of outsourcing, which proved to be unfeasible.
- **Hypothesis H3 is also accepted,** which is supported by the fact that the smaller the company is, the lower is the degree of using marketing outsourcing. Most of the external, knowledge-based services in the field of marketing are related to *promotion and other forms of marketing communications,* followed by *market research* activities.

Although, in this paper, the application of outsourcing has been discussed only on the level of an individual enterprise, its further analysis on a 'macro level' is also important. The outcomes of outsourcing could be important especially for undeveloped countries with cheap labour, as international outsourcing of both knowledge-based activities (Research & Development, customer support ...) and production becomes more intensive. Outsourcing of marketing is, definitely, part of the knowledge-based processes, which have a high potential for improving the competitive advantage of Croatian companies, as demonstrated by the high degree of companies already using specialized services in market research and marketing communication.

References

Belak, V. et al. (1999), 'Outsourcing and Insourcing in a Transitional Economy: The Case of Croatia', *Proceedings of the 10th International DAAAM Symposium*, 21 - 23 October 1999, pp. 35 - 36.

Boone, L.E./D. L. Kurtz (1997), *Contemporary Business – 1997 edition*, ZDA: The Dryden Press.

Bennett, P.D. (ed.) (1988), *Dictionary of Marketing Terms*, American Marketing Association, Chicago.

Citra, S. (2002), *Outsourcing: strategy or necessity?*, Marketing UP, Zagreb.

Gibson, V.M. (1996), *Outsourcing can save money and increase efficiency*, Benefits Administration.

Gravier, M.F. (1999), *Strategic Outsourcing: A Structured Approach to Outsourcing Decisions and Initiatives*, AMA Publications, New York.

Kotler, P. (1988), *Marketing Management*, Informator, Zagreb.

Kraker, F. (1995), *The Truth about Outsourcing*, Brian Roherty and Ian Robertson, Gower, Aldershot and Brookfield/VT.

Makar, B. (2006), *Research of the Importance of Outsourcing for Marketing Purposes*, MSc thesis, Faculty of Business and Economics Zagreb.

Marušić, M./T. Vranešević (2001), *Market research*, Adeco, Zagreb.

Prahalad, C. K./G. Hamel (1990), 'The Core Competence of the Corporation', *Harvard Business Review*, May - June 1990, pp. 79 - 90.

Previšić, J./Đ. Ozretić Došen (eds.) (2004), *Marketing*, Adverta, Zagreb.

Previšić, J./Đ. Ozretić Došen (1999), *International Marketing*, Masmedia , Zagreb.

Šestić, M. (2001), 'Outsourcing', *Informator*, No 4981, December 2001.

Zelenika, R. (1998), *Metodologija i tehnologija izrade znanstvenog i stručnog djela*, Faculty of Economics Rijeka.

Internet sources:

Engelke, W.D. (1996), 'Outsourcing perspectives', *The Virtual Times* [http://hsv.com/writers/engel/menu.htm] retrieved on 15.07.2009.

Samuel, P. B. (1999), 'The Long and the Short of it All', *Outsourcing Journal* [http://www.outsourcing-journal.com/mar1999-insight.html] retrieved on 15.07.2009.

[www.outsourcing.com]

[www.outsourcing-faq.com]

Nenad Brkić – Almir Salihović

Measuring Web Site Service Quality Using e-SQ and SDDS Criteria – Example of Central Banks in Southeast Europe

Introduction

The Central Bank is a key institution of every national economy, its basic goals being the stable growth of national product and a decrease in unemployment. It pursues these objectives by implementing the macroeconomic policy model it estimates to be the best for the country. Besides implementing the macroeconomic policy, the Central Bank often performs other functions as well, such as managing the foreign currency market, harmonizing international finance, and it is frequently also responsible for the task of supervising banking, i.e. the entire financial sector.[1] By performing its functions, the Central Bank is a true "generator" of a number of statistical and other data that allow state governments to perform high-quality econometric analysis and to make proper decisions in the field of economy.

The last decade of the 20th century and early 21st century have been witnessing the trend of economic financial globalization, where "transition countries" compete to attract direct foreign investment (FDI)[2]. A great part of the investors' decision on where they will invest depends exactly on statistical data, which are carefully examined by investors before making their decision. Such trends present a great challenge for Central Banks. Now, besides serving local decision makers, they must also provide timely and high-quality data for the international business community.

The question that arises is this: What is the role of the Internet in all this, and have Central Banks recognized the Internet as a tool they can use to improve their function? Since 1989, when Tim Berners-Lee and his colleagues from CERN patented the World Wide Web (WWW)[3] concept, the Internet has grown inconceivably. Converting data into an appropriate format and uploading it to a web site are a far faster and cheaper way of distributing information than monthly, quarterly and annual reports, which have to go all the way from text composing and page set-

---

1 Samuelson, P. A./W. D. Nordhaus (2000), *Economics*, 15th Issue, Translation, Mate, Zagreb, pp. 503, 514.

2 Bank for International Settlements (2004), 'Foreign Direct Investment in the Financial Sector of Emerging Market Economies – Executive Summary', *CGFS Publications*, No. 22, March 2004.

3 Griffiths, R. T. (2002), 'Chapter Two: From ARPANET to World Wide Web' [http://www.let.leidenuniv.nl/history/ivh/chap2.htm], Leiden University/NL.

ting, printing, packaging to distribution via mail. Still, some research conducted so far shows that they have not fully embraced the Internet. For instance, research conducted at John Hopkins University in 2000 revealed that out of 174 Central Banks worldwide only 123 (71%) had some form of web site, and 14 banks out of those that had a form of web presentation did not have any web site contents available in English.[4]

The goal of this research is to provide at least part of the answer to the question asked above. By combining one of the best known sets of criteria for measuring the quality of service provided over web sites, e-SQ[5], and the standard introduced by the International Monetary Fund (IMF) for disseminating statistical data (SDDS – Special Data Dissemination Standard)[6], the article will attempt to answer to what degree the present quality of service offered by these sites is close to or far from the desirable one.

The subject of research is the analysis of qualitative and quantitative elements of the region's Central Banks' web sites. By examining certain web site segments it will attempt to determine whether these sites satisfy the standards of web service quality, and whether the data on the sites has been prepared according to suitable standards.

The goal of this paper is to establish whether the management of Central Banks in the countries of the region sufficiently understand the importance of having a high-quality web site. The research will attempt to determine whether the design, quality and content of the web sites satisfies the standards expected from such sites. Based on the obtained results, differences between the required and obtained results will be defined and recommendations will be given for improving contents and quality of the web sites themselves.

Measuring Service Quality on the Internet

"e-SQ" – Electronic Service Quality

Measuring electronic service quality is still in the initial stages of development. According to Zeithaml, Parasuraman and Malhotra[7], the measurement of electronic service quality so far is limited and the number of papers on the topic is

---

[4] Hanke, S./Morgenstern, M. (2001), *What's Wrong With Central Banks' Websites*, John Hopkins University.

[5] Zeithaml, V. A./A. Parasuraman/A. Malhotra (2002), 'Service Quality Delivery through Web Sites; A Critical Review of Extent Knowledge', *Academy of Marketing Science Journal*, Fall 2002.

[6] The International Monetary Fund (1996), 'Guide to the Data Dissemination Standards: Module 1: The Special Data Dissemination Standard', May 1996.

[7] Parasuraman, A./V. A. Zeithaml/A. Malhotra (2004), 'E-S-QUAL: A Multiple Item Scale for Assessing Electronic Service Quality', *MSI Reports*, Marketing Science Institute.

very small. Extensive research on the traditional service quality has been conducted for over twenty years, while the research on the quality of service provided by web sites is of a more recent date. The greatest number of quality-measuring scales has been developed within the business itself, either by companies themselves or by consultancies. According to the definition offered by the mentioned authors, *E-ServQuality (e-SQ) is the extent to which a web site facilitates the efficient searching, purchasing and delivery of products and services.* As opposed to the standard SERVQUAL model (SQ), in e-SQ, mostly due to the very nature of technologies that have to be used in order to "visit" a web site and to the information the web sites contain, expectations held by Internet service users are not as great as in the SERVQUAL model. Although the Internet and technologies used when accessing the Internet have progressed significantly and become far more user friendly than a few years ago, access to the Internet still requires specific equipment and a certain degree of computer literacy.

By subliming results of a number of researches, Zeithaml, Parasuraman and Malhotra identified the following criteria used by web site users when assessing web sites and the quality of service they provide:

1. Availability of information and content
2. Ease of use and usability
3. Privacy
4. Graphic style
5. Fulfilment/Reliability
6. Other criteria

Special Data Dissemination Standard (SDDS)

Special Data Dissemination Standard (SDDS) were established in 1996 by the International Monetary Fund (IMF) as a guide for member countries that are, or might seek, access to capital markets through the provision of a range of economic and financial data. In combination with the General Data Dissemination System (GDDS), these standards should increase the availability and timeliness of disseminating comprehensive statistics and thus enhance the process of developing sound macroeconomic policies[8]. The SDDS are also expected to contribute to the improved functioning of financial markets.

Since the process of web site analysis covers exactly the countries of the region that are undergoing a transition process and that are attempting to attract for-

---

[8] IMF: 'Dissemination Standards Bulletin Board – Overview Page', [http://dsbb.imf.org/Applications/web/overview/]; IMF: 'Dissemination Standards Bulletin Board – Four dimensions of data dissemination'; [http://dsbb.imf.org/Applications/web/sddsdimensions/].

eign investors, particularly in the financial market field[9], having sound statistical data becomes a priority for each of the states. It is for this reason that SDDS was selected as a supplement to e-SQ, so that we could use both basic elements with which the quality of web site service is measured, and see whether the information (in this case statistical data) contained on these web sites is adjusted to international standards.

SDDS identifies four elements of data dissemination:

- Data themselves: coverage, periodicity and timeliness;
- Access by the public;
- Integrity of the disseminated data;
- Quality of the disseminated data.

Specifics of Measuring Quality of Service Provided by the Web Sites of Central Banks of Southeast European Countries

Methodological Remarks

The paper analysed web sites of the following Central Banks:

1. Central Bank of Bosnia and Herzegovina – www.cbbh.ba
2. Bank of Slovenia – www.bsi.sl
3. National Bank of Croatia – www.hnb.hr
4. National Bank of Serbia – www.nbs.yu
5. National Bank of Macedonia – www.nbrm.gov.mk
6. Central Bank of Montenegro – www.cb-mn.org
7. Central Banking Authority of Kosovo – www.cbak-kos.org.

The research used the method of content analysis. Data were gathered by visiting web sites of chosen Central Banks and browsing their content in order to find out whether they have all the required elements in accordance with the questionnaires we formed, based on the defined research methods: The "e-SQ" criteria defines six categories of assessing the quality of web site service: information availability and content, ease of use, privacy, graphic style, reliability and other criteria. Based on these six categories, a questionnaire was developed with a total of 55 questions.

For the research to be complete, the content of Central Banks' web sites was tested by an additional questionnaire, where the questions were mostly derived from the SDDS standard[10]. This questionnaire consists of 27 questions.

---

9 Bank for International Settlements (2004), 'Foreign direct investment in the financial sector of emerging market economies – Executive Summary', *CGFS Publications,* No. 22, March 2004.

10 The International Monetary Fund (1996), 'Guide to the Data Dissemination Standards: Module 1: The Special Data Dissemination Standard', May 1996.

Research Results

Information Availability and Content

All seven institutions from the region that are involved in monetary policy have their own web presentations. Web information is regularly updated in five cases (71.4%), while in the remaining two updating is somewhat rarer, and will therefore be treated as partial.

The presentation of the basic institution information is well done – all the web sites have sections describing the basic functions the institution performs, with five examined sites having very extensive data (71.4%). Since Central Bank operations are, as a rule, defined by law, all the sites consider the access to legal regulations as very important and this data is available on the banks' web sites. Besides, if the bank is involved in any activities of the banking supervision type, legislation regulating this area is also available on the site.

Information relevant for Central Bank operations and activities are of high quality, and all the sites include statistical data, data from the banking supervision domain and data on the financial sector health. The only exception in this case is the Central Bank of BH (CBBH), which has no data on banking supervision, but that is acceptable considering that the CBBH is not in charge of banking supervision and that aforementioned data are available on the sites of Entities' banking agencies. The site design had in mind communication with the public, and consequently all sites include a news section. Admittedly, the "news" is clearly indicated only on two sites (28.5%), while the others have news included within press releases. Otherwise, PR activities are well represented. All sites provide press releases, and six also include speeches and presentations (85.71%). Besides, all sites offer the option of downloading quarterly and annual bank reports and bank newsletters. All sites include useful links, although they are clearly indicated only on five sites (71.4%), while they were not clearly indicated on two.

With respect to additional data on the state of the economies they represent (e.g. credit rating stock exchange reports), results are somewhat different. Not on a single web site could we find even the basic data on investment terms and conditions, or steps necessary to start a business. Some other economy data, such as stock exchange reports, could partly be found on every web site, but as part of a statistical bulletin, e.g. the annual report or a press release, which in turn required extensive site searching, downloading and reading of annual reports, which are mostly rendered in PDF, which is not suitable for easy search. Credit rating and stock exchange reports were found in six of the seven cases (85.71%); however, only in one case were these data prominent and easy to find (14.28%).

With respect to languages, all the sites are available in English; moreover, the site of the Kosovo Banking Authority was primarily made in English, presumably due to the specific organization of the institution in the province. Still, only five sites (71.4%) have a well-developed English part, which agrees well with the local version. On the remaining two, there is a great discrepancy between the site content in the local language and the English page. On one site, there is even a great difference in available links between the local and the English version.

In terms of communication between users and the institution, all the web sites list traditional methods of communication (mailing address, phone number), and the available e-mail address; two institutions (28.57%) also offer both e-mail address and online contact forms. As for feedback, results are significantly different. A reply to the test e-mail, the content of which was described earlier in the paper, was sent only by four Central Banks (57.14%). The replies were sent in the one (fastest reply) to five day (slowest reply) range. On average, the reply arrived three days after the query, which is very slow, since it is taken that the normal time for a reply to an e-mail query is up to 24 hours[11]. Thus, only one Central Bank (14.28%) met e-mail communication standards.

Finally, this part also explored whether Central Banks' web sites allow downloading of forms that will serve the site users and that will facilitate communication between the bank and users. This option was found on three sites (42.85%), and the forms found served different purposes. The Croatian National Bank offers the option of downloading forms for submitting statistical data. CBBH offers the possibility to download forms for applying to the registry of credits and transaction accounts, while the Bank of Macedonia allows the downloading of application forms for internships.

Ease of Use

Standardized navigation is present on all the examined web sites, with that on two sites (28.57%) the navigation on the local and English version differs.

The usable option of a site search was found only in one case (14.28%). A search was also carried out on two more sites, but did not work. In one case, the search link simply did not work, while in the other, no query yielded any results. One site, which did not offer a search function, provides an interesting solution that allows finding one's way on the site, i.e. an index with terms. A click on a term shows links to all the documents where this term is listed.

A site map was found in five cases (71.42%); unfortunately, only one site (14.28%) allows the adjustment of fonts according to user's needs, and only this site allows opening documents from the site in a printer-friendly format. No site

---

[11] *Internet Retailer*, 'Slow response to E-mail queries will become a chief source of customer loss' [http://www.internetretailer.com/internet/marketing-conference/87181-slow-response-E-mail-queries-will-become-chief-source-customer-loss.html].

offers advanced options of adjusting the site appearance according to user's preferences, and no site offers a subscription to mailing lists.

All the sites offer the option to download documents in various formats. The most frequent format is PDF[12], which is present on all the sites; this makes sense since it has already been said that all the Central Banks provide various publications such as annual reports or laws. Due to its small size compared to the amount of data and easy printing, PDF is an ideal format for providing such publications on the web, and is particularly appreciated by the owners of slower web connections. The second most represented format is XLS[13], which was found on six sites (85.71%). Such a high percentage was expected since all the sites release statistical data and Excel is the most wide-spread software for tabular calculations, very popular among people involved in statistics. In two cases (28.57%), ZIP files[14] were also found, used in cases when it was necessary to reduce huge files or simply make an archive for a number of related files. On one site (14.28%), files were found in the MS Word format (DOC), and in the same number of cases a related file format for showing text documents – RTF[15] was found. Placing text documents and data tables in online databases allows their easy use and handling; however, such an option was found only on one of the sites covered by the research (14.28%). On two sites (28.57%) links or input forms for external databases can be found, but they are not integrated parts of the site. It should be noted that one web site adds the option of the so-called web service, i.e. script that allows automatic copying of the content from one to another web site and its updating on each change; this site also offers WAP service, i.e. a site adjusted to reading on mobile phones, although this option is available only for the exchange rate.

Privacy

Only one of the tested web sites includes a Privacy Statement (14.28%).

As for the remaining sites, three (42.85%) have only a Disclaimer, i.e. a statement refusing responsibility in case the use of the web site material causes potential damage to the user's computer, and in one of these three cases the Disclaimer claims that the bank guarantees the accuracy of data, which are examined only within the bank's network.

In five cases (71.42%), the Copyright is provided referring to the permission to use and reproduce the data on the web site.

---

[12] PDF – Portable Document Format, Adobe Systems Inc. [www.adobe.com].
[13] XLS – Microsoft Excel, Microsoft Corporation [www.microsoft.com].
[14] ZIP – WinZip Corporation [www.winzip.com].
[15] RTF – Real Text Format, Property of Microsoft Corporation, 1987.

Graphic Style

Two sites use state symbols (28.75%), and in both cases these are state coats of arms. All the tested web sites also have a highly visible bank logo, and the corresponding colours, which are used in all parts of the site. Only in one case (14.28%), it was registered that the bank logo was not prominent in all the parts of the bank's web site.

Although it was not prominent in the questionnaire, a general impression on the web site design was recorded within the assessment. According to the replies we received in the banks' e-mail messages, and the data found on their web sites, in five cases (71.42%) the site was designed in-house, while two banks used outsourcing.

Reliability

In the review process, sites were tested for so-called "dead links". In three cases (42.85%) there were no such links, i.e. the site maintenance was good. In two cases, links were found, but since this happened only once or twice per site, this was not considered a problem. However, on two sites (28.57%) a number of dead links were found and, interestingly, on one of the two sites most of the dead links were found in the English version of the web site.

Pages under construction were found in three cases (42.85%), and the same as in the dead links case, in two of the three recorded cases this was limited to only one or two cases per site, so that this cannot be considered a problem. However, in one case (14.28%) pages under construction were found a few times, mostly in the English part of the site.

Five of the seven tested web sites (71.42%) displayed correctly in the most popular web browsers. Out of the two remaining cases, differences in display were found in one, but the errors registered did not cause any troubles when viewing the site content – at one point the dark background did not show on the web browser, so that it was difficult to read white letters against a white background; however, the site could be used normally. In the second case, there were problems with "pop-up"[16] sub-links, which displayed very poorly in one of the browsers.

Other Criteria

In four cases (57.14%), the web site domain was simple and easy to remember. We took it that the easiest domain to remember in this case is [www.name oftheinstitution.countryextension], with the name of the institution abbreviated to no more than five letters (e.g. www.cbbh.ba), and without using hyphens and dots. In the remaining three cases, one has the domain name unnecessarily extended by

[16] Additional (sub)links that appear upon a click or when passing the mouse across the main link.

adding the 'gov' sub-extension, and in the other two the domain names were unnecessarily cut by a hyphen in the domain name (www.cb-cg.org and www.cbak-kos.org). Besides, the consistency of the last two domains is very questionable, since the authors of these web sites used commercial domains 'org' instead of the national domains. The reason for the Kosovo monetary authorities to choose the 'org' domain is probably the current status of Kosovo, while in the case of Montenegro it is because the country has not yet obtained its national domain. Actually, the process of winding up the 'yu' domain is not over yet, so that Serbia and Montenegro are still to obtain their respective national domains.

Four web sites (57.14%) out of the seven tested are properly listed at the head of the search results in the most popular search engines. The remaining three sites did not list in all the search engines, but the level of error was low – each site had only one recorded case when an Internet search engine could not find it, and this can therefore be considered a satisfactory result.

Statistical Data Categories

As noted in the methodological remarks, statistical data are reviewed and analysed using SDDS standards. It should be noted that three sites (42.85%) explicitly state that the data were prepared in accordance with SDDS standards.

Viewed by data categories, data on the economy real sector (national account, production index, labour market, price index) can be found on all the web sites. 75% of all the released data is in the tabular form (HTML or XLS), while 25% data was found in the form of publication, i.e. in PDF.

In the case of fiscal sector data (operations of central government or public sector, central government operations and central government debt), 81% of the required data could be found on the web sites, while 19% data was provided partially. 71.5% data is provided in the tabular form (HTML or XLS), while 28.5% data was found in a form of publication, i.e. in PDF.

With respect to financial sector data (analytical accounts of the banking sector, analytical accounts of the Central Bank, interest rates, stock market), the required data were found in 89.3% cases. In one of three cases where not all data were found, one of the Central Banks had partial data on interest rates because its monetary policy does not include the setting of the discount rate; in the second case when the data were partially available the bank had only the data on the securities it issues itself, while in the third case no stock market data were found. Identically to the economy real sector, 75% of all the provided data is in the tabular form (HTML or XLS), while 25% data was found in the form of publication, i.e. in PDF.

External sector data (balance of payments, foreign currency reserves, trade exchange, international investment position, exchange rates) were found on all the sites, although on one site that declares the publication of data according to SDDS standards, data on exchange rates were not found in the section devoted to the statistics according to SDDS standards. 77.14% of all data was found in the tabular form (HTML or XLS), and the rest was found within publications, i.e. in PDF.

Finally, the last data set required by SDDS is the population of the country, which was published in four cases (57.14%), while in three cases these data were not found. In case of BH, the data are published as an estimate.

Quality of Statistical Data Presentation

For easier viewing, it was desirable for each category of data to have its own page. This was recorded in two cases (28.51%), while in one case it was partially allowed. In the remaining four cases (57.14%), all the data are found within a single page or link.

When working with huge time series data, one of the desirable options is to allow browsing these time series. Unfortunately, this option was available only in one case (14.28%). Out of the remaining six tested sites, three (42.85%) have data in the PDF format, and the remaining three (42.58%) in the XLS format, which prohibits any meaningful search from the site itself.

Since it was only one web site that allows a search of statistical data series, only this site offered the option to export the obtained search results into a form that could further be used through its direct import into databases. Three formats were offered: HTML, CSV[17] and PX. Another web site also offers the option of exporting data into CSV format, although the option is limited only to the exchange rate.

SDDS provides for the existence of an Advanced Release Calendar, i.e. the schedule of updating the existing statistical data with new series, which in turn facilitates navigation for people who track the publication of data series. In case of web sites analysed for this research, the Advanced Release Calendar was published in four cases (57.14%). As opposed to Advanced Release Calendar, information on updating or revision of data could be found on all the sites.

Explanations of the format the data are provided in could be found in three cases (42.85%). Information on data revision by relevant government institutions was not found.

Upstream Channel

Internet-based reporting, i.e. the possibility to use two-way communication over the Internet and allow the upload of, e.g. input data in the field of statistics, i.e. upstream channel, was not found on any of the analysed web sites. Only in one case (14.28%) was it confirmed, through the e-mail query, that the bank plans to

---

17 CSV – "Comma Separated Value", a format used for exchanging tabular data between unrelated applications.

introduce this option, and that it currently offers a download of a small application for preparing and submitting data that performs this role.

Besides, only one (the above-described) bank also offers the option of applying for a username and password, and accessing parts of the web site beyond the public domain.

The questionnaire checked whether the banks offer the possibility to download forms for filling in and submitting statistical data, which can be considered an alternative to Internet-based reporting. This possibility is offered only by one bank (14.28%); when combined with the number of banks that offer any form related to Internet-based reporting, this means that only two banks (28.57%) offer any form of help or possibility to submit data.

Comments on the Research Results

With respect to the strategy of data presentation on web sites, it was good to see that all the Central Banks are presented on the Internet. It is impressive that 71.42% (five) banks used their own resources when designing web sites, and that the sites could fairly easily be found on Internet browsers. Still, overall impressions on the level of quality of web presentations of banks are very different, and the difference in quality recorded between individual sites is large.

Still, before giving individual assessments, one should see what the averages offered. Primarily, the information/content side of the sites is good. All contain sound data on the institutions they represent, as well as data, i.e. documents on related information, the type of laws that regulate the operations of Central Banks.

All the sites include a news section, or a section devoted to press releases. On 85.71% sites speeches and presentations could be found. 91.5% data required by SDDS could be found on the sites; 5.04% data was partly present, while 3.36% data could not be found. 42.85% tested sites point out that data are prepared in accordance with SDDS. What is not good is that 23.52% data is published only within statistical bulletins, i.e. in PDF, which is completely useless for any importing into calculation programmes and databases.

Data on the sites were updated regularly, although on two sites (28.57%) it could be observed that data were a few days old, but still within more or less acceptable limits.

Far poorer results were obtained in finding information on the state of the economies they represent, which are not a direct product of Central Bank operations, such as credit rating, stock market reports, etc. These data are published only partially, and only as part of publications, of a bulletin or annual report, which made finding them far more difficult. Only in one case could information of this type (credit rating) be found easily.

Definitely the weakest point of these sites is the two-way communication. Form download is available only in three cases and none of the sites offers the possibility of subscription to mailing lists. Besides, no web site offers the possibility to upload data directly into the database. Only one site offers the download of a small application that allows statistical data submission. The fact that this option was not found anywhere cannot be considered a big "minus", since such a way of submitting statistical data requires the source of data to be appropriately equipped as well, to have an appropriate Internet connection, trained staff, etc., which is hard to expect, particularly in this region, where the IT structure is just being built.

What represents a far bigger problem is the percentage of responses to e-mail/online form questionnaires listed on web sites. Responses were received only in four out of seven sent e-mails (57.14%), and only one of them in a reasonable, 24-hour period. As stated at the beginning of the article, support and communication with users beyond mere information presented on a web site, play a big role in assessing the service quality.

The part that deserves a separate assessment is the ease of using the sites. Five of the seven sites (71.42%) were developed in a simple HTML format, which does not provide a possibility of creating interactive elements that make it easier for visitors to find their way. Thus, the operational site search was found only in one case, while on two sites the search function was found but did not work. Only in one case is it possible to adjust the font size according to user's needs, and in the same number of cases one can get a printer-friendly form. The option of making a customized view version adjusted to each user does not exist in any case. In searching statistical data, only one site offers a database that can be searched, and from which data can be exported in a form of usable formats. The format in which statistical data are published are explained only in three cases (42.85%). In general, it can be concluded that the analysed sites are still far from user friendly, and as such do not offer a good-quality service to their users.

The privacy policy is also very poorly represented on the sites. Only in one case does the policy exist and is published on the site, while in the other cases it is reduced to copyright and disclaimer statements.

The analysis of graphic style on the sites used standard questions related to the design consistency, proper use of graphic symbols, having in mind the mission of the institutions the sites represent. Still, answers to these questions are only part of the general impression of the site, since real impressions of the quality differ greatly. While in a few cases graphic design is truly impressive, and the content has been arranged in a very clear way, on some sites the opposite is true – completely unprofessional design with poor organization and use of graphic elements that really give a poor appearance to the entire site and a bad image to the institution. Although it is nice to say that the whole site was "made using our resources", sometimes it is still better to leave it to professionals and opt for outsourcing.

Site reliability is another category with "mixed" results. Three sites do not have dead links (42.85%), while on two they appear only rarely. In two cases it is repeated, which does not leave a good impression of the site. Central Banks are too serious a form of institution to afford such errors, the more so since there is a number of tools on the web design market that can rapidly search the entire site for dead links. The conclusion about the dead links is also true of the pages under construction. On two sites (28.57%) it happens only sporadically; however, on another two the 'under construction' occurrence was observed a few times. Interestingly, on all the analysed sites the greatest number of these occurrences was observed in the part done in English. Better results were registered when opening sites in the most popular browsers. Only on two sites (28.57%) was it observed that they do not open properly in all the popular browsers. Besides, problems recorded on one site were minor and did not affect viewing of the site, but in the second case the change of browser caused big problems with correct reading of the site.

Conclusion

The analysis of web sites covered by the study revealed that only the Bank of Slovenia site met information and technical standards, and that only this site implements currently available technologies in a high-quality manner. This resulted in a site that satisfies the needs of a Central Bank and its web site users in the best possible way. The key advantage of using the new technology is that on the site users have, at their disposal, a series of tools that allow easy and comfortable work on the site, which certainly ensures high rating for service quality. Naturally, this site is not perfect either – it could implement a mailing list, there is no option to use the web site as an entry point to gather statistical data, there is no trace of pages adopted for opening on mobile phones. Still, all things considered, the site deserves a high rating.

Other Central Banks' sites are below this standard. This is particularly true of the technologies the sites were developed in, since all the sites use outdated web technologies, which are extremely static and offer almost no possibility for implementing tools that could allow users easier navigation. No site has a proper search option, which means that it is extremely difficult to find your way around when visiting these sites. The "leant-on" databases found on two sites, and the "agreeable surprise" in the form of WAP and web service of the National Bank of Macedonia will not improve the impression that users of these sites are left to themselves and good luck when looking for data on these web sites.

Even if one can have some understanding for the fact that, due to the lack of staff and work overload it is difficult to find enough time for extensive projects of site redesign, some occurrences this research came across proved to be unacceptable. Thus, crude errors were found such as dead links, pages under construction, incorrect scripts, pages that do not read well in all the browsers, non-optimized graphics that read slowly on modem connections. The design seen on some sites is a story for itself, as it is done completely unprofessionally and is inappropriate for an institution such as a Central Bank.

The same can be said of the unused potential of information technologies on the sites analysed within this project. With the exception of the Bank of Slovenia, no Central Bank offered a simple way of viewing and searching statistical data, nor a way to directly download or export data, of the RSS feed[18] type. Most data offered on the sites are, at best, provided in the form of MS Excel documents, which has to be downloaded from the site in order to be potentially used for later calculations. In the second most frequently observed case, data are published in a still worse, PDF format, which is simply unusable for anything but reading and printing, and the user can thus only retype the found data. All this points to the fact that for relevant individuals in the Central Banks the Web is still only a secondary way of data dissemination, subordinated to classic bulletin printing. Actually, all the found formats of data provision on web sites point to the fact that they are derivatives of printed publications or data that were primarily prepared for the person in charge of Desktop Publishing (DTP). Data disseminated in such an impractical form have a negative impact on the web site quality.

All the above leads to the conclusion that the troublesome web sites of Central Banks in the region and the way of data presentation on them result from the banks' information policy. Due to the mission and delicacy of the work they do, Central Banks rarely change the organization and ways they do their business. Slow change adoption is also strengthened by the fact that the staff employed in Central Banks is frequently older than average, which means that the resistance to changes and adoption of new technologies is far more prominent than in companies with younger staff. The social dimension is also frequently prominent, i.e. the fact that a change and automation of work processes would inevitably lead to the extinction of a certain number of jobs, which would put the banks' managements in an unpopular position of downsizing which, in turn, has very negative connotations in the region. Still, regardless of all the reasons cited above, sooner or later these banks' management will have to face this need and adjust the information flow in their respective organizations in accordance with world standards. This will ultimately result in greater efficiency and production of data in polyvalent formats that can be used for designing high-quality web presentations. Finally, this study showed that by implementing e-SQ criteria for measuring service quality and SDDS, the countries' central financial institutions could achieve a relevant grading of their respective sites quality and significantly improve the quality and way of presenting data on them. In this way, they improve the quality of service they provide for interest groups, and generally improve the information on economic trends in their respective countries.

[18] RSS = Really Simple Syndication, a format used for publishing series of data that are frequently changed, such as stoch exchange data, exchange rates, blogs.

References

Bank for International Settlements (2004), 'Foreign direct investment in the financial sector of emerging market economies – Executive Summary', *CGFS Publications*, No. 22, March 2004.

Hanke, S./M. Morgenstern (2001), 'What's Wrong With Central Banks' Websites', John Hopkins University.

Parasuraman, A./V. A. Zeithaml/A. Malhotra (2004), 'E-S-QUAL: A Multiple Item Scale for Assessing Electronic Service Quality', Marketing Science Institute, MSI Reports 2004.

Samuelson, P.A./W. D. Nordhaus (2000), *Economics*, 15th Issue, Translation, Mate, Zagreb, pp. 503, 514.

The International Monetary Fund (1996), 'Guide to the Data Dissemination Standards: Module 1: The Special Data Dissemination Standard', May 1996.

Zeithaml, V.A./A. Parasuraman/A. Malhotra (2002), 'Service Quality Delivery through Web Sites; A Critical Review of Extent Knowledge', *Journal of the Academy of Marketing Science*, Fall 2002.

Internet sources:

Griffiths, R.T. (2002), 'From ARPANET to World Wide Web' [http://www.let.leidenuniv.nl /history/ivh/chap2.htm], Leiden University/NL.

IMF, 'Dissemination Standards Bulletin Board-Overview' [http://dsbb.imf.org/Appli cations/web/overview/].

IMF, 'Dissemination Standards Bulletin Board-Four dimensions of data dissemination' [http:// dsbb.imf.org/Applications/web/sddsdimensions/].

Internet Retailer, 'Slow response to E-mail queries will become a chief source of customer loss', [http://www.internetretailer.com/internet/marketing-conference/87181-slow-respons e-E-mail-queries-will-become-chief-source-customer-loss.html].

Zdeslav Hrepić

Exploring the Role of Pen-based Computing in an Advancing Knowledge Society

Introduction

The ubiquitous presence of computing technologies in the education process and their overwhelming potential for information exchange make advances in this field promising tools for development of a knowledge-based society. A relatively recent milestone in this domain was marked by the wide commercial availability of Tablet PCs and a fast growing number of Tablet PC-specific software products, most notably the Microsoft Windows XP Tablet PC Edition, first introduced in 2002 (Microsoft Corporation 2007).

Tablet PC is a notebook-type computer that can be operated with a stylus in addition to a keyboard or mouse. It owes its added educational utility primarily to the capability of recognizing and displaying handwritten input. This advantage is especially important in fields where hand annotation, formula writing, graphing, schema sketching, or free drawing play an important role. These fields include all sciences, mathematics, a variety of engineering fields, and art. This wide range of areas in which Tablet PCs may play a significant role calls for a serious exploration of the educational value of this hardware.

In accordance with this view, Fort Hays State University (FHSU), initiated a mobile computing programme in the fall of 2005, with the intention of investigating and promoting effective ways of using Tablet PCs in teaching and learning at the university-wide level. After two years of experience, we report on the implementation venues and results of this programme from the perspective of a physics instructor who was part of the initiative from the beginning of the programme.

Exploring the Utility of Tablet PCs in Education

The investigation of the educational use of Tablet PCs does not have a long history, and research literature addressing this question in 2005 was scarce. Thus it was necessary to determine what an instructor can accomplish better, faster or to achieve greater student satisfaction with pen-based hardware than would be possible in a traditional classroom setting. Also, it is necessary to consider, i.e. determine the optimal instructional approach in different scenarios or scenario combinations such as:

- Instructor has a Tablet PC but students do not.
- Instructor and all students have Tablet PCs.

- Classroom is equipped with a wireless infrastructure.
- Tablet PCs are equipped with software enabling real-time communication among all the devices.
- An online course management system is available for utilization.

In this paper we will examine these educational scenarios, present successes and pitfalls that we experienced while implementing them, and show some quantitative results obtained while implementing these strategies in a Physical Science course for non-science majors and in a Modern Physics course for physics majors. While presenting our results and experiences, our aim is to provide a template for employment of the best practices at institutions in the Alps-Adriatic region and also to make it possible to avoid some of the possible pitfalls in implementation. As one might expect, more advantageous and reliable solutions are, in principle, also more costly. For this reason we will also explore low-cost options that, for limited purposes, worked adequately.

Scenarios of the Educational Application of Tablet PCs

Scenarios with one Tablet PC and with Online Course Management System

1. Instructor uses a Tablet PC. During the spring semester of 2005, and before the mobile computing programme was implemented at FHSU, the author used a Tablet PC in instruction – but at this time students did not have Tablet PCs. In this scenario a Tablet PC was used as an electronic chalkboard in teaching introductory physics. The instructor took advantage of slides prepared in advance that contained diagrams, pictorial representations of experimental setups, written problems and photographs of relevant phenomena.

In addition, he wrote derivations and solved problems in real-time on the screen instead of on the chalkboard. This enabled electronic recording of all of the lectures and lecture files which where regularly posted on the online course management system (CMS) called "Blackboard™."[1] The advantage of this approach was that students were able to pay attention to the lecture with the understanding that all the notes would be available to them at the end of the class session. This was especially beneficial for students who were not able to come to class. The disadvantage was that skipping the class became less troublesome for less ambitious students. Also, because students did not have to take notes – and at the same time were not typically engaged in the process of co-creating the content (for example through collaborative activities) – it was not always easy for them to stay focused and on task in this setting.

---

[1] Note: In this paper we use the term "Blackboard" to refer to The Blackboard Academic Suite™.

2. Instructor shares a Tablet PC with students. In order to remedy the negative effect of this non-interactive mode of teaching, we employed the wireless network. In this setup it was possible to project the screen of the Tablet PC onto a large classroom screen from any place in the room and without a physical connection between the computer and the projector. In this situation it was possible for the instructor to present a problem to students and then walk out to any student in the classroom and request that s/he solve the problem. While doing that, the solution was projected on the large screen so the class could see it. As in the previous scenario, only one Tablet PC was used in this scenario as well. However, the level of the students' attention dramatically increased because any of them could be called upon to solve a problem at any time.

Scenarios with Tablet PCs in the Hands of the Instructor and all Students with Online Course Management System

In the spring semester of 2006, as part of the campus mobile computing initiative, FHSU obtained several sets of Tablet PC carts. With these, we had a sufficient number of Tablet PCs to hand out, one to each student in classes not larger than 30. In this setup we again progressed through several stages of advancement toward a more efficient use of this technology.

1. Students and the instructor use Tablet PCs that are not wirelessly networked. It did not take long before we realized that having a Tablet PC for each student is not much of advantage unless they are wirelessly networked and unless there is a way to exchange inputs among devices. In small, upper level class settings for physics majors it was possible to project different computer screens at different times by gathering students around a large conference-type table and by sharing the projector, i.e., by passing the projector cable among the instructor and students. This was another way to accomplish the higher attention level, but this time with multiple Tablet PCs. However, the time and effort spent on cable manipulation made this situation far from optimal. Also, as it is, this scenario is practically impossible in classes larger than about 10 students. It became clear that a wireless network and interactive software are necessary companions for the effective use of Tablet PCs in teaching.

2. Students and the instructor use wirelessly networked Tablet PCs. With wireless infrastructure in place and with Tablet PCs in the hands of all students, the question became how exactly to capitalize on this combination of advanced technology for effective instruction? What kind of software is needed to facilitate the learning process and what (possibly new) teaching strategies will be optimal in this setting?

In order to answer these questions, the physics department faculty at FHSU defined three guiding principles for the implementation of this hardware and (yet to be found) software combination:

- Engagement: as opposed to passiveness
- Collaboration: as opposed to individual work
- In-class learning: as opposed to coming to the classroom to find out what information should be learned and/or memorized later

These three guiding principles together with available hardware defined some new teaching strategies. For example, we envisioned students working in groups – each on their respective Tablet PC screen – in a way so that anything that any of them writes or erases reflects simultaneously on the screens of their partners. The instructor on the other side would have the ability to monitor the work of each group and would scaffold or correct the process accordingly. At the end of the session students would be able to exchange the files with their results.

Implementation principles and teaching strategies such as this one served as a basis for defining the properties of the desired software application, famously named "the killer app". The "killer app" would serve to:

- enable *selective* streaming of inputs (files, text, drawings, pictures, sound) in all directions in a real and virtual (online) classroom,
- enable instructor and participants to select with whom to work in breakout sessions,
- enable individual groups to work either on the same or a different problem – so that markups show up simultaneously on all screens within the group AND not elsewhere,
- monitor students' individual screens showing a participant list and each student's current activity,
- enable the instructor to pick one file (student solution) at a time in order to either show it to the rest of the class or to give a targeted feedback – or both,
- enable student groups to exchange files of their work.

Although our search for the "killer app" was very comprehensive (it included software packages such as Microsoft's Live Meeting™, Groove Virtual Office™, Blackboard Virtual Classroom™, Microsoft One Note™, UW Classroom presenter™, Lotus Virtual Classroom™ and CrossTec SchoolVue™), our expectations were met only when we tried the DyKnow™ Vision and Monitor software package (DyKnow 2007b). Below we present features of the DyKnow software that make it a unique application. DyKnow is a commercially available product, but for our discussion it is important to mention that there is another similar and freely available software package called Ubiquitous Presenter (2007) developed at the University of California at San Diego. The Ubiquitous Presenter shares all of the main features with DyKnow, but lacks some of the fine tunings and is slightly less user-friendly. However, at this point it can be used anywhere and at no cost.

Utilizing Tablet PCs Accompanied by DyKnow Software

DyKnow Vision software is designed to promote the kind of interactive classroom instruction that we wanted to implement. The software has been successfully deployed at all educational levels, including the pre-primary (Lindroth 2006), the tertiary (Roland 2005), and in a variety of academic fields ranging from mathematics (Hubbard 2006) and computer science (Berque et al., 2004) to special education (Exter/Ochoa 2006). A growing number of studies show beneficial effects of the software use on student learning and attitudes. Reported benefits include better learning and retention of concepts, higher levels of student engagement, higher rates of homework completion, and fewer absences (Rockman et al. 2005).

DyKnow software has a variety of features that work toward creating a dynamic learning environment. In this paper, in order to present the advantages of DyKnow software implementation, we group software features into three major categories or sets. Each of these feature sets then defines a new and more dynamic level of classroom usage of the software. If we calibrate a single instructor's use of Tablet PC as a baseline level of capitalizing on Tablet PC versatility, DyKnow software offers the following three distinct steps above that level, each facilitated with one set of software features:

- Feature set 1: New dynamics of note taking
- Feature set 2: Multiple channels of real-time feedback
- Feature set 3: All in control: Students in charge of the teaching/learning game

Each of these sets is an upgrade toward creating a more interactive learning environment, and together they can be employed very productively. Below we elaborate on the advantages of each of these three feature sets.

Feature set 1: New dynamics of note taking. DyKnow works in a way that instructor's annotations (or slides prepared in advance) are wirelessly – and in real time – automatically transmitted to the whole audience. In this way, students can take notes and write clarifications on top of and in addition to instructor's materials rather than spending time on blind copying. This feature cuts class time spent unproductively copying instructional material either onto the chalkboard (by instructor) or into the students' notebooks. This way the role of students as "human copy machines" (DyKnow 2007a) is eliminated. Time can instead be spent on analysis and discussion of the topic. This feature also adds to the accuracy of students' notes and effectively resolves the frequent dilemma of whether to concentrate on note-taking or on following the instructor. In addition, the software records the pen strokes so students can later review annotations as they appear in the order in which they were written. This feature is very helpful for reviewing problems solved in class.

Feature set 2: Multiple channels of real-time feedback. There are four distinct channels of real-time feedback that DyKnow features. They enable effective implementation of formative assessment and can also be used for summative testing. These channels are: (1) "students' status" through which students indicate their level of understanding as high, medium and low; (2) a chat feature through which students can submit a written message to the instructor or to the rest of the class; (3) a pooling option used to elicit multiple-choice answer distributions within the classroom and (4) the slide submission, which enables submission of hand-written solutions to numerical problems or submission of open-ended answers to questions.

These four feedback channels together make it possible for students to be heard by the instructor without using their voices in class. To the instructor, these channels offer all benefits of formative assessment, which include student engagement, immediate feedback, adjusting of teaching well before the exam and according to the specific needs of his/her students. Finally, they facilitate interactive learning and peer instruction (especially in large enrolment classes where those forms of instruction are particularly difficult to accomplish).

Feature set 3: All in control: Students in charge of the teaching/learning game. In this mode of learning, a group of students share the same slide and students within the group compose (ink) annotations together on that slide. This way they can either solve a problem collaboratively or perform a group investigative activity.

This final feature set offers unparalleled interaction opportunities, ranging across group problem solving, collaborative experimental investigations, interaction and discussions within the group, and class-wide brainstorming, and automatic result sharing. Also, while groups work on their problems, the instructor can monitor progress of each group from his own screen, thus intervening and scaffolding as deemed necessary.

These three described sets of the software features, when working together and in synergy, bring about the three goals of instruction that we set forward for usage of this technology: engagement, collaboration, and in-class learning. In the next part of this paper we show results obtained during DyKnow implementation in two introductory physics courses.

Research Questions and Methodology

This study evaluated results of DyKnow software implementation in the teaching of two college level introductory physics courses. The first course was Physical Science, a concept-based introductory physics course for non-science majors. DyKnow was implemented in this course in the summer of 2006 (S06) for the first time and on a pilot basis. The research questions in this initial deployment were:

1. What are the positive and negative aspects of using Tablet PCs and DyKnow software as perceived by students/users?
2. What are student's recommendations for future use of Tablet PCs and DyKnow software in that same course and in other courses?
3. After the pilot study, we conducted more structured research during the fall of 2006 (F06). In this semester, DyKnow was deployed in a calculus-based, modern physics course for physics majors. Both courses were offered at Fort Hays State University, one of the six public universities in the state of Kansas, USA. In addition to research questions investigated during S06, in F06 we sought to answer these additional questions:
4. Does usage of Tablet PCs combined with DyKnow software affect students' test scores?
5. Given the choice of utilizing different levels of technology involvement in instruction, what are the students' preferences in terms of the instruction/presentation mode?

In order to answer the above research questions – as pertaining to introductory college-level physics courses – we used multiple surveys during the S06 and F06 semesters as well as baseline test scores collected during F05 of the modern physics implementation – at that time without DyKnow software.

Results and Analysis

Results of Study in Physical Science Course (Summer 2006)

Two anonymous surveys were administered at the end of the S06 semester. In the first one, we elicited students' attitudes about the software and the various aspects of its usage. The results are shown in Table 1.

These results show a high level of student satisfaction with the software. A large majority of students agreed with the general positive aspects of the software usage (90% and 100% respectively), while at the same time disagreeing with the general negative aspects (between 80% and 100% in different questions). Similarly, in the students' views, DyKnow enhanced their learning (90%) and facilitated their interaction both with the instructor (100%) and with their fellow students (80%).

The impact that DyKnow had on student motivation was also considerable with seventy percent of students being more attentive when DyKnow was used and another fifty-six percent being more motivated. In a similar way, students highly recommended the future usage of DyKnow software and Tablet PC in the Physical Science course and other on-campus courses, as shown in Figure 3 with all answers being in the "Yes" category. One should note that students' recommendations were elicited in another survey, thus the difference in the number of respondents.

Table 1 **Students' end-of-semester evaluation of DyKnow software in Physical Science course (Summer 2006)**

Category of DyKnow Evaluation	General Positive Aspects		General Negative Aspects			Cognition			Communi-cation		Motivation	
Statement: Using DyKnow …	…was enjoyable	…made learning more fun	…was very challenging	…was very frustrating	…was a waste of time	…helped me take better set of notes	…facilitated my learning	…enhanced my understanding of the course material	…enhanced my interaction with classmates	…enhanced my interaction with the instructor	I was more attentive when DyKnow was used	I was more motivated when DyKnow was used
Agree and Strongly Agree		0						0				
Disagree and Strongly Disagree												
N (out of 10 total)	0	0	0	0		0	0	0	0		0	

Figure 2 **Student recommendations for future usage of DyKnow software and Tablet PCs obtained in Physical Science course (S06)**

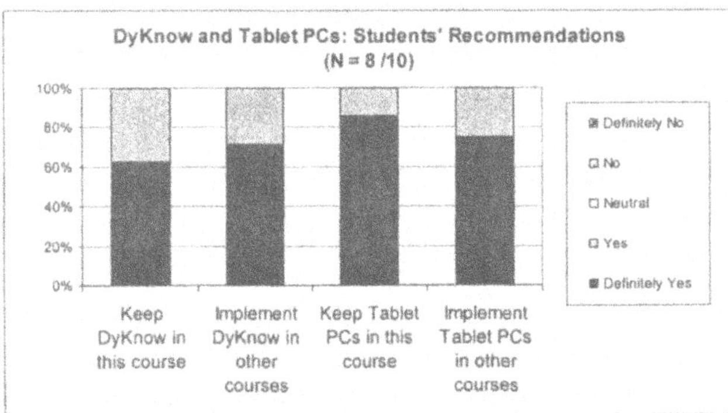

Results of Study in Modern Physics Course (Fall 2006)

Encouraged by the positive results obtained in the Physical Science course, DyKnow was implemented in the modern physics course for physics majors – a sophomore level, calculus based course (Hrepic 2007). We again elicited students' preferences and attitudes related to DyKnow software and Tablet PCs through multiple anonymous surveys administered at different times of the semester. Results corresponding to those obtained in S06 are shown below.

Table 2 Students' end-of-semester evaluation of DyKnow software in Modern Physics course (Fall 2006)

Category of DyKnow Evaluation	General Positive Aspects		General Negative Aspects			Cognition			Communication		Motivation	
Statement: Using DyKnow …	…was enjoyable	…made learning more fun	…was very challenging	…was very frustrating	…was a waste of time	…helped me take better set of notes	…facilitated my learning	…enhanced my understanding of the course material	…enhanced my interaction with classmates	…enhanced my interaction with the instructor	I was more attentive when DyKnow was used	I was more motivated when DyKnow was used
Agree and Strongly Agree	8	7	1	3	0	6	8	5	8	7	4	3
Disagree and Strongly Disagree	1	2	8	6	9	3	1	3	1	2	5	6
N (out of 10 total)	9	9	9	9	9	9	9	8	9	9	9	9

Table 2 indicates highly favourable results in this course as well, although in some aspects less favourable than in the Physical Science course. In both cases all but one of the students reported that using DyKnow was enjoyable and facilitated their learning. Again, the majority of students agreed with positive statements about DyKnow usage (between 78% and 89%) and disagreed with negative statements (between 67% and 100%). Also, a large majority of students stated that DyKnow enhanced their interaction with the instructor (78%) and their classmates (89%). In this course, DyKnow did not appear to make as large a difference in terms of students' attention and motivation.

Thirty three percent of students were more motivated when DyKnow was used and forty-four percent were more attentive. It should be mentioned that in the modern physics course, DyKnow was used consistently, so students' comparisons were between DyKnow usage in this course and other courses in which the programme was not used. In the Physical Science course, DyKnow was used in every other class session due to the limited number of licenses available at the time, so, in that case, students were comparing the same course with and without DyKnow usage.

In the Modern Physics course, students' recommendations for Tablet PC and DyKnow usage again were very favourable with no negative comments, although in this course, certain percentages of students were neutral with respect to their recommendations. Results are shown in Figure 3.

Figure 3 **Student recommendations for future usage of DyKnow software and Tablet PCs obtained in Modern Physics course (F06).**

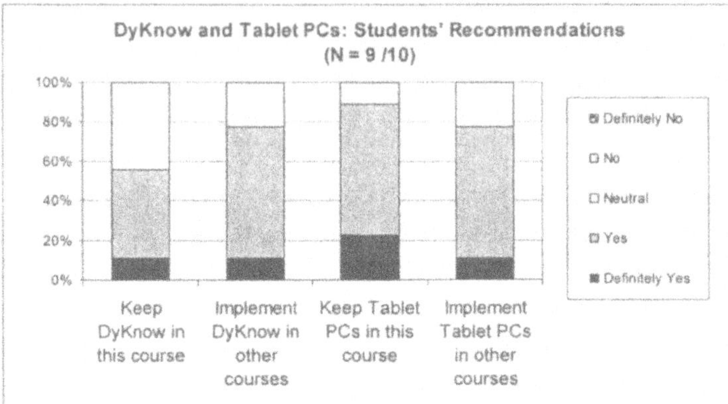

In order to answer the research question related to test scores, we compared students' test results in F05, which served as a baseline data set, with test results collected in F06. The same instructor taught the Modern Physics course in both semesters. In addition, the same textbook was used and the content covered was the same. The scope and complexity of test questions were also the same, although administered problems were different. This difference added to the validity of obtained results since it eliminated the possibility that students had the advantage of taking identical tests administered the previous year. In each of the semesters three tests were administered. Also, one of the tests was repeated in each semester in order to encourage further learning and deeper understanding. Table 3 shows the results obtained in each of the two semesters (Hrepic 2007).

Table 3 **Comparison of test results in Modern Physics course in F05 (without DyKnow) and F06 (with DyKnow)**

	F05 (N=13)		F06 (N=10)		
	Average (%)	SD (%)	Average (%)	SD (%)	P(T<=t) one-tail
Initial test results	71.31	13.04	80.70	16.51	0.1035
Repeated test results	75.78	10.54	82.53	15.92	0.1635

As presented in Table 3, the average test results were 9.39 percent (almost a full grade) better in F06 for the initial test and 6.75 percent for the repeated test. However, because of the small samples, the difference was not statistically significant at 0.05 level. The statistical significance was determined with an independent samples t-Test, assuming equal variances. The equality of the variances was established with Levene's test.

Finally, we gave students the opportunity to express their preferences for different modes of instruction, by independently rating each of them on a scale between 1 and 10, with 10 representing the best alignment with their preference (Hrepic 2007). Four major modes were offered in the survey, two of which utilized DyKnow software and another two which did not:

- *"Chalkboard"* – Instructor writes on chalkboard, and students take notes on paper (Note: This is the traditional presentation mode, and does not involve any technology).
- *"Blackboard™"* – Instructor writes on Tablet PC screen, and students take notes on paper. At the end of instruction, instructor posts his notes on Blackboard™. (Note: Blackboard™ refers to The Blackboard Academic Suite™ – an online course management system).
- *"In-class writing with DyKnow"* – Instructor writes derivations on DyKnow slides so writing also appears on student screens – as it is written. (Note: This mode fully utilizes opportunities of both DyKnow software and Tablet PCs.).
- *"Pre-prepared slides with DyKnow"* – For the most part, the instructor pre-prepares the slide content and sends a whole slide at one time with a follow-up explanation. (Note: this mode differs from the previous one in that derivation is not done in the class. Rather, it is prepared in advance and only explained in the class.)

The results obtained in this survey are shown in Table 4. All ten students took the survey.

Table 4 Students' preferences of different instructional modes

Rate instruction modes individually (Scale 1 - 10):	1&2	3&4	5&6	7&8	9&10	Average (Scale 1 - 10)	SD	Mode	Median	Rank per Average (out of 4)	Model Facilitated by DyKnow
1. "Chalkboard"	3	1	3	2	1	4.6	2.9	1	5.5	3 / 4	No
2. "The Blackboard™"	4	0	2	4	0	4.6	3.0	1	5.5	3 / 4	No
3. In class writing with DyKnow	0	0	2	4	4	8	1.5	7	8	1	Yes
4. Pre-prepared slides with DyKnow	1	2	0	3	4	6.9	2.9	9	7.5	2	Yes

These results indicate students' preference of DyKnow-based teaching settings when compared to the other two options. DyKnow-based teaching modes had higher average scores, smaller standard deviations, and much higher modes of answers. Between the two DyKnow based strategies, students preferred the dynamic usage of the software, with in-class writing of the course material.

Conclusions

In order to develop or advance a knowledge-based society, it is imperative to investigate options and venues offered by emerging computing technologies in improving education in general and in facilitating information sharing. This study explored a variety of different instructional settings and teaching strategies based on usage of Tablet PCs and interactive learning software such as DyKnow. We investigated the utility of this hardware and software combination in teaching two introductory physics courses at Fort Hays State University, a public university in the state of Kansas, USA. Results obtained in both courses (concept-based Physical Science and calculus-based Modern Physics) show students' high level of satisfaction with both Tablet PCs and DyKnow software. The majority of students in both courses recommend that Tablet PCs and DyKnow software be used in the future – in courses they took, as well as in other off-campus courses.

In the Modern Physics course – in which we conducted a more comprehensive study – students' test results showed improvement in the F06 semester when DyKnow was used compared with the previous semester (F05). The difference was substantial (one grade), but due to the small sample, not statistically significant. Furthermore, students in this course on average clearly indicated a preference for DyKnow-based instructional modes when contrasted with other, more traditional teaching settings.

Based on these results, we can highly recommend that institutions in the Alps-Adriatic region consider implementation of Tablet PCs and interactive learning software in teaching. The only major disadvantage of the implementation is the cost of Tablet PCs which are still more expensive than regular laptops with similar processors and memory performances. However, the expense of purchasing Tablet PCs will likely be the main, if not only, financial expenditure associated with the implementation of this technology. This is because wireless networks already exist in many institutions. Although DyKnow software is a commercially available product, there are other, freely available programmes that have all the core functionalities of DyKnow which are available for users any-where in the world (Ubiquitous Presenter 2007).

In the end, we suggest conducting further studies related to the educational value of Tablet PCs and interactive learning software with different, larger populations and in different academic areas.

References

Berque, D./T. Bonebright/M. Whitesell (2004), *Using Pen-Based Computers across the Computer Science Curriculum,* Paper presented at the 35th SIGCSE Technical Symposium on Computer Science Education, Norfolk/VA.

Exter, M. E.,/T. A. Ochoa (2006), 'Interactive Assistive Technology: A Preliminary Analysis of the Use of DyKnow Vision and Wacom Graphire3 4x5 USB Tablets in a Special Education Teacher Preparation Course', in D. A. Berque/J. C. Prey/R. H. Reed (eds.), *The Impact of Tablet PCs and Pen-Based Technology on Education: Vignettes, Evaluations and Future Directions,* Purdue University Press, West Lafayette.

Hrepic, Z. (2007), 'Utilizing DyKnow Software and Pen-Based, Wireless Computing in Teaching Introductory Modern Physics', in *Proceedings of 30th Jubilee International Convention MIPRO, Conference on Computers in Education (2007),* Opatija, Croatia.

Hubbard, J. (2006), 'Use of Pen-Based Technology in Calculus Courses', in D. A. Berque/J. C. Prey/R. H. Reed (eds.), *The Impact of Tablet PCs and Pen-Based Technology on Education: Vignettes, Evaluations and Future Directions,* Purdue University Press, West Lafayette.

Lindroth, L. (2006), 'Blue Ribbon Reviews', *Teaching Pre K - 8,* 36/5, p. 25.

Roland, J. (2005), 'Reviews - DyKnow Vision and Monitor', *The ISTE (International Society for Technology in Education) journal of educational technology practice and policy,* 33/3, p. 38.

Internet sources:

DyKnow (2007a), Company Information [http://www.dyknow.com/company/] retrieved on 3.09.2007.

DyKnow (2007b), Dyknow Vision and Monitor [http://www.dyknow.com/] retrieved on 3.09.2007.

Microsoft Corporation (2007), Windows Xp Tablet PC Edition [http://www.microsoft.com/windowsxp/tabletpc/default.mspx] retrieved on 3.09.2007.

Rockman et al. (2005), A Case Study of DyKnow Vision: Conversations and Observations That Demonstrate Its Educational Potential [http://www.dyknow.com/products/more/North%20Daviess%20case%20study%20-%20FINAL.pdf] retrieved on 20.01.2007.

Ubiquitous Presenter (2007) [http://up.ucsd.edu/] retrieved on 3.09.2007.

CASES FROM THE ALPS-ADRIATIC

Gunhild Sagmeister

Graduates in a Knowledge-based Society

The Meaning of the Term 'Knowledge Society'

When societies are characterized as 'knowledge societies' – what does it mean? Thinking about several labels for society like 'industrial society', 'leisure society', 'service society', 'information society', this has different backgrounds. Industrial society has the meaning, that industry is the basis of the economy and determines the work of most of the people. This is, in an alleviated sense, true for the term service society, conveying that a growing part of the working population is occupied in the service sector. Speaking of leisure society or information society is an indication of trends. Leisure has become an important part of life for more people in the last 30 years than before, and information – using the new technologies – is pervading more and more fields of every day life. So is knowledge, and this is not new. The growing relevance of knowledge for everybody started no later than the industrialization, when people needed a qualification for occupation, gained through formal education. Where, in former times, implicit knowledge and informal learning processes were the basis for survival, formal education became more and more important and the investment of time needed for a special position in work is still growing. To gain access to a higher position it is not enough to have learned a lot, one has to prove this with certificates. In this sense formal knowledge is necessary for the individual to be allowed to work as an expert. People with lower qualifications have more and more problems to enter the so called labour market. (Kößler 2006)

The growing importance of expertise for the creation of intelligent products and services resulted for some authors (e.g. Willke 1998) in seeing knowledge as the fourth factor of production, besides capital, labour and land. Knowledge, of course, is more than facts and information, it includes experience.

Facts and information though are developing a more and more ephemeral character: The process of research and developing new findings is so fast, that five years after graduation from university most of the facts learned there have become obsolete. The newer curricula therefore emphasize qualifications like 'learning to learn' and so called key qualifications, important for work requirements like teamwork or leading people – students have to be able to develop knowledge, not only to gather facts.

Thinking this aspect through, the growing demand for continuing education is a consequence for people living in a so called 'knowledge society', in an attempt to remain a part of this society. As research shows, participation in continuing education is higher for highly educated people in elevated positions than for those working on lower levels – so the stimulative nature of the knowledge society prefers university graduates (cf. Bolder 2006).

A second challenge regarding knowledge is the question of how to make use of it, for both – the individual and the enterprise as well for society as a system. The person has to be able to apply his/her knowledge, which demands willingness and motivation, initiative and analytical competence, to only mention some important aspects. The enterprise has to make the best of the capacity of its employees, which means putting the right person in the right place, but also a lot of communication and teamwork. The development of new knowledge makes it necessary to continuously follow further training and courses to keep the qualifications up-to-date.

Taking into account the global economy and the demands on mobility and flexibility for the enterprises and the employees, an additional demand comes to the fore: Changing structures on the side of the enterprise often lead to only short periods of occupation at the same company – but the person takes the knowledge with him/her, and the employer loses it, if he/she has not built up an efficient knowledge management system, making sure that it will remain available.

These few aspects regarding some theoretical aspects of 'knowledge society' lead to some empirical findings of an EU-Project, in which Austria participated [1]. The main questions to be discussed are:

- Are graduates able to use their knowledge?
- Are the working situations demanding professional knowledge?
- Did graduates follow further training?

---

1 *The Flexible Professional in the Knowledge Society– New Demands on Higher Education in Europe.* The REFLEX project focused on three broad and interrelated questions: (1) which competencies are required by higher education graduates in order to function adequately in the knowledge society? (2) what role is played by higher education institutions in helping graduates to develop these competencies? (3) what tensions arise as graduates, higher education institutions, employers and other key players each strive to meet their own objectives, and how can these tensions be resolved? The project developed a series of instruments designed to provide the information required to answer these questions. These instruments are: (1) a country study highlighting the main structural and institutional factors that shape the relation between higher education and work in nine European countries; (2) a qualitative study on graduate competences in the knowledge society; (3) a survey of higher education graduates in these countries. The REFLEX project was financed as a Specific Targeted Research Project (STREP) of the European Union's Sixth Framework Programme. The project involved partners from fifteen countries (Austria, Finland, France, Germany, Italy, the Netherlands, Norway, Spain and the UK plus Belgium-Flanders, Czech Republic, Portugal, Switzerland, Japan and Estonia that have received funding from national sources). A parallel project using large parts of the REFLEX methodology is being undertaken in Russia and Latin America (Mexico, Colombia).

How Demanding are the Working Situations?

Labour situations of graduates differ very much regarding the demand for knowledge, the degree of utilization of knowledge and skills in current work and the appropriateness of the field of study for this work. Of course, a distinction may also be drawn, if the person is self-employed and if she or he is working in the public or private sector. The graduates cope with different situations in various ways, which has an influence on the development as an expert in the working situation. Looking at the variables describing their expertise and constructing groups, the following types may be distinguished:

Table 1 Expert role in the working situation

ITEMS	Types (based on Latent Class Analysis)[2]		
	I (53%)	II (22%)	III (18%)
Field of study most appropriate for this work	Exclusively own field/ own or related field	Completely different field/ no particular field	Exclusively own field/ own or related field
Type of education most appropriate for this work	Master degree or higher	Bachelor or no higher education	Master degree or higher
How much time does it take to become an expert in this kind of work	At least 3 years	2 years maximum	2 years maximum
To what extent are knowledge and skills utilized in your current work	To a great extent	To a low extent/ not at all	To a great extent
To what extent does your current work demand more knowledge and skills than you can actually offer	To a low extent/ not at all	To a low extent/ not at all	To a low extent/ not at all
Type	***Professional Expert***	***'Jobber'***	***Flexible Professional***

Three out of five types show relevant percentages and may be described as follows. The *first type* may be characterized as **professional expert**; most of the people in this group are graduates in Business Administration. Graduates voting this way are slightly more frequently self employed and more likely to be male. In this group more engineers are to be found. Especially physicians, but also architects, teachers and psychologists tend to be professional experts. Regarding physicians and teachers it has to be taken into account that these professions are required to complete a postgraduate training programme before being allowed to work in this capacity.

The *second type* also works in the private sector and is not self-employed, but for her (more female)/his current work a lower level of education and another field of study or no particular field would be appropriate, so his/her knowledge

2 Latent Class Analysis tries to categorize answers into different types. In this case five classes were statistically identified, but only three with a higher percentage, which are shown in the graph.

and skills are not utilized to a high extent. This seems to be a **precarious labour situation**. He/she graduated mostly in Humanities or Education and Teacher Training or in Social and Behavioural Sciences.

The *third type* is an **expert** as well, although not to the same extent as the professional expert, because the time needed to become familiar with the work tasks is two years at the most. This group is not very specific, the only possible characterization to be made is this: members of this group most probably work in the fields of business administration or law, or as social scientists. Managers as well as another group of engineers show more of the profile of this flexible professional type.

Extent of Responsibility at Work

A high grade of professionalism is closely connected to a high level of responsibility – so the graduates were asked about their responsibility in different dimensions. Looking at the extent of responsibility in their work, there are some differences to be seen (cf. Figure 1 below).

Figure 1 Responsibility for ...

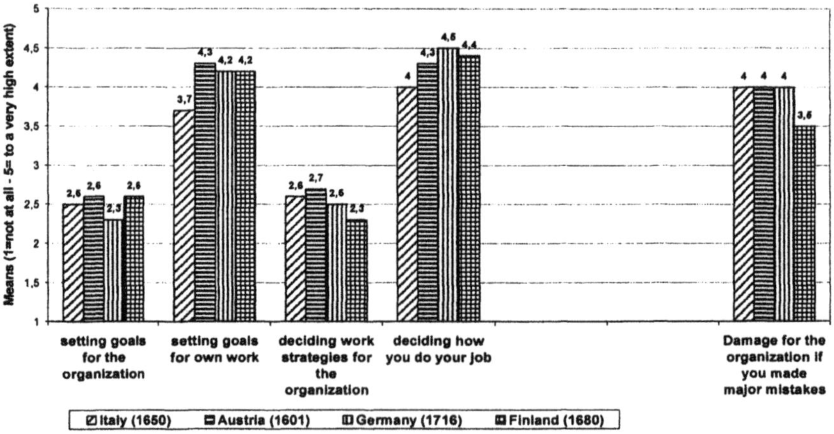

The most important area of responsibility is – not surprisingly – the own frame of work. Both types of professionals decide how they do their work and set their goals more or less on their own. Both seem to have some opportunity to take decisions for the organization, but not yet to a great extent. The jobbers, on the other hand, show much less responsibility in all respects.

Expert Roles in Other European Countries

Taking the variables defining the expert roles and looking at how far such types are to be found in other European countries, the following picture arises:

Figure 2 Professional role

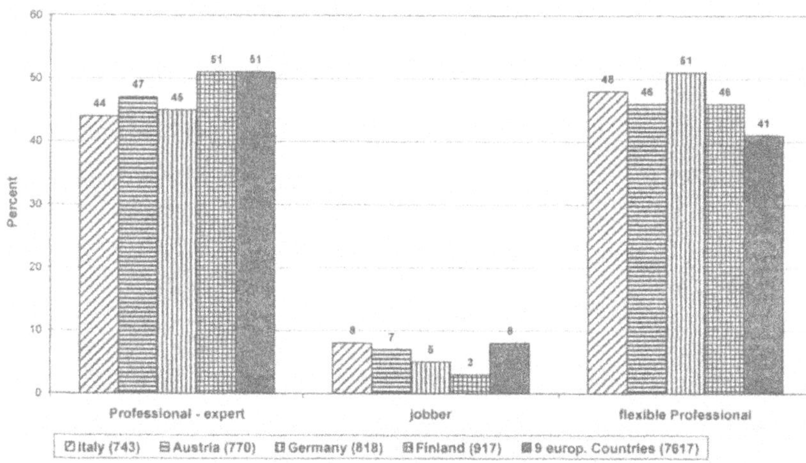

The professional expert is nearly as common as the flexible professional, only few people face a working situation not really requiring their expertise. While Italy and Germany seem to have more occupational situations demanding more flexibility-aspects, in Finland a more focused professional expertise seem to be slightly more important. Austrian graduates show a more or less balanced situation.

Required Competencies

Consequently the required competences at work are much higher for graduates working as professionals than for those working in lower jobs – the only exception is the ability to work with the new communication technologies, which is necessary in nearly every job. Also the ability to work productively together with others is required from all.

Are there different requirements regarding competences comparing Austria and Italy?

Figure 3 Highly required competencies – Austria and Italy

Austrian professionals seem to face higher requirements than Italians regarding knowledge of their own discipline in both expert positions. The demand regarding the rapid acquisition of new knowledge and the ability to work together with others is nearly the same in both countries. In Italy the flexible professional has to assert his authority more, but at the same time should be willing to question his own and others' ideas to a higher extent than the Austrian colleagues – this might be an indication of different working cultures. Differences may be caused by the size of the enterprise and if it is a global player or not, which makes it necessary to deal with people coming form various cultures, working in another situation.

Evaluation of Study Programmes

Another part of the explanation might come from the study programmes in the different countries – what are the specific strong and weak points?

Figure 4 Strong points of the own study programme

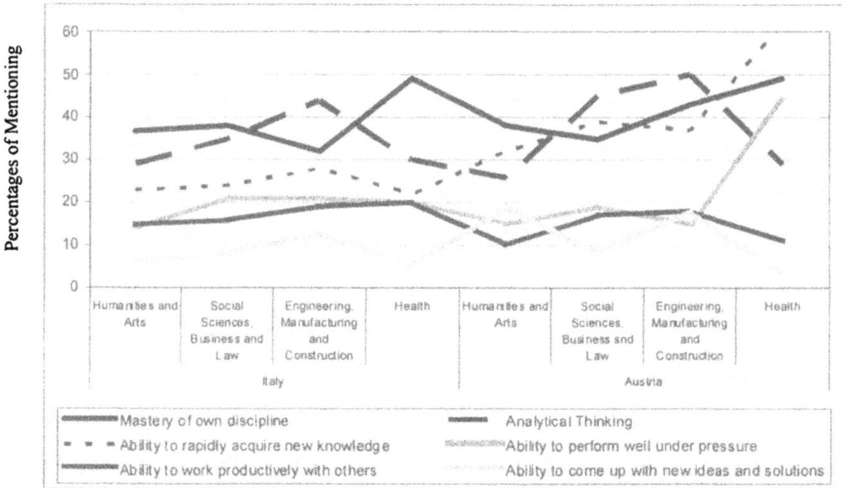

While in Austria the ability to rapidly acquire new knowledge is more often mentioned as a strong point of the completed study, especially regarding health studies, where new research results are crucial, Italian graduates in general are more reticent about pointing out strengths, and if so, they stress mastery of their discipline and analytical thinking – on a very similar level as the Austrians. The creative aspect of developing new knowledge (indicator: the ability to come up with new ideas and solutions) seems not to play such an important role in university studies as could be expected in a knowledge based society. For Austria, this aspect was stressed more than in Italy, especially in study fields like Engineering and Humanities. Nevertheless this is mentioned as one of the weak points of their study, as the following graph shows, but even more by graduates of health studies.

Looking at the mentioned weak points, the graduates of both countries identify a deficit in language competences. This result is not really new – former graduate studies showed this lack as well (cf. Guggenberger/Kellermann/Sagmeister 2001), but it becomes more important, working in globally acting enterprises. Austrians in addition would like to have more ability to present as well as to negotiate effectively – here a correspondence might be seen to the required competences. Italian graduates have these competencies and they are highly required.

Figure 5 **Weak points of the study programme**

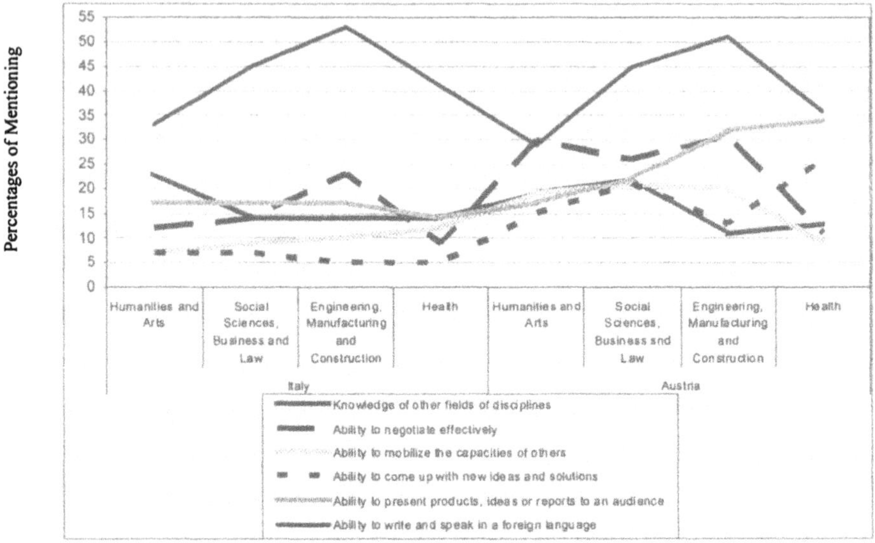

Here the question arises, how does the organizational side look?

The Extent of Change and Innovations in the Working Organization

One of the most central questions in the REFLEX Project was the extent of changes and innovations in the working situation. To estimate the change and innovation process the following questions are relevant: has a major change in the own work tasks or a reorganization taken place since the graduate started working in the current employment; what is the extent of innovations and is the organization at the forefront when it comes to adopting innovations, new knowledge or new methods?

Out of the six types identified by the LCA-Analysis five show a relevant number and are to be found on a dimension between conservative and highly innovative with greater changes taking place in the organization.

The *first type* may be characterized as a *conservative* 'business as usual' company. The study fields of graduates working in such organizations are more likely to be Education, Teacher Training or Humanities.

The *second type is very similar*, but innovative in regard to adopting knowledge and methods. Both more often belong to the public sector, namely education and health.

Table 2 Types of more or less innovative working situations

Items (original wording)	Types (based on Latent Class Analysis)[3]				
	I (32%)	II (19%)	III (16%)	IV (15%)	V (14%)
Changes taken place in your organization since you started working there: major change in my own work tasks	No	No	Yes	No	Yes
Changes taken place in your organization since you started working there: reorganization	No	No	Yes	No	Yes
Aspects extent of innovation: product or service	To a low extent	To a low extent	To a low extent	To a great extent	To a great extent
Aspects extent of innovation: technology, tools or instruments	To a low extent	To a low extent	To a low extent	To a great extent	To a great extent
Aspects extent of innovation: knowledge or methods	To a low extent	To a great extent	To a low extent	To a great extent	To a great extent
Adopting innovations by organization	Mainly a follower	Mainly a follower	Mainly a follower	Mainly at forefront	Mainly at forefront

The *third type* of working situations is interesting, because graduates working in companies characterized in this way say that changes have taken place in the last few years, but the organization is not really innovative. As these companies have more people working in them and the scope is more international than local or regional, it might be, that these companies belong to an international organization, which is reorganizing the structure top down for more economical reasons, but not operating very innovatively.

The *fourth type* is just characterized the other way round: *highly innovative, but no recent structural changes*. The companies are large (more than 1.000 employees) and operate internationally.

People working in a *highly innovative working situation (type five)* come from study fields like Engineering or Business Administration. They tend to estimate that the appropriate level of education for their job should be at least a master's degree, while those working in a not very innovative situation without big changes more often think a lower degree would be fitting as well.

So it is not surprising, that graduates working in an innovative enterprise have more often followed a work related course during the previous year (especially Austrian graduates). Comparing the working status, self-employed graduates characterize their working situation as highly innovative much more frequently than others. While the more conservative working situations, showing low innovative initiative operate more regionally, the innovative types act more internationally, belong to the private sector in the field of real estate agency, consultancy and also production (engineers). The flexible organizations compete

---

3 The Latent Class Analysis contains six classes, but only five with higher percentages.

mainly by quality, the more conservatively oriented tend to compete more by price.

Of course, these different working situations have an impact on the role of the graduates: In the innovative enterprises they more often supervise staff members and play a role in introducing new knowledge, methods and technologies. Their professional expertise is much more in demand: They advise colleagues, keep them informed about new developments and establish professional contacts outside the own company much more than graduates working in more conservatively acting enterprises.

As how innovative are the working organisations described in different countries?

The extent of innovation in the working organization, where graduates are employed, in their view shows a very similar picture across all the countries involved in the project. As can be expected, main innovations affecting their work place are in the areas of 'knowledge and methods' or 'product and services'. In this regard Austria and Italy show the same situation, while innovation in the area of technologies seems to be more common in Italian enterprises.

Does innovation influence the use of knowledge and the role graduates play in their working situation?

Figure 6 Use of knowledge (extent to which statements apply)

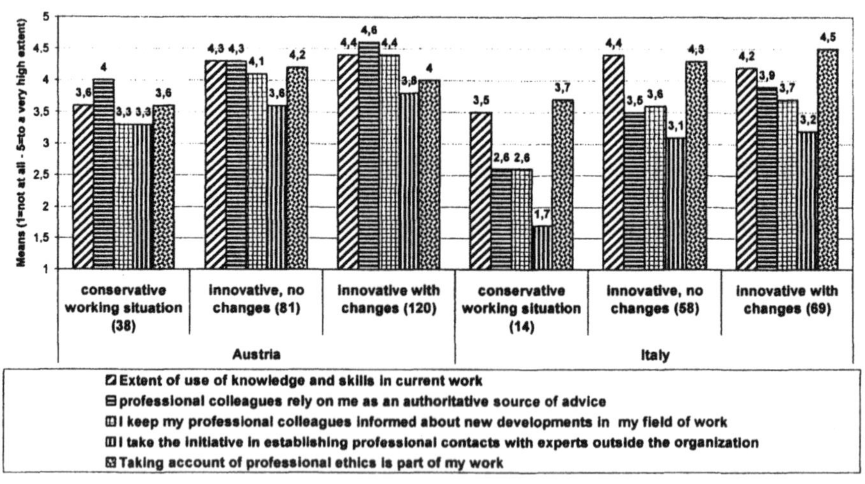

It is not surprising that the use of available knowledge of the graduates is given more in innovative working situations, where young people bring newer knowledge. But are they already accepted in their professional role, giving advice and informing colleagues about new developments in their field of work? In Austria this seems to be much more the case than in Italy, especially regarding initiatives in establishing contacts with experts outside the organization – graduates could make use of their connections with study-colleagues. Young professionals in Italy, working in innovative organizations, on the contrary emphasize more taking account of professional ethics – may be for them it is more important to become accepted as somebody belonging to the group of professionals.

Are there Consequences for Further Learning Strategies from these Differences?

It might be a consequence of being highly demanded in the work environment, that continuing education is seen as a matter of course. So, how do the graduates in the different situations follow their career – do they continue their education?

The professional experts were more likely to have followed work-related courses in the previous year than flexible professionals. Italian graduates show the same behaviour, but on a lower level of participation – maybe the lower extent of responsibility does not motivate them in the same way as seems to be the case for the Austrian professionals. If one thought that 'jobbers' participate more in continuing education to enhance their career – this is not the case everywhere, as the following graph shows.

Figure 7 Reason for following work-related courses

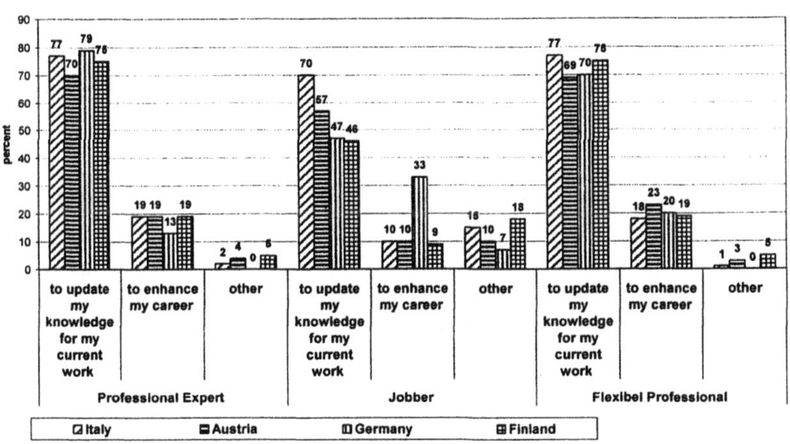

German graduates follow this goal, while Italians try to update their knowledge. This was an important reason for Austrian graduates as well. The most interesting result is that the professionals join courses to update their knowledge for the current job. This may be interpreted as an indication that the demand in the job is high. Although most of the graduates said that their work does not demand much more knowledge than they can offer – but without further learning this could become the case very quickly. Especially Italian graduates seem to face this, German professional experts as well, more so than the Austrians.

Conclusions

Coming back to the term of the 'knowledge society', these results make evident that there is an interactive relation between knowledge and products, service and technologies. Knowledge helps to be creative and develop new ideas. Development of new products and technologies is both: result and basis of new knowledge and further research.

Being allowed to take responsibility not only for one's own work, but for setting goals for the organization and being involved in the development of strategies, earning appreciation inside and outside the organization, seems to motivate the professionals to keep developing their competencies – a positive result for both sides, the person and the organization.

For the system of higher education the evaluation five years after graduation indicates shortcomings in foreign language competencies nearly everywhere and in most of the studies. To varying extents the balance between knowledge of the field of study and key qualifications could be improved. Regarding the transition to work the option to become self-employed could be brought into better view during the studies.

References

Bolder, Axel (2006), 'Weiterbildung in der Wissensgesellschaft. Die Vollendung des Matthäus-Prinzips', in U. H. Bittlingmayer/U. Bauer (eds.), *Die "Wissensgesellschaft" Mythos, Ideologie oder Realität?*, VS Verlag für Sozialwissenschaften, Wiesbaden, pp. 431 - 444.

Guggenberger, Helmut/Paul Kellermann/Gunhild Sagmeister (2001), 'Wissenschaftliches Studium und akademische Beschäftigung. Vier Jahre nach Studienabschluss. Ein Überblick', Unpublished Research Report, Klagenfurt.

Kößler, Reinhard (2006), 'Skeptische Anmerkungen zur Formbestimmung von "Arbeit" und "Wissen"', in: U. H. Bittlingmayer/U. Bauer (eds.), *Die "Wissensgesellschaft" Mythos, Ideologie oder Realität?*, VS Verlag für Sozialwissenschaften, Wiesbaden, pp. 353 - 372.

Willke, Helmut (1998), *Systemisches Wissensmanagement*, Lucius & Lucius (UTB Wissenschaft) Stuttgart.

Gabriella Rigoni

The Function of ERDISU of Trieste within a New Concept of the Right to Higher Education in the Alps-Adriatic Area and the Adriatic Euroregion

Introduction

Before tackling the subject of the function of the ERDISU[1] of Trieste, the regional body for supporting the right to higher education, within a new concept of the right to higher education, I would like to give just a short description of the cultural, technical and scientific background in which this institution works.

After a specific law was approved in 1963, Friuli Venezia Giulia became one of the five Italian regions with a special statute (i.e. regions empowered with a particular territorial jurisdiction). Friuli Venezia Giulia was awarded greater autonomy, which allows the Regional Administration to introduce its own laws on specific subjects agreed on with the National Government.

The region is divided into four provinces: Trieste, Udine, Pordenone and Gorizia. The regional capital is Trieste. The resident population is 1.216.016 (as at 31/12/2006).

Friuli Venezia Giulia is a region which, thanks to its highly favourable geo-political and economic position, has a historical vocation to international trade and has a balanced industrial structure made up mainly of small and medium enterprises and with a significant tradition in the fields of science and innovation. The region hosts a highly advanced scientific system, based on competences and know-how in fields ranging from physics, pharmacology, and chemistry to nanotechnology and bioengineering.

Thanks to these favourable factors and to the availability of highly qualified human resources it is an area with great innovative ability. The region has always focused on supporting research and industry development and features an enviable quality of life and a low unemployment rate. This factor makes the territory particularly attractive.

Universities and Other Important Advanced Education, Training, Research and Technological Institutions

Friuli Venezia Giulia hosts three universities and features prestigious research institutions, science and technology parks, business incubators and technology transfer services.

---

[1] ERDISU = **E**nte **R**egionale per il **DI**ritto e le opportunità allo **S**tudio **U**niversitario

In *Trieste* there are two Universities: The University of Trieste which has twelve faculties and the International School for Advanced Studies, which was the first Italian university to offer the PhD degree. It represents one of the leading scientific institutions in Italy and is a noted centre on the international stage. Other important advanced education, training, research and technological institutions in Trieste are: ICTP – International Centre for Theoretical Physics, which is a research and international co-operation centre in the field of physics and mathematics; the Area Science Park, one of the most important multisector Science and Technology Parks in Europe. It is the greatest research structure in Friuli Venezia Giulia and hosts institutions such as CBM, the Consortium for the Centre of Molecular Biomedicine, ICS-UNIDO International Centre for Science and High Technology of the United Nations Industrial Development Organization, Elettra – Synchrotron Light Laboratory for basic and applied research activities in the fields of physics, chemistry, life and materials sciences. MIB School of Management, a business school for advanced management training which offers courses from an international perspective and conducts research in the main areas of international management.

In *Udine* there is one University, a well-established and constantly growing reality, with ten faculties and 16.407 enrolled students (as at 31.07.2007). The "Luigi Danieli" Science and Technology Park is the centre for research and technological transfer of Udine University.

In *Pordenone* we can mention the CRO, Oncology Reference Centre, one of the six Italian national oncology centres operating in cancer research and the Pordenone technological Pole supporting competitiveness of local enterprises.

In *Gorizia* there is the International Institute of Sociology (ISIG) and other departments of both Trieste and Udine Universities. The Gorizia Technological Pole is an Area Science Park structure which promotes growth and generates co-operation aimed at innovation in accordance with the needs of the territory.

Lisbon Objectives

The role of the Regional Authority and public administration is extremely important in the economic and social growth, as through the formulation of various initiatives and strategies it can accelerate the process of attaining the objectives of a knowledge economy set out by the Lisbon strategy.

The *employment situation* in Friuli Venezia Giulia (FVG) shows a positive trend. In 2005 the employment rate in Friuli Venezia Giulia (63.2%) was higher than the Italian average (57.6%) and in line with the EU-27 average (63.3%) – the Lisbon objective for 2010 is 70 percent. The unemployment rate in the region (4.1% in 2005) ranks better than both the Italian average (7.7% in 2005) and the EU-27 average (9.0% in 2005).

The *number of graduates in science and technology* in Friuli Venezia Giulia is also positive: In 2005 the value was 13.5 compared with 10.9 (Italian average) and 12.9 (EU-27 average). The indicator "Tertiary graduates in science and technology" includes new tertiary graduates in a calendar year from both public and private institutions completing graduate and post graduate studies per 1000 of population aged 20 - 29 years, an age group that corresponds to the typical graduation age in most countries.

Still unsatisfactory however is the *gross domestic expenditure on research and development* financed by government and by industry in Friuli Venezia Giulia. Public expenditure on research and development in our region is higher than the Italian average, but is still much lower than the EU average.

In 2003 gross domestic expenditure on R&D as a percentage of GDP (gross domestic product) in Friuli Venezia Giulia was 0.64, compared with 0.58 (Italian average) and with 1.9 (European Union – 25 countries).

The strategic lines of the Regional Authority focus on the realization of a knowledge society and a knowledge economy with a lot of interventions. Let us mention some of them:

- financing Universities in FVG
- financing selected research projects submitted by research centres
- financing technological transfer and technical assistance to enterprises
- financing large research projects of regional interest, such as renewable energy, biodiversity in agriculture, environmental protection etc.
- venture capital for university spin-off companies
- projects for local development of mountain areas
- territorial marketing to strengthen competitiveness.

This list can give us an idea of how the Public Administration can help all actors and stakeholders involved in the process of transforming the economic system of FVG from an economic model based on the manufacturing industry to a model based on knowledge (service economy with high knowledge content).

The Function of ERDISU Trieste and ERDISU Udine, the two Regional Bodies for Supporting the Right to Higher Education

It is within this social and cultural context that the two regional bodies for supporting *the right to higher education* work hand in hand with the universities and the other scientific institutions and are therefore actors in a knowledge society.

Article 34 of the Italian Constitution establishes the principle of the right of individual citizens to higher education: "All those who can prove the necessary competency and commitment have a right to pursue the highest levels of education, regardless of their financial means."

The possibility of attending university and obtaining a degree through a regular course of academic study is guaranteed by a series of services promoted by the so called "right to study", which in Italy is governed by National Law No. 390 dated December 1991. The State has established a set of rules for optimizing and organizing the entire system of services, distinguishing between the duties of the University and those of the Regions as a result of the devolution of administrative powers.

In the Autonomous Region of Friuli Venezia Giulia the Regional Law No. 12 of 23 May 2005 within the national legal framework governs the principles, aims and interventions of the two regional bodies for supporting the right to higher education: the ERDISU of Trieste and the ERDISU of Udine. They are public institutions with administrative, managerial and accounting autonomy and are under the control of the Friuli Venezia Giulia Region. ."

The *main objectives of their interventions* are:

- to remove social and economic barriers that limit the access to academic education,
- to reduce academic desertion fostering interventions that help the students to become integrated in the University community and in the new environment,
- to enhance academic retention improving the higher education offer through services and activities for all students and promote academic achievement and progress towards graduation.

The concept of the right to higher education was traditionally considered as a series of interventions such as financial aid, accommodation and restaurant services based on precise criteria related to income and merit and consequently reserved for deserving but financially disadvantaged students according to the constitutional principle aiming to overcome social and economic barriers to post-secondary education.

This concept has changed over the years, as it has become increasingly necessary to promote opportunities that help the generality of students to integrate into academic and social life. The ERDISU of Trieste has already begun to rethink its role, introducing activities and projects that go beyond basic assistance.

Main Services Offered by ERDISU Trieste

Study grants – ERDISU assigns study grants to students with low income and who meet specific merit criteria. It also provides a service for fiscal assistance to students who have to prepare documentation proving their economic situation.

There is a high percentage of non-EU students (Albanian, Croatian, Lebanese, African, Chinese etc.) benefiting from ERDISU grants (473 in the academic year 2006 - 2007, out of 2040 grants assigned, i.e. 21,4%) and services.

Student Residences – ERDISU provides an accommodation service for non-local students studying at the University of Trieste and at the Trieste Conservatoire. A certain number of rooms in the residence halls are reserved every year for foreign students spending a study period at the University of Trieste within the Erasmus Programme.

In Trieste ERDISU has three halls of residence with 463 beds in all. Most of them are in single rooms, but there are also 60 small flats for one or two persons. 15 rooms are specially equipped for disabled students and 137 rooms (i.e. 30% of total number) were assigned to non-EU students in 2006 - 2007. Three more halls of residence in Trieste are under reconstruction at the moment and will offer about 470 rooms in all when they are finished.

In Gorizia ERDISU has a hall of residence in a historical palace with 45 beds in completely renewed single and double rooms. Two rooms are specially equipped for disabled students and 14 (i.e. 31% of the total number) were assigned to non-EU students in 2006 - 2007. In all halls of residence there are common and multi-purpose rooms: kitchens, computer rooms, TV-rooms, conference rooms, libraries etc. *The monthly rate* paid by students varies according to their economic situation, and ranges from a minimum of 80 EUR per month for a single room to a maximum of 120 EUR per month for a one-room flat. The rooms are assigned every year to applying students on the basis of precise income and merit criteria and according to room availability.

Contributions towards accommodation costs – As there is not sufficient space for all applying students in the halls, ERDISU pays a yearly contribution to students who rent a room or a flat and meet the established income and merit criteria. There are two kinds of contribution: *1.200 EUR* per year for students with the lowest economic level foreseen for this service and *600 EUR* per year for students with a higher economic level.

Grants for degree thesis – Students at the end of their university career who want to prepare their degree thesis spending a study period abroad or in Italy outside of Friuli Venezia Giulia, Veneto and Trentino Alto Adige can apply for a grant if they meet the economic and merit criteria established. The amount of the grant is: *1.600 EUR* for study periods abroad and *800 EUR* for study periods in Italy.

Contributions for international mobility – Students who meet established economic and merit criteria have the right to a contribution integrating the international mobility grants assigned within EU mobility programmes, i.e. Erasmus, or also non-communitarian mobility programmes. The contribution amounts to *500 Euro* per month for a maximum of 10 months with an additional reimbursement for travel expenses.

Restaurant services – Restaurant service in the form of low-cost meals to students is provided by ERDISU both through own restaurants and through structures that have an agreement with ERDISU Trieste. In Trieste there are two central student restaurants serving about 1.800 meals a day. Students of dislocated faculties, such as Medicine or those studying at the International School for Advanced Studies or at Area Science Park have access to the canteens of these structures. Restaurant service is provided also in Gorizia (two structures), in Pordenone and Portogruaro.

The cost of one full meal is covered by the student on the basis of his income situation. There are three income brackets:

- 1,55 EUR for students in the lowest bracket,
- 3,10 EUR for students in the intermediate bracket,
- 4 EUR for students in the higher bracket.

Transport cost allowance – ERDISU Trieste has recently signed an agreement with the three public transport companies of Trieste, (Trieste Trasporti), Gorizia (APT) and Pordenone (ATAP) to reduce transport costs for all students enrolled at the University of Trieste: Students can buy an annual or a monthly bus pass with a 50 percent reduction on the full price, while the remaining 50 percent is covered by ERDISU through a contribution by the Regional Authority.

Library, audiovisual media service and internet connection – In one of the student residence halls ERDISU provides a library service where students can read or borrow national and foreign newspapers, magazines as well as audiovisual means. In the residences there are PC rooms with internet connection.

Cultural and recreational activities – ERDISU promotes cultural and recreational activities financing initiatives carried out by student associations (expositions, conferences, debates, theatre and music activities, courses etc.). These cultural and recreational events organized are open to everyone.

MOVE Project – This is an international mobility project, which has been promoted by ERDISU since 2000 with the objective of both enhancing the international dimension within the framework of regional research and educational activities and fostering a constant exchange system between University and enterprises in terms of research and high-standard training.

The project is financed by the Regional Authority, by the University of Trieste and by private companies and institutions. It is open to all students who meet established merit criteria, regardless of their income situation. The income situation of the applying students is taken into account only to determine the amount of the grants, which vary from a minimum of 500 EUR per month to a maximum of 1.000 EUR per months.

Up to 2008, 295 mobility grants have been financed for traineeships carried out throughout Europe by graduates and undergraduates of Trieste University. ERDISU has signed 230 traineeship agreements with foreign host structures.

The Future of ERDISU

These are the main activities that ERDISU of Trieste carries out at present, but the institution has already begun to rethink its post-secondary education policy and to realize this new concept of the right to higher education.

On the one side, ERDISU is planning to strengthen its traditional mission of providing accommodation with a strategic view, attracting relevant national and international actors in the field of science, culture, sports etc. On the other hand, ERDISU is working to develop new services, activities and collaborations, introducing interventions aiming at enhancing all students' opportunities to pursue and achieve high-quality education and training.

Our participation in Klagenfurt at the international symposium in September 2007 is due first of all to the organisation's desire to widen its range of action and broaden contacts with other actors, to establish new collaborations, to learn from the experience of others and share views on subjects of common interest in a transnational context.

Projects for the future focus on enhancing international mobility throughout Europe, on cross-border collaborations especially within the Alps-Adriatic area and the Adriatic Euroregion as a platform for cultural, scientific, technological co-operation and exchange.

A transnational collaboration through co-ordinated interventions to sustain students on undergraduate, graduate, doctoral and research levels would therefore represent a strategic instrument as the result of a joint project.

ERDISU is planning not only to reconstruct residences with large capacities in Trieste, but also to run new ones, in order to improve the host capacity and the attractiveness of the region for graduates and undergraduates coming from abroad for a study or research period, a traineeship or for other sports and cultural events.

An example is a residence in Gorizia, which was once a boarding school run by nuns and is now almost abandoned or anyway certainly underused.

This structure has an auditorium, large luminous learning rooms, a conference room, 116 bedrooms, DSL-connection, a large garden and parking spaces. What makes it even more interesting is its strategic position alongside the border between Gorizia and Nova Gorica, near the University campus and the hospital. It could become a meeting house for international events, a residence for master courses, educational and cultural cross-border activities.

The objective is to set up a study network of experts working in centres of excellence for higher education, research etc. as well as experts working in structures of logistical support providing residences, restaurants, grants for students, teachers and researchers. This network should work in strict collaboration with the regional territory and its resources in order to contribute to outline possible development strategies, to define social standards for transnational areas, focusing special attention on youth.

Gordana Forčić – Bojana Ćulum

Civil Involvement in the Knowledge Society – The Case of Volunteering in Primorsko-Goranska County (Croatia)

Introduction

Various research studies describe volunteering as one of the strongest elements in developing and shaping democratic changes in every society. Furthermore, volunteering affects the economic development of a country. The authors of this paper deal with issues regarding the research of volunteering in Croatia. They also give an overview of the most important results of the only comparative research conducted in Croatia (in one of its counties) with the time distance of five years. The results show a slight increase of citizen engagement in volunteer activities. Low frequency of volunteering and negative attitudes of the younger population continue to represent key challenges for all the subjects involved in promoting and developing volunteering.

The results confirm a need to further develop and improve volunteering in such a way that all the segments of society (the state, local and regional government, the media, civil society organizations, the business sector, educational institutions) have to continuously and simultaneously contribute to the development of volunteering in Croatia through activities in each of their domains in the following areas: acknowledging volunteer work, promoting and organizing volunteering, establishing networks and influencing public policy.

Volunteer Work – Contributing to Democratic Changes in Society

Volunteering is one of the strongest elements in developing and shaping democratic changes in every contemporary society. Furthermore, it allows citizens to engage in various citizen initiatives and make their contribution to developing their community and society in general by offering their free time, knowledge and experiences, enthusiasm and energy. According to the United Nations Economic and Social Council's report, "*volunteering is both a habit of the heart and a civic virtue. It is an action deeply rooted in the human spirit with a far-reaching social and cultural impact. Listening to, being concerned with and responding to the needs of others are evidence of the highest human motivation. Human beings help each other out of love and compassion. Yet, in its deepest spiritual dimension and symbolic meaning, volunteering is not simply something that we do for others. Our own values and humanity are at stake: we are what we give".*[1]

The concepts of volunteerism and volunteering are subject to different interpretations and understandings. These interpretations and understandings are tightly connected with tradition, cultural conditions and the social context of a particular country. According to a traditional understanding of volunteerism (unselfish service to others), Govaart and associates (2001) offer a contemporary understanding of volunteerism viewed through mutual support, delivering service and active social participation. In traditional societies mutual support is based on a natural human desire to survive or to live better, and is provided inside a close circle of people. Volunteerism in the form of delivering service is mostly connected with organized, often institutional contexts while active social participation, on the other hand, represents a form of people's self organization (based on participation principles) in solving problems. Volunteerism has recently started to be connected with the concept of leisure. Certain authors define or describe it as a free activity of an individual. Stebbins (1996) connects volunteering with the concept of serious leisure stating clear differences between the following types of volunteering: career and casual, formal and informal and occupational and non-occupational volunteering. The serious leisure model suits most those types of volunteering classified as formal and nonoccupational, i.e. those in which volunteers can pursue their careers.

The potential of volunteerism to find solutions to various social problems has become evident in recent years and many countries have come to appreciate volunteer contributions in both social and economic development. Volunteerism affects all levels, from education, environmental protection, social policy through the justice system by connecting the private domain of volunteers and a wider sphere of the public and business sector. It empowers individuals, builds a sense of solidarity, encourages participation, and safeguards vulnerable groups from economical, social and political marginalization. Numerous examples across the globe prove how volunteerism contributes to the development of human potential, raises citizen participation in social development and in turn strengthens social capital and social cohesion.

Conducting Research on Volunteerism in Croatia – Issues and Challenges

Results of different research studies conducted in developed countries and countries in transition never cease to point out the fact that volunteerism is an important part of social life and economic development. For example, if we focus only

---

1 From the United Nations Economic and Social Council's report: The Role of Volunteerism in the Promotion of Social Development; [http://www.worldvolunterweb.org/policy/international/reports/index.htm].

on the economic benefits of volunteering, we see that, according to the results of research carried out by the Institute for Policy Studies at John Hopkins University, Baltimore, USA in 1995, which included twenty-two countries, of which twelve were developed (Belgium, Finland, France, Germany, Ireland, Holland, Spain, Great Britain, Australia, Israel, Japan and USA), five were countries in transition (Czech Republic, Hungary, Poland, Romania and Slovakia) and five countries were Latin American (Argentina, Brazil, Columbia, Mexico and Peru), a total of 10.6 million volunteers added to the number of nineteen million employees, makes 6.9 percent of the total number of employees in the before mentioned countries employed in the non-profit sector.

Croatia seriously lags behind in doing research on the civil sector, and especially in conducting research on the benefits of volunteer work which is considered one of the stepping stones of civil society development. A question thus arises: *Why is it necessary to conduct research on volunteerism?* Considering it is well known that volunteering affects the stability of society and generates social capital, examining levels of citizen engagement in volunteer activities is an important source of information to governments, the media and to civil society organizations as well. Recent research studies on civil society in Croatia reveal numerous challenges for different social subjects to meet. In the report on *Civil Society Index in Croatia (2001, 2003 - 2005)* authors state a week citizen concern for social and community problems and testify that citizens do not feel obligated and responsible for solving problems and that they are not interested in within their immediate surroundings (Bežovan 2005). Furthermore, the concept of civic engagement with social problems is not a part of educational programmes and the Croatian socio-cultural background is more inclined to encourage passivity than inventiveness and confidence in citizens. This is confirmed by the results of a comparative study of values in which, among other things, it is stated how Croatia needs to make a substantial effort to overcome the existing level of solidarity and develop an effective system of social solidarity (Baloban 2005, p. 204). The results show a need for permanent strengthening of civic engagement with social and community problems in Croatian citizens. Volunteerism surely represents one of the mechanisms of the previously mentioned civic engagement.

Is volunteerism in Croatia recognized as having a social (and especially an economic) value? It is difficult to say, because of the lack of empirical data and indicators on the development and perception of volunteering in Croatia on both the local and national level. Even though continuous research has not been conducted in Croatia to provide relevant information for volunteer development, there are individual efforts of local civil society organizations on the one side, and certain international donor agencies on the other, aimed at designing and implementing research projects on volunteerism (volunteer frequency, types of volunteer activities, and public attitudes towards volunteering). As a result, there have been six research projects on the issues of volunteering conducted in Croatia. All the projects were carried out by civil society organizations because of the fact that the Croatian academic community has still not become aware of the significance and importance of conducting research on volunteerism. These organizations invest additional efforts in conducting research of the non-profit sector in order to improve their own analytical capacities and to offer answers to crucial public policy issues as well as urgent needs of the sector itself. Research studies conducted in other countries see volunteerism as a phenomenon worth researching in both the civil sector and the academic community. In recent years we can notice efforts made, for example in the EU, to collect comparative data on volunteering (Hal/Mejs 2005). Considerable contributions to this comparative dimension are offered by civil society organizations and networks on the European level who work in collaboration with relevant EU institutions in establishing a foundation for defining recommendations and measures for volunteer development.

Examining the Involvement of Citizens in Civic Initiatives by Doing Volunteer Work in the Primorsko-Goranska County

Research Methodology

The Association for Civil Society Development SMART conducted the research "Examining the involvement of citizens in civic initiatives by doing volunteer work" in 2001 – the international year of volunteers. The research was conducted in Primorsko-Goranska County and was the only such research conducted in Croatia[2]. The research showed the existence of a positive attitude towards volunteering of the respondents but a general negative attitude in their environment. Furthermore, a positive attitude does not guarantee actual involvement in volunteer activities. Citizens do not volunteer because of a difficult financial situation, value crisis and lack of information. According to research results, 43.7 percent of respondents have participated in some form of volunteer activities in the year 2000. A similar situation is found in countries where volunteerism is more developed (e.g. Great Britain). Differences arise when we look at volunteer frequency. As research results indicate, the largest number of respondents with volunteer experience participates in some form of volunteer activity once or twice a year. In Great Britain, on the other hand, volunteers in average participate in volunteer

2 The research was conducted only in Primorsko-Goranska County, under the professional supervision of Jasminka Ledić, PhD from the Faculty of Arts and Sciences in Rijeka. The research results were published in Ledić, J. (2001), Biti volonter/volonterka? – Istraživanje uključenosti građana u civilne inicijative u zajednici kroz volonterski rad, Rijeka: Udruga za razvoj civilnog društva SMART. This research earned the Association for Civil Society Development SMART, an award bestowed by the Croatian government in 2001.

activities five to seven hours a week. This was one of the crucial research findings which showed the importance of developing and promoting volunteering, especially because of the fact that the economic value of volunteering in Croatia has been seriously put into question. In addition, research results showed the need for doing continuous research of the existing situation in order to enable a quality and effective volunteer development in the whole county (and beyond) with adequate programmes and interventions. Five years later, SMART had decided to conduct the same research for two reasons: (I) so far comparative studies on volunteering have not been conducted in Croatia and (II) the repeated study will allow for further development of the infrastructure for volunteering in Primorsko-Goranska County. A *Questionnaire on Volunteerism* was used for research purposes on a sample of 500 respondents[3]. The research was based on the hypothesis that there would be a slight increase in volunteer frequency and positive attitude about volunteering in Primorsko-Goranska County in comparison with the first research. An additional hypothesis has been put forward which claimed that citizens would be willing to do volunteer work if there existed a certain level of infrastructure, reliable initiatives and organizations prepared to include volunteers in their activities.

Research Results – Are There Any Changes Five Years Later?

The analysis of respondents' general attitudes towards volunteering was based on eleven suggested statements in a questionnaire using a five-point Likert scale to determine the respondents' degree of agreement with the statements (1=strongly disagree, 2=disagree, 3=neither agree nor disagree, 4=agree, 5=strongly agree).

The analysis of results obtained from the 2006 research in relation to 2001 results show positive general attitudes towards volunteering and volunteers. In 2006 the respondents indicated their strong agreement with the statement that *"Engaging in voluntary activities helps meet interesting people"* (2001 M=4.13; 2006 M=4.2). They also strongly agreed with a statement that *"Volunteers can help solve problems in the local community"* (2001 M=3.82; 2006 M=3.87). These results can have a positive effect when it comes to involving citizens in different initiatives and activities which improve the life in local communities and strengthen social capital. Arguments support that there exist positive attitudes about volunteering and volunteers, which confirms the conclusion from the 2001 research that general positive attitudes on volunteering and volunteers are a cause for optimism because they enable the development of a systematic concern for volunteerism and volunteer encouragement (Ledić 2001). Statistical analysis shows a considerable impact of certain independent variables – age, gender, place of residence, profes-

[3] The questionnaire was composed with the professional assistance of Jasminka Ledić, PhD, supervisor of SMART's survey research "Examining the involvement of citizens in civic initiatives by doing volunteer work" from 2001.

sional qualification, financial status and membership in civil society organizations. The 2006 research confirmed the 2001 findings according to which women agree considerably more with positive statements in relation to men. The results from 2006 indicate that respondents with a lower and higher level of *professional qualifications* agree more with positive statements than the respondents from 2001. On the other hand, the respondents with a high level of professional qualification from 2006 disagree more with positive statements (contented with self and optimal leisure), which proves that the respondents of higher and high levels of professional qualifications from the 2006 research are more sceptical when it comes to volunteering than the ones in 2001. In 2006 research, as opposed to the 2001 research, the variable *financial status* proved to be a significant factor in determining attitudes about volunteering. It is interesting that the respondents of a financial status below average from 2006 have a positive attitude towards volunteering (more agree with affirmative statements which show a statistically significant difference) that the respondents of a better financial status. *Membership in organizations*, as can be expected, has proven to be an important factor in forming opinions about volunteering as was in the 2001 research. The respondents, members of organizations, in both studies have a significantly more positive attitude about volunteering, in relation to the non-members.

The respondents were offered sixteen statements in the questionnaire using a five-point scale to determine their personal attitudes, asking them to choose their degree of agreement with the statements about volunteerism in Croatia (1 = strongly disagree, 2 = disagree, 3 = neither agree nor disagree, 4 = agree, 5 = strongly agree). In the final, seventeenth section the respondents had an opportunity to make a comment and express their personal opinion.

In both the 2001 and 2006 research a relation can be noticed between estimated attitudes about volunteering and actual attitudes about volunteering in Croatia. In the 2006 research the respondents rated volunteering and volunteers as positive. When it came to estimating attitudes about volunteering in Croatia, the reasons they found the strongest for influencing a low interest in volunteering were inadequate promotion, disregard for the importance of volunteering and no stimulative measures on volunteerism offered and implemented by various social subjects, especially the government.

The highest score was given to the statement *"The state offers no stimulative measures on volunteerism"* (M=4.2). The statements *"Croatians know little about volunteer opportunities and its benefits"* and *"Schools do not realize the benefits of volunteering, so the children and the youth have no opportunities to learn about it"* were also given a high score (M=3.97) and were mentioned as reasons influencing a low interest for volunteering in Croatia. These results once again show a need for introducing subject matters on volunteerism in educational institutions (volunteer activities, electives dealing with volunteerism, etc.).

Figure 1 Differences in attitudes towards volunteering in Croatia between respondents from 2001 and 2006 research[4]

1. The social situation in Croatia has a negative effect on volunteering.
2. Upon completion of volunteer work, volunteers do not get certificates, credentials or recommendations, so people are not motivated to volunteer.
3. Nobody deals with volunteer promotion seriously.
4. **Croatians know little about volunteer opportunities and its benefits.**
5. Croatians do not volunteer because of a stereotype that volunteer work is less important.
6. People are passive and have no ambitions.
7. **The state offers no stimulative measures on volunteerism.**
8. People working with volunteers usually lack the necessary experience and knowledge so they treat their volunteers inappropriately.
9. **There are no opportunities to volunteer.**
10. **We spend a lot of time helping our family members so there is no time to help others.**
11. **Volunteer exploitation has a negative effect on volunteer motivation.**
12. Volunteering is sometimes associated with "shady" business so it is easy to doubt its integrity.
13. Volunteering does not get enough media attention (newspapers, TV, etc.)
14. Schools do not realize the benefits of volunteering, so the children and the youth have no opportunities to learn about it.
15. **Families do not realize the benefits of volunteering so they do not encourage it.**
16. People are not aware that volunteering offers opportunities for personal growth.

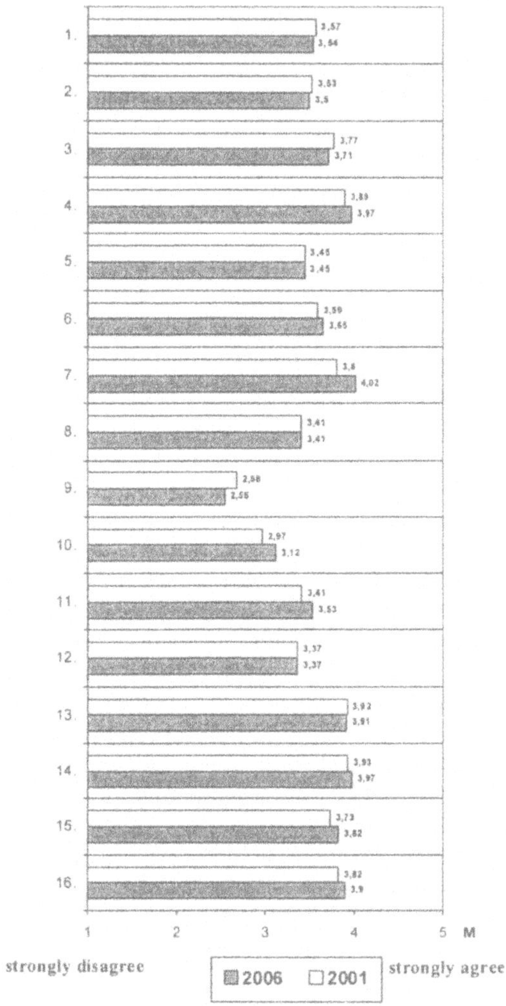

4 All statements in the graph in which a statistically significant difference was determined between respondents from the 2001 and 2006 research are marked in bold.

The importance of providing information on volunteer opportunities and volunteerism in general was recognized by the respondents. They strongly agreed with the following statement: *Volunteering does not get enough media attention (newspapers, TV, radio)* (M=3.91). The respondents gave a high score to the following statements as well: *People are not aware that volunteering offers opportunities for personal growth* (M=3.9) and *Families do not realize the benefits of volunteering so they do not encourage it* (M=3.82), mentioning them as reasons why people do not volunteer in Croatia.

The analysis of the results obtained from the 2006 research shows that the respondents found the lack of promotion in the family and the environment to be a crucial obstacle to volunteerism in Croatia, along with exploitation of volunteer work and no stimulative measures offered by the government. As opposed to the 2001 research when the basic/crucial obstacle to volunteerism was the overall negative situation in Croatia, the 2006 results are more directed towards a better organization of volunteering which is easier to influence and change making it then easier to develop mechanisms to improve volunteering. The seventeenth section gave the respondents an opportunity to add their own opinion on the reasons why people do not volunteer in Croatia if none of the offered statements applied to them. The questionnaires generated 87 comments which means that 17.4 percent of respondents gave comments on reasons why they think people in Croatia do not volunteer. The same approach to categorizing comments was used as in the 2001 research. Comments were categorized in clusters of similar comments in three basic groups: social circumstances, volunteer problems, etc. Each group was divided into clusters so we arrived at ten clusters in total.

One of the research objectives was to examine volunteer activities of Primorsko-Goranska County residents, which were then analysed according to the following categories: types of volunteer activities, frequency of participation in volunteer activities, focus of volunteer activities and volunteer experiences.

In 2005 45.8 percent of respondents had participated in some form of volunteer activity. Comparing this percentage with the results from the 2001 research, when 43.7 percent of respondents participated in some form of volunteer activity, we notice a slight increase.[5] In 2006 the largest number of respondents (45.4 percent) volunteered in associations which again confirmed the presumption that associations are the ones responsible for organizing volunteer activities and that their activities have a beneficial effect on volunteer promotion.

---

[5] The authors presume that this high percentage is in part a result of the research sample which consisted of a large number of respondents who declared themselves as members of an association (24.6%).

Table 1 Groups of comments on reasons influencing a low interest for volunteering in Croatia

GROUPS OF COMMENTS	CLUSTERS OF COMMENTS	2006: N=87 (17,4% of the total sample)		2001: N=309 (19,93% of the total sample)	
		N	%	N	%
SOCIAL CIR-CUMSTANCES	Personal circumstances	17	19,54	55	17,8
	Value crisis	10	11,49	41	13,27
	Social context	15	17,24	40	12,94
TOTAL		**42**	**48,27**	**136**	**44,01**
VOLUNTEER PROBLEMS	Lack of information, motivation and awareness on the benefits of volunteer work	9	10,34	63	20,39
	No cost reimbursements for volunteers	9	10,34	23	7,44
	Lack of interest for volunteering	3	3,44	20	6,47
	Negative attitude towards volunteer work	8	9,19	17	5,50
	Lack of volunteer regulation (organization)	6	6,89	14	4,53
	Inadequate supply of volunteer jobs	1	1,14	9	2,91
	Lack of corporate and institutional interest for volunteer engagement	1	1,14	3	0,97
TOTAL		**36**	**41,37**	**149**	**48,21**
OTHER	Other	9	10,34	24	7,77
TOTAL		**9**	**10,34**	**24**	**7,77**

Comparing results from the 2001 and 2006 research, a statistically significant difference was noticed only in church helping activities, where the respondents from 2001 help in the church more often than the 2006 respondents. Comparing data connected with working without compensation with the purpose of obtaining employment with 2001 results, when 4.9 percent of respondents opted for this type of volunteer activity, in spite of a slightly larger percentage (6.1%), we can still claim that a relatively low percentage of people connect volunteer work with one of the ways of obtaining employment. A more complex statistical analysis in relation to independent characteristics does not show a statistically significant difference in any of the activities of either research.

An important aspect that should be taken into account when examining volunteer activities is *volunteer frequency* which primarily points out the economic value of volunteer work. Results show no significant progress in relation to 2001. A slight progress can be seen in the 2006 category *several times a year* (2001 - 43.7%, 2006 - 47.1%), and *once a month* (2001 – 7.1%, 2006 – 8.4%).

Figure 2 The percentage of respondents who had volunteer experience and those who had no volunteer experience in the 2001 and 2006 research

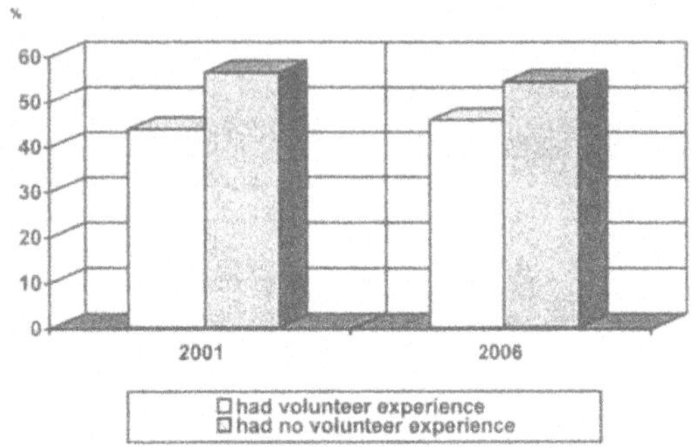

In relation to independent variables from the 2006 research, a statistically significant difference was noticed between respondents who are members of associations and those who are not. Members of associations reported participating in the specified activities every week and every day, while the ones who are not members of associations once every few years or once a year. Analysing certain independent variables (age, gender, place of residence, financial status, professional status, membership in associations) and comparing them in both sets of research did not result in significant differences in participation frequency.

With the next group of questions we wanted to examine respondents' opinions about activities which could improve volunteering and motivate people to volunteer. The respondents were offered ten activities or stimulative measures which could improve volunteering and motivate people to volunteer for them to grade on a scale from 1 to 5 (1 = would not improve volunteering; 2 = would improve volunteering slightly; 3 = would neither improve nor worsen volunteering; 4 = would improve volunteering; 5 = would greatly improve volunteering). In the eleventh segment, the respondents could add their own comment or suggestion. (See Figure 3 below.)

In accordance with the 2001 research, the respondents from the 2006 research also give high grades to all the recommended volunteer improvement measures, especially the ones which deal with finances. In 2006, the respondents gave the highest grade to *Offering advantage to volunteers upon employment would motivate people to volunteer* (M=4.16). A special emphasis was again put on measures dealing with volunteer cost reimbursements and offering advantage upon employment to volunteers. At the same time, 2006 respondents choose to rate *the need to implement stimulative measures on the national level to improve volunteering* to a significantly greater degree, which serves as an additional confirmation of the previously identified finding on attitudes about volunteering in

Croatia where the respondents see the lack of government stimulative measures as a reason why people do not volunteer in Croatia.

Figure 3 Differences in respondents' opinions on volunteer improvement measures between the 2001 and 2006 research[6]

1. **Offering advantage to volunteers upon employment would motivate people to volunteer.**
2. Offering better information on volunteerism (acquainting the public with the concept and importance of volunteerism) would improve volunteering.
3. Establishing special organizations for volunteer promotion would improve volunteering.
4. **Media attention (media campaigns) would have a positive effect on volunteering.**
5. Adequate supply of volunteer jobs would improve volunteering.
6. Reimbursing costs (of transportation, etc.) would motivate people to volunteer.
7. Professional training for organizations to accept and handle volunteers would improve volunteering.
8. **Offering and implementing stimulative measures on the national level to promote volunteer work would improve volunteering.**
9. Introducing subject matters on volunteerism and encouraging volunteering in schools would improve volunteering.
10. Corporate and public service openness to volunteer work would improve volunteering.

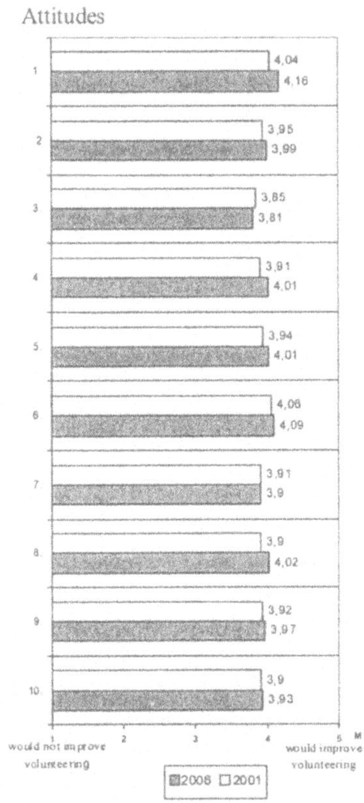

The largest number of comments in the 2006 research was given in the *Encouraging volunteering through the educational system* section – almost twice as many as in 2001. This could be linked to the previously identified finding on attitudes about volunteering in Croatia in which the respondents, according to most

6 All statements in the Graph in which a statistically significant difference was determined in respondents from the 2001 and 2006 research are marked in bold.

independent variables (age, gender, place of residence, professional qualification, professional status), saw the lack of attention given to volunteerism in families and educational institutions as reasons why people do not volunteer in Croatia. When offering volunteer improvement measures it has to be taken into account to initiate and implement them by all social sectors (government, public, business and non-profit sector) with the emphasis on government stimulative measures and implementing volunteerism in the educational system.

Volunteer management measures (better coordination of organizations to accept and handle volunteers and a better supply of volunteer jobs) were recognized by all respondents. This indicates the importance of a good and systematic approach to include volunteers in the work of organizations with a clear volunteer programme as an essential prerequisite which could motivate citizens to volunteer. Based on all these findings, it is evident that an additional hypothesis can be accepted – that citizens would be willing to volunteer if they were offered a certain level of infrastructure, credible initiatives and organizations willing to include volunteer in their activities.

Conclusions and Recommendations

The basic principle in proposing recommendations for improving volunteering is based on key research findings which indicate an existence of a positive general attitude towards volunteering and volunteers of Primorsko-Goranska County residents. Reasons why people choose not to volunteer in Croatia, according to the respondents, are a lack of promotion, inadequate recognition of the importance of volunteering and no stimulative measures offered by different subjects in the society (state, employer, educational institutions). Young people still have a negative attitude towards volunteering even though results obtained in certain segments (attitudes about volunteering in Croatia, volunteer improvement measures) show that young people from the 2006 research have a slightly more positive attitude towards volunteering. Even though a slight increase in volunteering can be notice in relation to 2001, a key challenge of volunteer frequency still remains which has not significantly changed since 2001.

In accordance with the results obtained from the research, we propose the following volunteer improvement measures:

- improve existing and develop new efficient mechanisms to improve volunteerism (offering and implementing stimulative measures by the government, business sector, educational institutions),
- increase visibility and recognition of the benefits of volunteer work through the media with an emphasis on promoting examples of good practice
- develop and design good volunteer programmes which would include all the elements of volunteer management and which would answer to different motivations and interests of different categories of people

- establish and develop mechanisms for motivating and including young people in volunteer activities
- increase volunteer frequency which manifests itself through the hours spent on volunteering by all categories of people
- establish effective mechanisms of monitoring volunteer activities in Croatia
- introduce subject matters on volunteerism in educational institutions

According to the before mentioned measures, all segments of society can continuously and simultaneously contribute to the development of volunteering in Croatia through activities in each of their domains on the following areas: acknowledging volunteer work (acknowledging its importance for society or acknowledging the volunteer service), promoting (volunteer values, its benefits and opportunities, as well as examples of good practice), organizing volunteering (developing the infrastructure for volunteer development), establishing networks (establishing connections between the volunteer community and different actors on different levels) and influencing public policy.

References

Bežovan, G. (2004), *Civilno društvo,* Nakladni zavod Globus, Zagreb.

Bežovan, G./S. Zrinščak/M. Vugec (2005), *Civilno društvo u procesu stjecanja povjerenja u Hrvatskoj i izgradnje partnerstva s državom i drugim dionicima*, CERENEO - Centar za razvoj neprofitnih organizacija, Zagreb.

Baloban, J. (ed.) (2005), *U potrazi za identitetom. Komparativna studija vrednota: Hrvatska i Europa*, Golden Marketing - Tehnička knjiga, Zagreb.

Ćulum, B. (2005), 'A zašto uopće "mjeriti" volonterski rad?' *civilnodruštvo.hr,* 2/2, pp. 6 - 7.

Forčić, G. (2007), *Volonterstvo i razvoj zajednice – sudjelovanje građana u inicijativama u zajednici*, Udruga za razvoj civilnog društva SMART, Rijeka.

Franc, R./V. Šakić et al. (2006), *Udruge u očima javnosti: istraživanje javnog mnijenja s osvrtima*, Acadamy of Educational Development, Zagreb.

Gaskin, K./J. D. Smith (1997), *A new civic Europe – a study of the extent and role of volunteering*, The National Centre for Volunteering, London.

Hal, T./L. Meijs/M. Steenbergen (2004), *Volunteering and participation on the agenda: Survey on volunteering policies and partnerships in the European Union,* CIVIQ, Utrecht.

Ivelja, N./D. Milinković/S. Škopelja (2004), *O volonterskom radu*, Udruga MI – Volonterski centar, Split.

Ledić, J. (2007), *Zašto (ne)volontiramo? – stavovi javnosti o volonterstvu,* Academy for Educational Development (AED), Zagreb.

Ledić, J. (2003), 'Volunteering in Croatia: Searching for a Younger Generation's Motivation', *University and College Level Third Sector Studies in Countries of Central and Eastern Europe*, pp. 63 - 79.

Ledić, J. (2001), *Biti volonter/volonterka? – Istraživanje uključenosti građana u civilne inicijative u zajednici kroz volonterski rad,* Udruga za razvoj civilnog društva SMART, Rijeka.

Milošević, I. (ed.) (2004), *Volonterizam i javne institucije,* Agencija za demokratski prosperitet – Zid, Podgorica.
Stebbins, R. A. (1996), 'Volunteering: A serious leisure perspective', *Nonprofit and voluntary sector quarterly*, 25/2, pp. 211 - 224.
Program suradnje Vlade Republike Hrvatske i nevladinog, neprofitnog sektora u Republici Hrvatskoj, 2000.
Radna verzija Nacrta prijedloga Zakona o volonterstvu (2005), Ministarstvo obitelji, branitelja i međugeneracijske solidarnosti, Zagreb.
Radni materijali Nacionalnog odbora za razvoj volonterstva.
United Nations (2000), 'The role of volunteerism in the promotion of social development', *Note by the Secretary-General,* United Nations E/CN.5/2001/6, 12 December 2000.
Žižak, A. (2004), 'Supervizija volontera', in M. Ajduković/L. Cajvert (eds.), *Supervizija u psihosocijalnom radu*, Društvo za psihološku pomoć, Zagreb, pp. 359 - 377.

Internet sources:
Council of Europe Recommendation 1496 (2001), Improving the Status of Volunteers in Society: a Contribution by the Parlamentary Assembly to the Year of Volunteers 2001, Council of Europe [http://www.cev.be/eudocuments.htm].
Izvješće gospodarskog i socijalnog vijeća UN-a (2001), *The Role of Volunteerism in the Promotion of Social Development* [http://www.worldvolunterweb.org/policy/international/reports/index.htm].
Nacionalna strategija stvaranja poticajnog okruženja za razvoj civilnog društva [http://zaklada.civilnodrustvo.hr].

EXAMPLES OF KNOWLEDGE UTILISATION FROM THE CORPORATE PERSPECTIVE

Vanja Sertić – Morana Fudurić

Moving Board as a New Marketing Communication Tool

Introduction

Archaeologists have traced the origin of advertising back to 3000 BC and the Babylonians. In fact, one of the first known methods of advertising was the outdoor display, usually with an eye-catching sign painted on the wall of the building (Robbs 2006). Today, 5000 years later, examples of outdoor advertising can be found in everyday life. From billboards, citylights, panels to new and innovative marketing communication tools such as Moving Boards.

The marketing industry is one of the fastest growing industries in the world, and the usage of more traditional ways of communicating one's message like TV, radio and newspapers is being replaced by new and innovative ways of marketing communication, among others Moving Boards. The purpose of this paper is to present the case of Moving Board[1], outline the pros and cons as compared to other means of advertising, and present research results on the efficiency of such advertising.

Idea in Motion

The Moving Board concept consists of multiple glowing mobile billboards that represent a complete and totally original approach to outdoor advertising. (Illustration 1) Moving Board makes it possible to display images and messages whenever and wherever desirable.

It can be used to display media normally hindered with restrictions (i.e. stationary billboards), and can be adapted to any market. Because of its unique look and versatility, Moving Board creates an attention-grabbing visual effect utilizing high-definition images placed on the front and back of the illuminated boards. Moving Board is appropriate for:

- everyday advertising
- launching new products and services
- promotions, new openings
- concerts, festivals, political campaigns
- shows and market auctions

---

[1] [www.moving-board.com] retrieved on 15.07.2009.

Illustration 1 Moving Board in action

The concept is protected worldwide – it is registered with the *World Intellectual Property Organization (WIPO, Geneva)*, the *Office for Harmonization in the Internal Market*, *Alicante Spain*, and with the *US Patent and Trademark Office*.

The benefits of Moving Boards – its possibility to become an integrated part of the environment and its flexibility – are being recognized not only in Croatia, but also by some of the world's leading organizations and companies (Germanwings, Adidas, Burgerking, Swatch, Foot Locker, 20th Century Fox etc.). This interest has led the company to open seven offices around the world – USA, Australia, New Zealand, Slovakia, Greece, Hungary and Eastern Europe (Croatia, Slovenia, Bosnia and Herzegovina and Macedonia).

Advantages and Disadvantages of the Moving Board

In order to reach consumers, advertisers employ a wide variety of media also known as media mix. The advantages of this approach become evident when we compare the efficiency, cost, noticeability, reputation, reach etc. of each separate media (Kesić 2003). Still, some media tools are more favourable than other. In the USA, the most popular media, as measured by the amount of ad spending, are television, newspapers, direct mail, radio, Yellow pages, magazines, the Internet, outdoor advertising etc.[2] It is significant that the growing percentage of budgets is spent on Internet advertising (26%), while the entire advertising market experienced a growth of (4.5%). This goes to prove that interactive marketing communication (and Moving Board can be seen as a part of this) potential, and its importance grow as we experience accelerating technological progress (Vlašić 2007).

[2] Research by Advertising Age, 2005.

In order to fully experience the advantages and disadvantages of Moving Board, we will construct a comparison based on the most frequently used media in advertising (Table 1).

Table 1 Most frequently used media in advertising

MEDIA	ADVANTAGE	DISADVANTAGE
Movingboard	• visual impact • mobility • human interaction • flexibility • low costs • integration	• control and measuring • range • weather conditions may compromise the campaign
Television	• demonstrates the product • wide range • video and audio • efficiency • dynamic and flexible • authority	• limited exposure • high costs • deteriorating ratings
Press	• reputation • trust, authority • low cost per reader • accessibility • longer life cycle	• costs • too crowded • fail to convey emotional images that build brand image
Radio	• efficient in reaching the target consumer • usage of audio effects • encourages imagination • range • selective • flexible (time and repetition) • lower costs compared to television	• does not ensure consumer's full attention • lack of visual perspective • fragmented audience • problem of buying radio time
Billboard	• lowest costs • 24h access • geographic and demographic flexibility	• control • location availability
Citylights	• good focus on the target audience • additional promotion options (audio) • geographic and demographic flexibility	• costs • measuring
Internet	• 24h access • interactive • exposure	• costs • measuring • limited ad quality

As demonstrated by Table 1, Moving Boards, as compared to other advertising media tools, have six key advantages. The three that stand out the most are human interaction, integration and flexibility. Human interaction leads to differentiation and better recollection and memory of the ads which is something no other advertising media tool can offer. In addition, the one-to-one relationship with current and potential consumers is something that people appreciate (Vlašić 2007). Integration is an advantage because during the day Moving Boards become a remarkable visual effect for pedestrians and drivers – there is no need to look up or away when you are walking or driving in order to see an add (which is the case with billboards, citylights and other types of outdoor advertising). In case of Moving Boards, the ad can literally be walking right next or in front of you.

The third advantage is that one can decide on the spot, depending on weather conditions and the number of people exposed to this kind of advertising, whether to change the walking route or not. This degree of flexibility makes the concept of Moving Board unique compared to other media (the number of publications, time etc. are set in the contract and therefore cannot be changed for a certain period of time).

As for disadvantages, range is something that can definitely be improved by increasing the number of "walkers" and better targeting methods. In addition, costs fall as the number of Moving Boards increases. Control and measuring problems are quite similar to those of billboards, citylights and the Internet. Weather conditions are by far the biggest problem that the company cannot influence, and can compromise the campaign to some extent (noticeability is smaller when the weather conditions are not favourable – rain, snow, etc. –, so the campaign is usually postponed).

Research Results

In co-operation with Moving-Board Ltd., Zagreb, the market research agency Puls conducted market research on the Effectiveness and Public Image of Moving Board illuminated panels. The survey was conducted by using the CATI research method (Computer Assisted Telephone Interviewing). The survey started on 24th of December 2005 and it lasted until 31st of December 2005. Five hundred people aged fifteen years and older were interviewed.

In order to measure the effectiveness and noticeability of the Moving Board media, it was necessary to determine the number of respondents that left the house during the day, as well as the number of people that visited locations during the campaign. It was necessary to define how many people had the chance to see the campaigns and who those people were.

The survey showed that 72 percent of people left the house during the day, but only 23 percent (113 respondents) visited targeted locations in the period from 10 a.m. till 10 p.m. One of the possible reasons why there was such a small percentage of people visiting the targeted location is the holiday season, when people prefer to stay at home with their families. Also, weather conditions were bad; heavy snow kept people in the house.

Table 2 Number of people that noticed the ad over the course of one day

	%	Frequency	Minimum	Maximum
Went out	72%	362	156.000	174.000
Noticed the ad during the day	14%	68	24.000	38.000

Survey results show that during the day, 14 percent of the people noticed the ads, i.e. that the minimum of 24,000 and the maximum of 38,000 people that are 15 years old and older noticed the ads (Table 2). During the seven day campaign, 235 people, i.e. 47 percent saw the campaign. In other words, results show that somewhere between 98,000 and 117,000 people (residents of the district where the campaign took place) noticed the campaigns (Table 3).

Table 3 Number of people noticing the ad over the course of seven days

	%	Minimum	Maximum
People noticing the ad (7 day period)	47%	97.000	117.000

The number of people who did not see the campaign, but who heard about it from friends, neighbours or colleagues is 86 (17%), which refers to a minimum of 31,000 people and a maximum of 47,000 people.

Respondents who did not visit the targeted locations, 421 interviewees, were asked if they had seen Moving Board ads in the period starting from 20th of December 2005. The results are presented by Figure 1.

Figure 1 Noticeability of Moving Boards among people not present on target locations

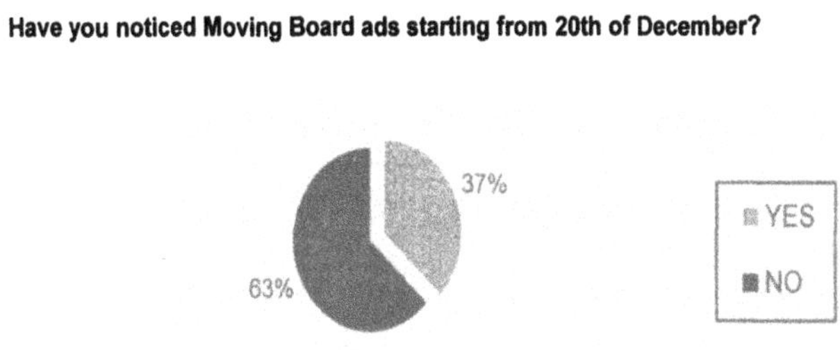

(N=421)

Respondents who had not visited target locations as well as those who had not noticed the Moving Board ads at these locations (265) in the period from 20th of December, were asked if they had heard of Moving Board media. The results are presented in Figure 2.

Figure 2 Recognition of the Moving Board media

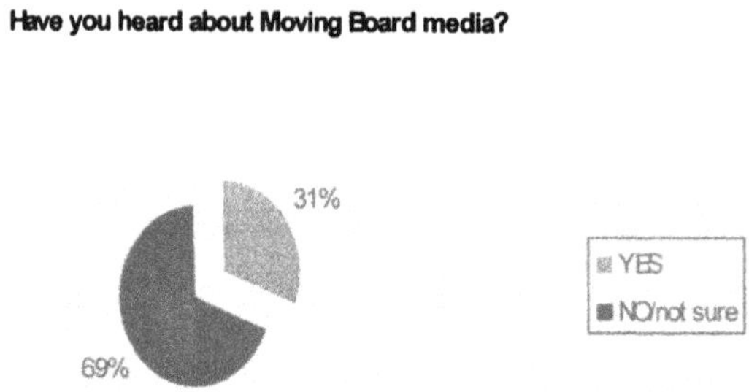

When all answers are considered, people who did leave their residence, as well as the people who did not, it is evident that 321 interviewees (64%) had heard about it or had seen the campaign. That is a high quota considering the fact that weather conditions were unfavourable during the campaign.

	%	Number	Minimum	Maximum
Number of people who have both noticed the ads and have heard about the Moving Board media	64,20%	321	136.231	155.731

As an answer to the question, which ads were noticed that day in the town, (the concept of Moving Board was not implied) the most frequently mentioned ad was the ad for Andol C, ads for Max Flu and a Coloseum-concert followed. For the second question the concept of Moving Board was implied. The most frequently mentioned ad was the ad for Andol C. The ad for Max Flu was the second most frequently mentioned while the ad for the Coloseum-concert was rarely pointed out. It is assumed that the Coloseum-concert ad was not remembered as much as two other ads because it was not advertised as much when compared to other two brands. Also, Pliva is a distinguished company whose brands are well known to most people, therefore Andol C and Max Flu ads were easier to notice, and were more likely to be remembered, especially Andol C, because Andol C, when compared to Max Flu is more renowned.

Public Opinion

The third topic covered in the survey is the public opinion regarding Moving Boards as an advertising media form. The interviewees were asked to rate this type of advertising on a scale form 1 to 5 (5 – I like it a lot, 1 – I do not like it at all). Results are presented by Figure 3.

Figure 3 Opinion on movingboard as an advertising media

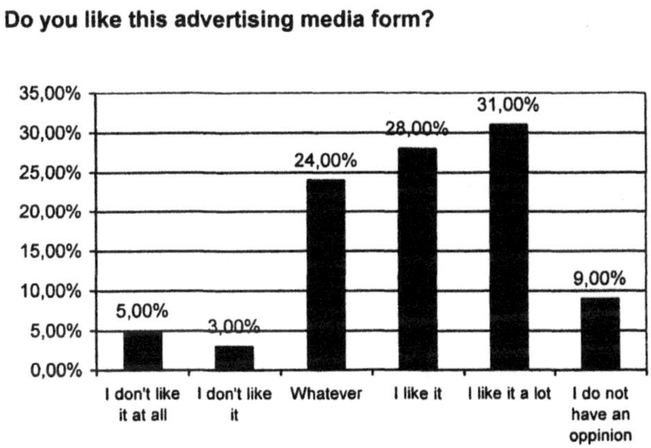

Respondents were also asked to compare Moving Board with other advertising forms. They were also asked to relate certain attributes that they associate with this type of advertising. They were asked to estimate whether this type of advertising is original, noticeable, acceptable, modern, cheap or with style (cf. Figure 4). The results can be explained by the fact that people are rather unfamiliar with this type of advertising, as well as the criteria and prices of other advertising media, including Moving Boards.

Most respondents find this type of advertising to be noticeable (86%). That fact supports the theory that illuminated objects in motion are much easier to notice. 67 percent of interviewees rated this type of advertising "with style", and only 42 percent rated it as cheap. Also, 41 percent people stated that they do not know whether this type of advertising is cheap. That is the only attribute that a significant number of respondents did not know whether to associate with the Moving Board or not. The reason why a small percentage of people rated the Moving Board ads as cheap, is because this type of media is still new on the market and people are not informed about the prices of this media and the prices of other media forms (TV, radio, city light etc.).

Figure 4 Opinion on the Moving Board, compared to other media

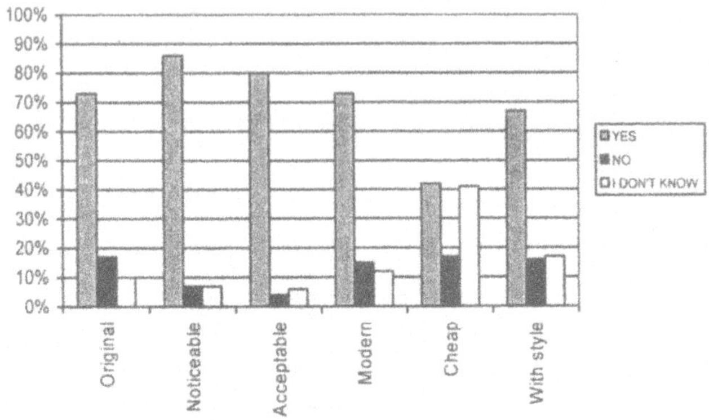

Conclusion

Trends show significant changes in the usage of advertising media tools – a growing percentage of the budget is being spent on Internet and other alternative ways of advertising. Moving Board represents an entirely new concept of advertising that brings the ad closer to potential consumers. Visual impact, mobility, flexibility, integration, low costs and especially human interaction make this new media interesting to some of the world's biggest companies and organizations that use Moving Boards for everyday advertising, launching new products, different kinds of events, shows and market auctions.

Moving Boards have been very well accepted among the public (86% claimed it is noticeable and 67% rated this type of advertising "with style"). Only 42 percent perceived it as cheap. 28 percent claimed they like this kind of advertising, and 31 percent said they like it a lot. What is most important, is that 64.20 percent of respondents have seen or heard of the ads which is a very good percentage if one considers the fact that this is a new concept still relatively unknown to the public. Based on the obtained results and the fact that the campaigns resulted in a growing interest in the promoted products, we can come to the conclusion that Moving Board is a media worth looking into, and with very good prospects for growth.

References

Kesić,T. (2003), *Integrirana marketinška komunikacija*, Opinio, Zagreb.
Vlašić, G./A. Mandelli/D. Mumel (2007), *Interaktivni marketing – Interaktivna marketinška komunikacija*, PeraGO, Zagreb.
Report on Effectiveness and Public Image of Moving Board, prepared by Puls Marketing agency for Moving-Board Ltd, Zagreb.
Internet sources:
[http://adage.com]
[http://encarta.msn.com]
[http://www.moving-board.com]

Josef Eltantawi

Kapsch and the Alps-Adriatic Challenges – Always one Step Ahead

Introduction

The global exchange of knowledge and goods has made our world faster, more transparent and more challenging. The continuous development of communications tools will make a decisive and lasting change in society. Transportation, manufacturing and organizational processes will be increasingly automated and accelerated. Environmental aspects gain ever more meaning. As one of Austria's renowned companies Kapsch has dedicated itself for the past 115 years to the exploration and application of new technologies, making a lasting contribution toward shaping the future and the development of a mobile and networked world.

Kapsch and the history of European telecommunications in the Twentieth century are inextricably linked. The development of the company since 1892 has been marked by growth and success: from a manufacturer of telephones to a system supplier for road traffic telematics and telecommunications. The Kapsch Group, headquartered in Vienna, Austria, has over 2.450 employees worldwide and is represented through subsidiaries, representative offices and financial interests on every continent. Close to our customers, individual solutions and the high quality of our systems are traditional strengths that have made the Kapsch Group one of the market leaders in the European traffic telematics and communications industries.

In the early 1990s, the Kapsch Group entered the road traffic telematics business. Through selected acquisitions, including the acquisition of the electronic toll collection division of Bosch Telecom, Germany (1999), and Combitech Traffic Systems AB, Sweden (2000), and following a reorganization of the Kapsch Group in 2002, the Company and its subsidiaries now form the road traffic telematics division of the Kapsch Group. Since 2002, Kapsch TrafficCom has gradually developed into an international road traffic telematics group by establishing subsidiaries and representative offices in various countries across the world, making selected acquisitions, including the acquisitions of DPS Automation S.A., Argentina (subsequently renamed Kapsch TrafficCom Argentina S.A.) in 2006 and VTI Industrials Pty, South Africa in 2007 and entering into strategic partnerships, including Kapsch Telematic Services GmbH, a joint venture company with its Portuguese partner Brisa, the largest Portuguese road operator, in 2005.

By creating efficient solutions for its clients, both in extensions of existing systems as well as the implementation of complete new ones, Kapsch TrafficCom has become the leading international supplier of road traffic telematic systems, products and services. The company develops and supplies Road User Charging (RUC) systems, traffic management systems, including traffic surveillance systems, parking and access systems (on-street and off-street) and traffic control systems. Only innovative products and proven technologies are utilized. Added to that are applications from leading manufacturers and the expertise of local specialists. These individual components are integrated together according to specific customer requirements into a comprehensive solution.

European Road Traffic

Europe has become a true single marketplace and industry heavily relies on the Europe-wide road network for commercial transport. Road transport has a central role to play in the continued health and growth of Europe's economy. Europeans expect goods to be delivered door-to-door to all corners of the continent, quickly and on time. Often road transport is the only answer to the demand for such high levels of mobility and flexibility – a situation that will remain despite increasing investment in other modes. The transport of goods between Member States of the European Union is set to increase by 50 percent between 2000 and 2020. Road transport – which already conveys 73 percent of goods on land – will undoubtedly take the lion's share of that expansion.

The road transport sector itself already contributes hugely to the European economy. It provides about 4.5 million jobs and generates a turnover worth about 1.6 percent of EU gross domestic product. And without an efficient, vibrant road transport system, other modes cannot function properly as most freight and passenger journeys begin and end with a trip on the road. Road transport therefore also plays a vital role in the development of Europe's integrated transport networks and intermodal transport solutions.

Road User Charging Systems

An efficient transport system is important for economic development, as transport costs are a significant part of the cost structure of the goods that a country produces or imports. If transport costs are unnecessarily high, then the country's products will not be competitive on international markets. Road transport costs include not only the cost of building and maintaining the road network, but also vehicle operating costs, which increase as roads deteriorate due to increased vehicle maintenance costs, and the costs associated with increased time in transit.

Consequently, it is imperative for the efficient operation of the road transport system that resources be available for timely road maintenance. This is just as much in the interest of the Ministry of Finance and of road users as it is to the road administrations and the Ministry of Transport. However, several European countries have experienced diminishing funding for road maintenance and rehabilitation. The severity varies from one country to another in terms of budget cutbacks, but frequently total road expenditures (including construction) amount to less than 0.8 percent of GDP. This ratio compares unfavourably to the 1 percent to 2 percent of GDP, generally considered necessary to adequately maintain the road networks and carry out a modest amount of construction.

This serious situation has led several countries in Europe to consider establishing improved, modern road user charging systems that provide more funds for maintaining and expanding their road networks. The use of such systems can also help decision-makers to take advantage of more private sector involvement in financing and operating highway assets. Experience in a number of countries has shown that road users are willing to pay for road maintenance, as well as expansion, if they can see that the fees and taxes that they pay result in improved road conditions. The preferable road user charges are those that link the charges most closely to the use of the roads. Generally, the most appropriate are charges for the use of the road space, and charges for the disproportionate damage caused by heavy vehicles.

The Eurovignette directive, adopted in 1999 and subsequently modified in 2006, establishes common rules relating to distance-based tolls and time-based user charges for goods vehicles over 3.5 tonnes. The aim of the legislation is to improve the way the internal market operates by reducing differences in tolls and charges across the EU.

Still, one major irritation for all drivers is having to queue at toll booths to pay charges. The problem is made worse on international routes as drivers of different nationalities figure out what they have to pay, sometimes in a currency they do not know well. Such conditions hold up journeys and cause congestion on busy routes, especially at peak times. Consequently, commercial tolling customers increasingly demand international interoperability.

Electronic Toll Collection (ETC) and Interoperability

Electronic fee collection is a complex business, involving the seamless interaction between technology and operations processes resulting in a financial transaction. During the last decade more and more Member States of the European Union opted for such systems to finance the construction of new infrastructure. The vast majority of these states apply electronic toll systems which are based on microwave technology, except for Germany where a satellite system based on GPS technology is in place. DSRC microwave is without a doubt the dominant technology found in electronic fee collection around the world.

Dedicated Short Range Communication (DSRC) is a short to medium range wireless protocol specifically designed for automotive use. It offers communication between the vehicle and roadside equipment and is a sub-set of the RFID-technology. This technology for Intelligent Transportation Systems (ITS) applications works in the 5.9 GHz band (U.S.) or 5.8 GHz band (Japan, Europe). Currently its main use is in electronic toll collection. The DSRC technology working in the 5.8 GHz band is a microwave solution that uses a simple, easily installable On Board Unit and communication points located throughout an interurban network. It is especially suitable for implementation in ETC systems since it offers reliable communication, high data security and fast transmission in all weather conditions, ranging from daytime temperatures exceeding 35° C to alpine conditions above 2000 metres. In addition 5.8 GHz microwave communication provides maximum accuracy and detection rates, the proof of toll liability and payment, thus supporting fairness in toll charging, proven and predictable operational capability and known performances.

As Europe moves towards a European electronic toll service, DSRC is recognised as the realistic means of achieving interoperability in Europe and paves the way for road user charging in the future. It is non-proprietary and offers the advantages of technical interoperability and availability of products from multiple sources.

The MEDIA Project

Although having one single currency in Europe, the payment of tolls still relies on local payment systems. Especially for international hauliers, the different systems in European countries interfere with the traffic flow. Either the toll has to be paid manually by credit-/petrol cards or cash, or the vehicle must be equipped with different OBUs from different EFC-Operators. For both, the user as well as the administrative staff, dealing with all statements and settlements is a cumbersome task.

For that reason the MEDIA project was launched more than two years ago in the Alpine Region. MEDIA stands for "Management of EFC DSRC Interoperability in Alpine Region" and is an interoperability initiative of tolling operators from the Alpine countries Austria, France, Italy, Slovenia and Switzerland. It has the objective to find and implement a concrete solution to enable tolls for heavy vehicles in the participating fee collection systems to be paid electronically and in an interoperable way.

All five involved Alpine countries have electronic fee collection systems installed which employ microwave DSRC technology. MEDIA has not defined a single technical product but a set of requirements. Any product, or mix of products, that fulfils the MEDIA requirements is acceptable as a technical basis for the service. This might, for example, be a combination of two on-board units that reside side-by-side on the windscreen. The required on-board equipment will be delivered to the customer through a single source, as part of the interoperable service.

Within the MEDIA project, every customer has a contract with a service company, named the Contract Issuer. For all aspects of paying tolls or fees in the participating systems, the Contract Issuer is the single point of contact for the user. The Contract Issuer prepares the on-board equipment with the required vehicle, payment and security data and gives it to the customer. The customer can use the equipment to automatically pay tolls and fees in all participating systems. The Contract Issuer pays the toll system operators on behalf of the customer, giving the system operators a payment guarantee. Finally, the customer receives from the Contract Issuer a single statement, or invoice, for all tolls and fees in the various systems, including a service fee for the Contract Issuer's services.

The idea of the MEDIA project and its service to the users was born from the desire to supply the customer and the user with an additional service. The operators do not expect an extra income through the application of roaming fees. The users are concerned to see an increment of safety and a reduction in congestion at the toll plazas. Therefore, the operators intend to maintain the user acceptance of the charging of fees through the extension of the quality of the service of the road infrastructure and of the fee collection itself. As an addition to this, two more issues strengthen the desire of the operators to realise the objectives of the MEDIA Project: 1) The operators have to fulfil a legal obligation for interoperability stated by the European Interoperability Directive 2) The operators potentially expect a reduction of the operational costs, if the market penetration of the common EFC service is high enough. This reduction should be obtained due to the increase of the share of EFC users, a reduction of the costs associated to the users, the development and operation of one common solution, synergies, scale effects and increased purchase power. The clear scope and advantages for the user within the MEDIA project is to be provided with one contract, one contact point, one invoice, one common service for different countries and one single process.

Once implemented, MEDIA will be the solution for a seamless freight transport in the MEDIA countries. No queuing at toll booths, no wasted administrative effort spent tracking all the records of a vehicle or user and all tolls will be charged through a single invoice by a single Contract Issuer. After the introduction of the Euro another single payment means will capture Europe.

Conclusion

Only by the continuous drive for and development of new technologies and system solutions will it be possible for Kapsch TrafficCom to ensure its current position on the world market. Kapsch is using all possible synergies and technological co-operations to create applicable and marketable solutions for our customers. Active in more than thirty countries on all continents Kapsch TrafficCom is especially engaged and focussed on the Alpine Region as a leading partner within the

MEDIA project. It is the common vision of the stakeholders to create a new contractual product for their customers in order to make traffic more efficient. With the constant and valuable support of various Austrian scientific institutions – especially the TU Wien, Joanneum Research Forschungsgesellschaft, Klagenfurt University and FH Kärnten – Kapsch is working very hard on the development of the technological base to make this vision come true.

Manfred Ruprechter

Knowledge Transfer and Knowledge Utility in the Alps-Adriatic Region

This article is based on insights drawn from the practical experiences of a company in Austria which manufactures roofing products in several Central and Southeast European countries, and sells these products using indirect distribution channels.

The practical use (integration) of knowledge that has been collected throughout many years of experience (a hundred and thirty years) in one country, and its transfer to the Alps-Adriatic region with local adaptations to the local market is the matter under discussion.

The company had to face conceptual and practical challenges in implementing sales strategies for its entire and massively-increased production capacity of hard roof tiling in the Alps-Adriatic region with the countries Austria, Croatia and Slovenia.

The following questions will be addressed in a comprehensive manner, using actual findings as examples:

- Why is it so important that knowledge transfer takes place?
- When does knowledge transfer take place?
- How does knowledge transfer take place?
- Where can all this knowledge be applied?

The prior situation indicated that the already existing production facilities in the countries of the former Yugoslavia were outdated. This was reflected in the exceptionally difficult working conditions of the employees and the often dubious quality of the wares produced.

Following the political changes in Croatia and Slovenia, the company has invested in modern production technology, as well as in administrative buildings, with practically all core factors being refurbished. Here follows a list of those core factors relevant to knowledge transfer and knowledge utility:

- Quality of the produced wares now at highest European standard
- Production capacity doubled or tripled
- Sales prices doubled
- Average income unchanged or slowly increasing
- Absolute revision of the initial going-in position

The social effects these changes have had on employees, the people in their immediate and proximate environments, and all other stakeholders of this extensive process, have not been analyzed here.

Method

The core question was: "*Which methodological approach can be applied?*", both to achieve the goals of the producer and to examine whether knowledge in marketing and sales can be transferred from an Austrian company with over a hundred and thirty years of experience to other countries at a one-to-one ratio.

From the methodological point of view each product decision of the customer follows certain determinants which need to be considered by the producer:

- How does one identify the decision-making processes?
- Which individuals/groups have an influence on the purchase decision?
- What are the motives behind the purchase decision?
- When, in the time-span of a project, is the purchase decision made?
- Do experiences exist with decision-making processes cross-border in the Alps-Adriatic region – are they valid and applicable?

In order to answer these questions, methodology to filter and create a structured depiction of the product decision-making processes has been developed.

Several "situations" that occur daily, whenever someone is interested in roofing, were simulated for the investigation. Building on these constructs, question sheets were devised, and were subsequently filled with responses provided by people occupying different positions in the industry. After working through the answers, new question sheets containing new questions were distributed. The results emerged from a complex system of questions, responses and analyses, as well as the subsequently derived questions, responses and correspondent evaluation. The methodology was developed by the author.

It is a search for trends. The quality of achieved results is dependent on the moderation of interviews with questionnaires, as well as the structure of expert respondents. In 2001/2002 about 20 experts of the branch in each of the three countries were interviewed.

Process of Product Decision

The results of the interviews revealed four main groups ("target groups") of influence on purchasing decision in the roofing branch. In the following each listed target group[1] is tagged with a number, behind which members of the same kind (e.g. "architects") are assembled, however across different countries. The per-

---

[1] Due to competition considerations the exact composition of the target groups cannot be made visible here.

centage in the following figures indicate how significantly different the influence of the target groups on the purchase decision is, however varying between countries, although at first glance the basic need ("roof over ones head") appears to be the same.

First the question: *"What individual/groups influence the purchasing decision?"* is addressed.

Figure 1 Austria: Impact on product decision by target group (%)[2]

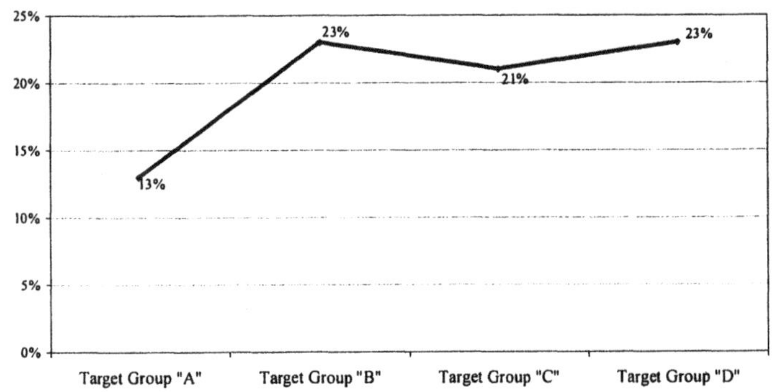

Figure 1 shows that in Austria four target groups explain about 80 per cent of the purchase decision, where three target groups dominate.

The next diagram addresses the question: *"How significant is this influence on the purchasing decision according to target group "A" in the countries of the Alps-Adriatic region?"*

Figure 2 Alps-Adriatic region: Impact on purchasing decision of target group A (%)

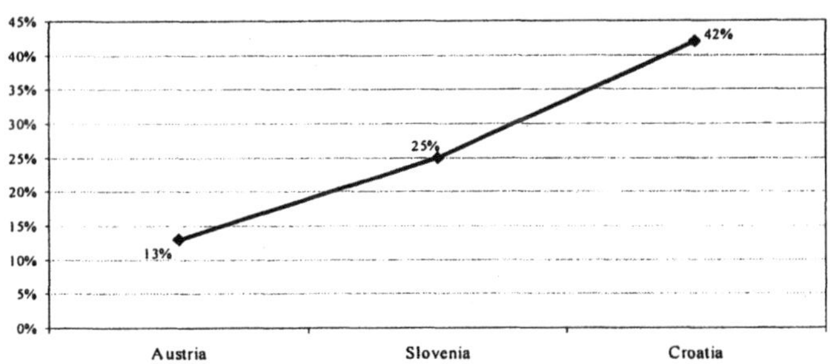

2 Percentages do not add up to 100 because only main target groups existing in all three countries are considered.

The impact of target group "A" on the purchasing decision across the various countries in the Alps-Adriatic region translates to a bottom-up influence difference of about three times comparing Austria and Croatia (Fig. 2).

The next diagram concerns target group "B": *"How significant is this influence on the purchasing decision according of target group "B" in the countries of the Alps-Adriatic region?"*

Figure 3 Alps-Adriatic region: Impact on purchasing decision of target group "B" (%)

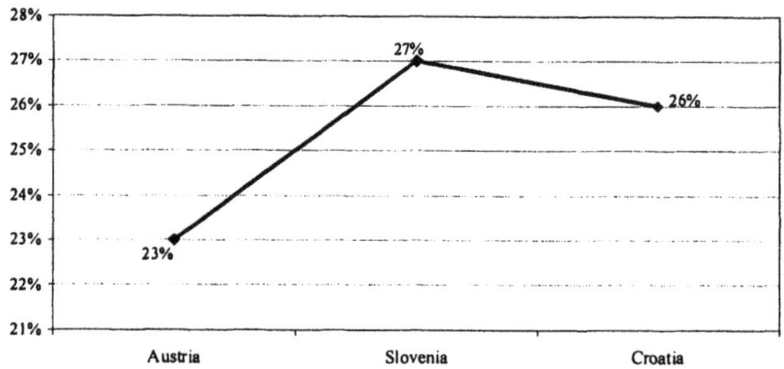

For target group "B" the main difference of impact on purchasing decision is between Austria and Slovenia (Fig. 3).

The following diagram addresses the question: *"How significant is this influence on the purchasing decision according to target group "C" in the countries of the Alps-Adriatic region?"*

Figure 4 Alps-Adriatic region: Impact on purchasing decision of target group "C" (%)

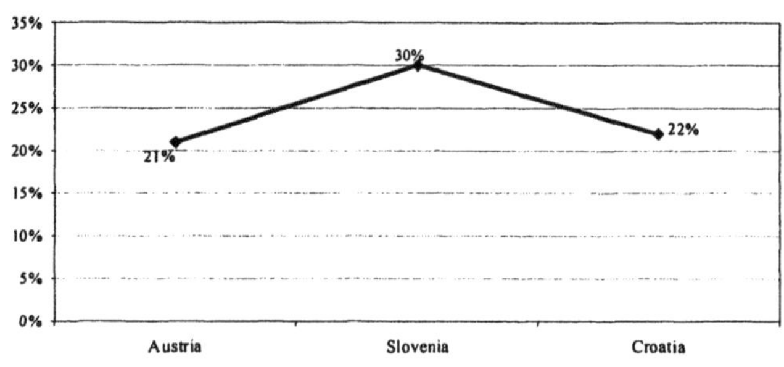

Particularly interesting appear to be the impact differences of target group "A", "B" and "C" between Austria and Slovenia, neighbouring countries which usually are considered to have very similar business cultures.
Figure 5 shows not only the main four target groups but also a residual category ("E") in a comprehensive chart of the three countries.[3]

Figure 5 Impact on purchasing decision of all target groups by country (%)

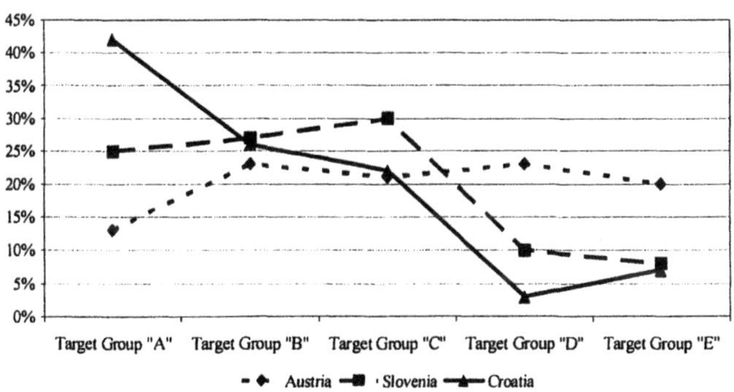

These results raise the following important questions for the company:

What would happen if...

- ...knowledge about the market in Austria were simply transferred on a one-to-one ratio to Slovenia and Croatia?
- ... the allocated marketing budget were not optimal and efficient?
- ... the field sales force did not occupy their singular and pro-rated time with the "right" target groups?

After having found out who is influencing purchasing decisions and to what extent, the question of the motives is raised.

The following three figures address the question: *"What are the motives behind the purchasing decision of individual target groups?"*

3 Target group "D" has to be taken carefully with respect to Croatia because of political circumstances during the investigation. Nevertheless, it is included in the comprehensive chart (Fig. 5) but with a hypothetical correction to give the reader a complete picture.

Figure 6 Austria: The most important criteria for the purchase decision Target group "A" – according to the number of namings

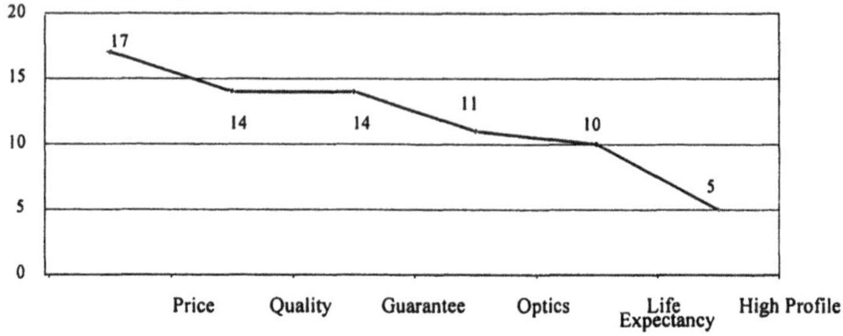

In Austria the expert interviewees of our study believe that the main variables for the purchasing decision of target group "A" are "price", "quality" and "guarantee", the least important "life expectancy" and "high profile".

Figure 7 Austria: The most important criteria for the purchase decision Target group "B" – according to the number of namings

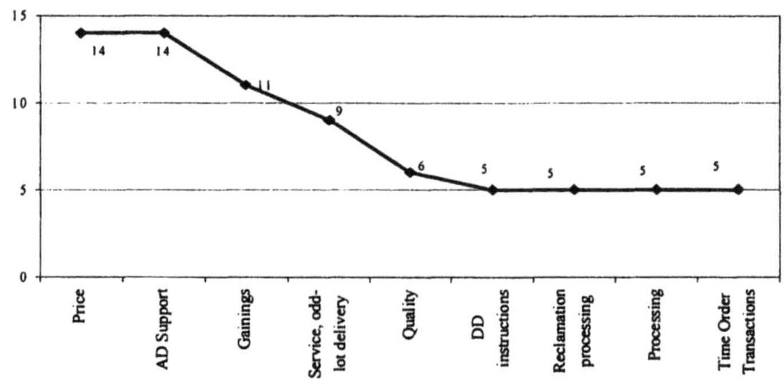

Figure 8 Austria: The most important criteria for the purchase decision Target group C – according to the number of namings

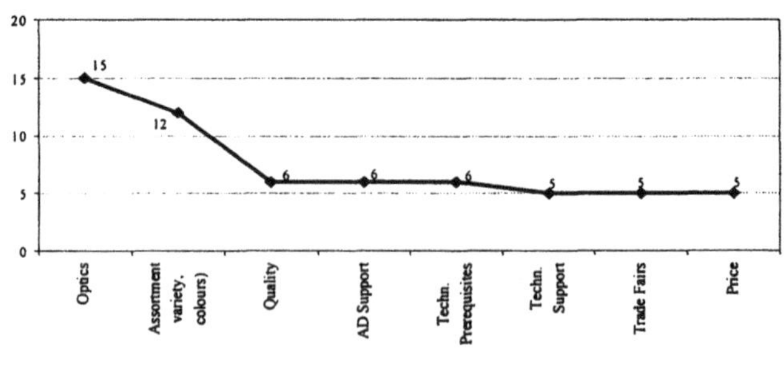

"Why" specific target groups do decide on a certain roof solution differs considerably according to the experts interviewed. This is basically the message of the previous three figures.

What would happen if...

- ... through marketing and advertising, the same message were conveyed to all target groups?
- ... the various audiences in the individual target groups felt themselves misunderstood?
- ... communication were not optimal and efficient?
- ...the target groups could not be motivated to contact the company?

In construction every business usually follows four phases: planning phase, call for proposals, allocation, building construction. This has an influence on the internal and external sales structure. To know what decisions are made in each phase has a decisive influence on the success.

The following diagram addresses the question: *"When, in the time-span of the project process, is the purchase decision made?"*

Figure 9 Proportion of the product decision according to project status (%)[4]

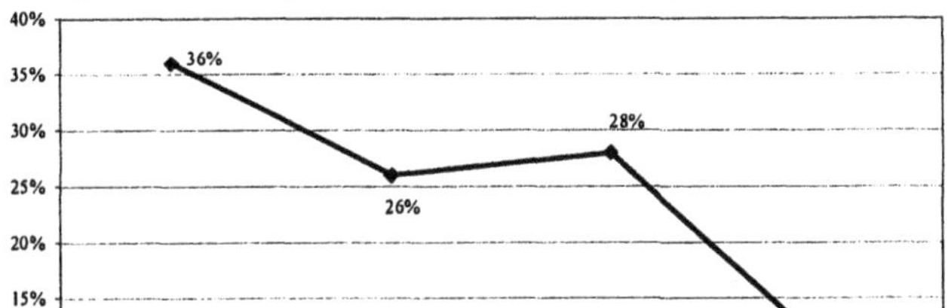

The results are clear, nearly 90 percent of the purchasing decisions take place in the broader planning phase (planning, call, allocation), which has some implications for the company, such as:

- Is this a clear indication that materials and tools useful in the planning phase should be made available to target group?
- What would happen if no tools were made available in the planning phase?

[4] Again, due to competition considerations, the country of origin of this data cannot be revealed.

- Would the decision makers choose these tools or go with a company providing better support?
- Would access to target groups be optimal and efficient?

Conclusion

At the beginning of this paper, several key questions were posed. Based on the market research, the following notions may serve as their answers.

Why is it necessary for knowledge transfer to take place? By absolutely revising the initial going-in position (e.g. takeover and reconstruction of a plant), present knowledge and resources are often insufficient to set and reach new goals.

When does knowledge transfer take place? It is assumed that, in general, a very similar business situation and demand exist in the Alps-Adriatic, but that the decision making process is not the same everywhere.

How does knowledge transfer take place? Knowledge transfer has taken place simply by asking questions. Knowledge of the basic functioning of the market in the respective country is generally present. However, the "tools" and people needed to sum up this knowledge, process it and disperse it are by and large lacking.

Wherein lies the use of knowledge application? The use lies in the precise and efficient access gained to the respective target groups and their decision makers. By means of appropriate content, they generally feel "understood". This situation helps foster trust and supports open dialogue. In fact, trust and the open dialogue resulting from it are (among others) two of the most important factors contributing to subsequent success.

On the basis of the demonstrated results, it is clear how important knowledge transfer is. The available resources of the company, in regard to people, capital and time, can thus be efficiently used to the full satisfaction of all the participating stakeholders. The insights as to *which congruence of global competition* exists between Austria, Croatia and Slovenia and *which national anomalies* are relevant for the purchase decision process have thus contributed toward goal-orientation and suitable action of the company according to the respective market.

CASES OUT OF REGION

Gerhard Strohmeier

Higher Education Institutions in Cross-border Co-operation – The Vienna Region and Western Hungary

Introduction

The central question for this article is the role universities and colleges play in cross-border regional development in the "Vienna Region" and Western Hungary. Changes within the system of higher education in Austria and Hungary have resulted in two conflicting strategic orientations. On the one hand, international competition between universities and the so called Bologna-Process within the EU are leading to increasing specialisation and the search for excellence in science and research at a global level, while the local and regional impact of universities plays a minor role. Various other EU-strategies, national science policies, regional development institutions and organisations for regional science and innovation transfer on the other hand stress the importance of higher education institutions in local and regional development. Can both the process of internationalisation in higher education as well as capacity building for regional development be successfully mastered by the universities? What are the challenges and what are the chances?

The article is based on findings of the INTERREG IIIA Joint Project UniRegio between Austria and Hungary that took place from 2005 to 2006. The Austrian partner was the University of Klagenfurt, the Hungarian Partner was the Centre for Regional Studies at the Hungarian Academy of Science. UniRegio investigated the strategies of the universities in the Vienna Region (Vienna, Lower Austria and Burgenland) towards regional development and the opinions of regional development professionals from the region about the role universities play in regional development.

Higher Education Institutions in the Vienna Region and Western Hungary

The Vienna Region is defined by three Austrian Provinces: Vienna, Lower Austria, and Burgenland. There are nine universities and five *Fachhochschulen*[1] in Vienna, with a total of about 5,000 faculty members, teaching 135,000 students.

---

1 Fachhochschule can be translated into "Technical College", or "Management School". These institutions offer various specialised study programmes with a focus on practical training for industrial, administrative and management jobs. In Austria they have been established since 1993. Cf.: Lorenz Lassnig, et al. (2003), 'Review des Auf- und Ausbaus des Fachhochschulsektors', Studie im Auftrag des Bundesministeriums für Bildung, Wissenschaft und Kultur, Endbericht, Wien.

Lower Austria's most important higher education institutions are the "Danube-University Krems" and *Fachhochschulen* in Krems, St. Pölten, and Wiener Neustadt with a total number of about 10,000 students and 1,000 staff. There is one *Fachhochschule* in Burgenland with locations in Eisenstadt and Pinkafeld and about 1,200 students; its faculty numbers about 400.

This shows a concentration of higher education and research institutions in Vienna, while the peripheral Austrian province and region Burgenland has only few science and research institutions. In addition to this highly centralised and unequal distribution of higher education facilities there is a strong concentration of research institutions in Vienna, including a total of 250 non-university research institutes. Vienna comes in fourth place among European cities regarding the number of employed in research and development, concentrating more than 50 percent of all the research expenditures in Austria.

Western Hungary (Györ-Moson-Sopron, Vas, Zala) has three small universities, the Western Hungarian University in Mosonmagyarovar, Szechenyi Istvan University of Györ, and the Western Hungarian University in Sopron; each with branches within the region. The largest university in Western Hungary is the University of Györ with 7,000 students and a faculty of 300.

The border region of Western Hungary pictures a variety of small players in the field of higher education and research, leading to a dispersed landscape of universities and research institutions. There are also several university branches of various Hungarian universities located in the region leading to a widespread competition among universities and their branches, competing for students, financial resources, and reputation in the region. It reflects one of the problems of the higher education system in Hungary: many very small institutions competing in a complex market. There are, for example, twenty-six faculties for economy registered with several branches all over Hungary.

Regional Development Strategies and Institutions in the Vienna Region

The municipality of Vienna has put a strategic development focus on science and research: In its city marketing it presents Vienna as the Austrian centre for science and research and defines science and research a special field of urban policy[2]. In the city's planning documents science and research, higher education and human resource development play a leading role in the city's economic development. Vienna hosts a variety of research & development funds and organisations, which concentrate on support for the local economy. The strategic goals are a competitive and innovative industry, a good supply in human resources to meet the standards in international science and industry competition. Vienna has been

2 STEP05, Stadtentwicklungsplan für Wien 2005, p. 121 [http://www.wien.at/stadtentwicklung/step].

rather successful in promoting research & development up till now; e.g. in biotechnology and the creative industries cluster.

Lower Austria has a complex landscape of organisations to promote regional development: there are transfer-institutions to connect science and research with the regional economy, there are institutions for economic development, also supporting local and regional enterprises with programmes for innovation and capacity building; and there are *Regionalmanagements* with various tasks, such as human resource building, to mention one among others.

The Burgenland has several regional industrial innovation centres and a *Regionalmanagement* too.[3]

Regional Development in the Strategies of the Higher Education Institutions on a Programme Level

With few exceptions regional development is not mentioned in strategic documents, such as the mission statements of the universities in the Vienna Region. It plays very little role in the general positioning and profiling of universities. *Fachhochschulen*, however, concentrate in general on local and regional needs of economy and society. In the Austrian law on *Fachhochschulen* a regional assessment of the demands is obligatory before a *Fachhochschule* is set up; so regional demands have to be considered from the beginning.[4]

University units, such as departments and institutes, are more or less oriented towards the regional environment according to their subject. Departments for Regional and Urban Planning, Landscape Planning and Design, Geography and Regional Economy, for example, connect to their regions in manifold ways: they do research and consulting in the region, teach about the region, and student's papers and theses consist of local and regional topics of interest.

Fachhochschulen do very little research, but they co-operate with local and regional research institutions. They are of great importance for capacity building in a region and qualify students in a very flexible mode for the needs of the local industry. Co-operation with the local and regional industry works well on different levels: there is even an organisation in Lower Austria that focuses on improving communication between industry and higher education institutions, the *NÖ-Bildungsgesellschaft*.

---

3 An overview by Hannes Schaffer in 'Regionalmanagements in Centrope-Regions' [http://centrope.info/static/files/baerdtneu/Regionalmanagements_in_Centrope_Regions.pdf].

4 Fachhochschule can be translated into "Technical College", or "Management School". These institutions offer various specialised study programmes with a focus on practical training for industrial, administrative and management jobs. In Austria they have been established since 1993. Cf.: Lorenz Lassnig, et al. (2003), 'Review des Auf- und Ausbaus des Fachhochschulsektors', Studie im Auftrag des Bundesministeriums für Bildung, Wissenschaft und Kultur, Endbericht, Wien.

Higher education institutions expect more networking between universities and regional development institutions in the future, especially networking based on personal communication. They expect more relevant regional development projects to come up with multilateral co-operation (banks, enterprises, research institutes, training institutions). Regional development strategies should be co-ordinated with universities and *Fachhochschulen.*

More activities towards regional development are expected, but there are several obstacles: There is a growing lack of financial and time resources, and transdisciplinary co-operation is seen as extremely time consuming. Differences in language and communication cultures between universities and regional development professionals are obstacles too for efficient co-operation. Some of the interviewed faculty have also questioned if the kind of knowledge the universities have to offer really serves the needs of regional development, respectively if it is the task of higher education to support regional development.

The question of improving university co-operation in regional development projects, in cross-border projects and in the co-ordination of study and training programmes is answered sceptically: Cross-border (Austria and Hungary) co-operation between universities is not easy in a time of growing competition. Different legal and organisational structures also hinder university co-operation. But the main problem is seen in deficits in university management capacities. Faculty engagement in internal affairs – such as career-building or organisational development – is making external activities less important. External activities in regional development are not explicitly encouraged by the university management, there are no incentives to engage in regional co-operations. Regional co-operations in general are not mentioned in the mission statements of the universities and their departments.

The Role of Higher Education Institutions in the Strategies of Regional Development

The main result of the interviews with regional development professionals: A good supply of a qualified labour force and human resources is considered essential for a competitive region. The Vienna region has a comparatively good system of institutions to qualify and train its labour force, but there is – due to the high concentration in Vienna – a very uneven distribution of higher education institutions within the region. Regional development agencies stress the need for universities or university-branches and *Fachhochschulen* also in peripheral regions. One regional management professional of Burgenland: *"We need every higher education institution involvement we can get in the region".* The impact of higher education is not only seen in the output such as an academically trained workforce or innovative research results, but also as a local employer, creating jobs and consuming goods in the local economy. Students usually come from the region, attend schools there and tend to look for jobs in the region after graduation. Higher education institutions in this process can diminish brain-drain from peripheries into the urban centres, if they adopt study programmes according to the needs of the regional economy and co-operate with institutions in development projects.

Professionals in regional development value both universities and *Fachhochschulen* highly, but they tend to see a very distant relationship between the universities and the region. They see universities struggling to be successful in international competition, concentrating on fields of global interest and specialising in international and global research. This should not necessarily conflict with activities for and within regional development, but in practice it does. There is very little institutionalised co-operation between universities and regional development institutions, and if so, only in specialised topics of planning and spatial development with departments and faculty in this field.

Regional development professionals value higher education institutions as impulses for innovation and as bridges across borders ("They are international windows to a region"). There is a high demand for co-operation with universities to create innovative milieus in the region: therefore it needs more mutual information and improved means and communication structures. Networks and regularly scheduled meetings between higher education faculty and regional development professionals are suggested.

But these proposals are shadowed by a pessimistic view: structural problems, such as lack of (time)resources, highly complex organisational problems for both the regional development and the higher education institution sides and growing international competition in the higher education system are seen as relevant obstacles to co-operation. Universities avoid presenting themselves as "regional universities" and so do not actively take part in regional projects.

Of significance are language problems and the type of research that is needed in the region – practical results in a short period of time – against the standard character of research seen in universities – abstract theoretical research in a longer conceptual time frame.

Obstacles for Co-operation of Higher Education and Regional Development Institutions

Higher Education

Organisational changes at universities led to larger units. Larger units are more difficult to manage, resulting in more resources bound to organisational development, and leading to less engagement towards the socio-spatial environment.

New management structures tend to create more centralised structures and strategic goals. Individual activities towards the region still take place but are not encouraged by central university management and in general not considered in evaluation.

The universities' socio-spatial situation consists of two driving forces, international orientation and centralising forces. Research and knowledge production takes place at an international and global scale. The academic community sees its peers spread out globally along their fields of research and teaching. The EU tries to strengthen a "European Research Area" and its research funds are international. Second, there is a strong pull-effect towards the already existing centres of science and research. The higher the threshold for financing research projects, the more complex partnerships research require, the greater the pull-effect: "Birds of a feather flock together" means the centralised concentration of research institutions, while suburban, rural and peripheral regions are continuously losing capacities.

Another important obstacle is the growing specialisation of research and the splitting up of disciplines into sub- and sub-sub-disciplines. Research questions and results are communicated in small groups of scientists spread out all over the world. They do not communicate their research in the region due to a lack of understanding and usability of research results in the region.

Regional Development

Regional development as a field of growing importance within the EU is connected with a high variety of institutions: Many different institutions are active in the field with similar mission statements, tasks and goals[5]. There are governmental, intermediate and private institutions engaged; they are funded internationally, by EU-funds, by national or regional funds and by regional companies. They are active in economic consulting and development support, in qualifying and capacity building, in technology transfer, innovation support, and in research and development projects. Most of their tasks are consulting, networking and assisting in project development. Some of them are competitors, who in general do not act along co-ordinated strategies.

It is difficult for higher education institutions to obtain a good overview over who the best partners for engagement in regional development could be.

Regional development is highly dependant on the political strategies of a region or province. If there is a political focus on science and technology, it is easier to connect to higher education than if this is a neglected field of policy. It is also related to governance structures in a region: If there is a complex network of institutions involved in regional decision making, higher education institutions often are part of. If, on the other hand, there is a highly centralised political deci-

5 Amin, A./N. Thrift (1994), *Globalization, Institutions and Regional Development in Europe*, Oxford University Press, Oxford.

sion making structure, it can turn out to be a serious obstacle for the involvement of higher education institutions in regional development.

One of the obstacles is related to the expectations regarding the kind of support from universities: Regional development professionals demand contextual knowledge and easily transferable results from research. They, in general, are neither able nor willing to engage themselves in a long research process or in applying research results.

Chances for Co-operation Between Higher Education and Regional Development Institutions

Higher Education Institutions

Universities in Austria are confronted with new requirements in negotiating their demands for public funds. They have to define their financial needs in so called *Leistungsvereinbarungen*, which means an outcome related contract of achievements and budgets. In the *Leistungsvereinbarungen* universities present their achievements for society. Regional development could be an important target: universities produce public goods, such as human resources and human capacities for societal development.

EU-strategies for science and research set goals for the improved dissemination of research in society explicitly in regions. In the 6th Framework Programme (FP), the EU started the focus on "Regions of Knowledge" and this seems to continue in the 7th FP. That means improved financial incentives for regions, research institutions and higher education to engage in regionally defined projects.

And last but not least, international examples show win-win-situations in regions, where the contribution to regional development was defined as one of the strategic focuses of universities and colleges, such as in Scandinavia[6], Great Britain, and the USA. Some examples show the importance of this field of activities also in the respective organisational structures of higher education institutions. Special management capacities such as vice-rectors are bound to improve the contact between the higher education institution and its region[7].

---

6 Hudson, Christine (2006), 'Regional development partnerships in Sweden: a way for higher education institutions to develop their role in the process of regional governance?', *Higher Education*, Vol. 51/Nr. 3, Springer Verlag, New York.

7 For example: Finnish universities like the Oulu University have one vice rector for the relations to the region. The University of Oulu explicitly states in its mission statement: "The mission of our university is to advance the education and material well-being of Northern Finland by being a high level international science university of state-of-the-art research." [http://www.oulu.fi/english/].

Regional Development

The European regions are in the process of strengthening their knowledge-base. Strategic positions such as in the so called Lisbon-Process define regional development as "knowledge-based" development. Science and research together with capacity building are strategic focuses for European regions in the Structural Funds Programmes. Regional development professionals in this process should get closer to the higher education system and the research institutions within their region, closely linking their activities to these institutions.

Regional networks, technology- and science-transfer institutions are growing and become increasingly important in regional development. They can open access to universities and their departments and institutes, and organise communication and co-operation. Chances to involve universities in regional development are higher the more these institutions are part of regional networks.

The trend towards a science and technology based society is a chance for regions to integrate higher education institutions in regional development processes. Science and technology nowadays is becoming an important part of everyday-life even in the remotest regions. The challenge in peripheral regions is to integrate this trend actively in regional development policy. There are significant examples in the Nordic countries[8].

Obstacles to an Efficient Human Resource Building: Different Types of Knowledge and Capacities

Universities can basically build human resources in two ways, by enhancing the knowledge of people and by increasing capacities. To transfer knowledge is the traditional understanding of teaching and training: Students are trained and specialised in various fields of knowledge by a faculty that acquired expertise through research, theoretical reflection, and communication. But there are various kinds of knowledge. Knowledge produced and transferred in and by higher education institutions is in large parts different to the knowledge needed in regional development. Research in this field shows the importance of a new learning approach to enhance special knowledge for regional development[9].

---

8 The regional development organisation *Glesbyggdverket* in Sweden has set up a strategy to support science and high technology institutions in Middle and Northern Sweden also by enforcing co-operative activities between the regional companies and the University of Lulea.

9 Heintel, Martin (2005), *Regionalmanagement in Österreich. Professionalisierung und Lernorientierung*, Wien, pp. 158f. Heintel presents three types of competences ("Sozialkompetenz, Wissenskompetenz, Projektkompetenz") and models of knowledge building for regional development. See also earlier works: Holzinger, Elisabeth et al. (1999), *Qualifizierungsmodell Raum und Gesellschaft*, Wien; Holzinger, Elisabeth et al. (1998), *Regionale Wissensbasis*, Wien.

A similar problem turns up in capacity building. Human competencies are very complex preconditions for action; they include e.g. social skills, innovative attitudes, creativity, intrinsic motivations, instincts and strategic abilities. The more complex societies, political and social situations are, and the more complex socio-spatial developments tend to be, the more necessary these capacities are in professional action.

What kind of knowledge does regional development require? What capacities enable professionals to contribute to regional development?

Academic Knowledge and Local Knowledge

Scientific knowledge is basically abstract knowledge: theoretical knowledge that can be standardised and applied in any context, such as in the medical paradigm, where the knowledge a medical professional has acquired has to work with any human body, or with the chemist, whose formulas have to work in Australia as well as in Lithuania. In opposition to this, regional knowledge has a strong contextual foundation: it has been created and it is used in local contexts. Contextual knowledge is strongly connected to specific local and regional action settings, to natural and societal conditions.

Universities have to consider this difference when they are co-operating and working in local und regional contexts. Especially when working with small companies, with rural institutions, with small and medium farms, they have to adapt academic knowledge to local and regional contexts. This means to contextualise the knowledge – integrate it in practical action – and to change from academic to everyday language, to "translate", which means to use a language of common understanding rather than a highly specialised academic language[10].

But what exactly is contextual knowledge? I am referring to Ulf Matthiesen, whose *KnowledgeScapes* shed some light on this subject. Matthiesen distinguishes eight kinds of knowledge, based in everyday practice and everyday life taking place in socio-spatial historical contexts. Knowledge of everyday life "represents the *essential deep structure* for more specialised and expertise-oriented knowledge forms"[11]. The knowledge that builds regional knowledge is based on the Knowledge of Everyday Life: Local Knowledge, Milieu Knowledge and Institutional Knowledge.

For universities it is difficult to connect to these knowledge forms. To create and communicate relevant knowledge in regional development, they would have

---

10 The language problem in transdisciplinary work was a major issue in the Austrian Cultural Landscape Research Programme. Cf.: Loibl, Marie Céline (2005), 'Vorstellungen von Wissenschaftlern und Wissenschaftlerinnen für die Zusammenarbeit mit Praktikern', in Franz Radits et al. (eds.), *Gemeinsam Forschen – Gemeinsam Lernen*, Innsbruck, pp. 103f.

11 Matthiesen, Ulf (2005), 'KnowledgeScapes', IRS Working Paper, Erkner, p. 5 [http://www.irs-net.de/download/KnowledgeScapes.pdf]

to turn abstract scientific approaches and theoretical positions into practical contextual knowledge. But locked in a system of international specialisation of publishing records and citation indices local knowledge in the milieu of a region is a different (language-)world.

Capacities for Regional Development

Regional Development started as a field of professionalisation in European regions about twenty years ago[12]. Regional Development Agencies, Regional Managements, Regional Consulting are examples for its institutionalisation. Hundreds of jobs were created in this field, with high demand on the qualifications of professionals in these jobs. .

To act professionally in the complex structures of a region and its regional development processes requires more than academic knowledge: it needs social and political skills and instincts, innovative and creative capacities. These skills and capacities are not easily built up in schools, colleges and universities. Next to a sound knowledge-base, consisting of different forms of everyday knowledge and expert knowledge, they need practical experience combined with *Knowledge of Reflection*[13]. Social and political skills are based on the ability to reflect on the identity of people and social situations and on the ability to develop an attitude of self-reflection. Innovative and creative capacities are the competencies most difficult to train. They are very deeply connected with the ability to take on a critical position towards the "normal" structures and activities in everyday life, to reflect upon the traditions and to think in a non-traditional way.

Are universities able to train these social and political skills, innovative and creative capacities? Yes, they are! Only to a minor extent it is the scientific knowledge of a discipline, but it is much more the ability to combine different theories, to connect disciplines to each other, and to connect the academic knowledge with other fields of society, that builds competencies for professional action. We can call this the creative use of science, interdisciplinarity and transdisciplinarity.

Universities that attempt to contribute to regional development have to focus on these three characteristics of innovative scientific work. Creative use of science means the courage to extend beyond the academic methods and theories by

---

12 One of the early conceptions leading to a professionalisation of regional development in Europe: Scheer, Günther (1983), 'Eigenständige Regionalentwicklung: Ziele, Strategien und Erfahrungen mit einem neuen Konzept regionaler Entwicklungsarbeit', *Österreichische Zeitschrift für Soziologie*, 3/1983, pp. 135f. Also: Mose, Ingo et al. (2004), 'Neue regionale Entwicklungskonzepte für periphere ländliche Räume. Das Beispiel der schottischen Highlands & Islands', *Raumforschung und Raumordnung 62*, 3, pp. 206 - 216.

13 Schön, Donald A. (1983), The Reflective Practitioner. How Professionals Think in Action, Basic Books.

relating to non academic, local knowledge settings. This was exemplified on an epistemological level by Paul Feyerabend and on a methodic and methodological level by Barney Glaser and Anselm Strauss[14] (see also the discussion of a "post-academic" science by Arno Bammé[15]).

Interdisciplinarity is no longer uncommon in academic language and, in the meantime, abundant in methodical statements, although the organisational structures of higher education institutions are still built according to disciplines. But the difficulties of interdisciplinary work can not only be perceived at the organisational level alone. It demands a new understanding of competencies for scientific and practical work: reflecting upon different world views and concepts and having communicative competencies to connect different concepts and languages[16].

Transdisciplinarity extends academic work to other systems of society. Regional development involves several societal systems and subsystems. If higher education units want to contribute to regional development, they have to opt for transdisciplinary work, which means being aware of different knowledge bases and forms of different systems and managing the communication between them[17].

Conclusion

Structural obstacles to efficient contributions in capacity building for regional development of higher education institutions can be found at an organisational and at a communication level: deficits in management structures and different forms of knowledge, different language and communication styles.

Recent developments have opened up chances for improving co-operation between higher education and regional development institutions:

- The societal impact of universities is considered in evaluating academic output and achievements.
- Dissemination of research results has become an increasingly important criteria for scientific work.

---

[14] Feyerabend, Paul (1975), *Wider den Methodenzwang* (Against Method. Outline of an Anarchist Theory of Knowledge), Frankfurt/Main; Glaser, Barney G./Anselm L. Strauss (1967), *The Discovery of Grounded Theory. Strategies for Qualitative Research*, Chicago.

[15] Bammé, Arno (2004), Science Wars – Von der akademischen zur postakademischen Wissenschaft, Frankfurt/New York.

[16] Godemann, Jasmin (2005), 'Zum Verhältnis von interdisziplinärer Zusammenarbeit und Kompetenz', in Franz Radits, et al. (eds.), *Gemeinsam Forschen – Gemeinsam Lernen*, Innsbruck, pp. 123f.

[17] One of the approaches to communicate between the higher education system and other systems in society is "Intervention Research". Heintel, Peter/Larissa Krainer/Ina Paul-Horn (2004), *Hintergrundtheorien zur Interventionsforschung*. Klagenfurt.

- Regional development strategies are based more and more on knowledge production: Learning regions, regions of knowledge are key words for the improved use of science and research in development strategies.

János Rechnitzer – Melinda Smahó

Cross-border Co-operation of Higher Education Institutions in Western Hungary

Introduction

The demand for foreign higher educational training has been changing relatively quickly with Hungary's European Union accession. Hungarian students have more and more opportunity to study at different European universities and colleges. This process is strengthened further by the Bologna-Process and the introduction of the credit system. It follows, that the interest is growing for the Austrian institutions, mainly for those located in the Austrian-Hungarian border region. West-Transdanubian higher education institutions are exposed an increasingly strong competition that makes it necessary for them to build up institutional cross-border co-operations.

The aim of the Hungarian Unirégió project was to explore the existing cross-border co-operations of West-Transdanubian higher educational institutions (located in counties Győr-Moson-Sopron, Vas, Zala) and to define their possible future directions. In order to reach these goals we weighted up and analysed the higher educational potential and the cross-border relations of universities and colleges on the Hungarian side of the border region. Beside collection and analysis of statistical data, we carried out thirty-three interviews with higher educational institutions' and regional administrations' leaders, as well as conducted a survey of 1300 students. In this article we would like to present some of our research results, focusing on the main characteristics of the West-Transdanubian higher educational potential, the cross-border co-operations of the institutions and their possible future directions.

Tertiary Education in West-Transdanubia

There are almost 33,000 students and approximately 1200 teaching staff in West-Transdanubia (Table 1). In 2008, the seats of two universities and one college could be found within the region (Figure 1). The biggest university of the region is the University of West-Hungary, with its seat in Sopron. Four of its total of ten faculties, namely the Faculty of Forestry (NYME-EMK), the Faculty of Wood Sciences (NYME-FMK), the Faculty of Economics (NYME-KTK) and the Faculty of Benedek Elek College of Pedagogy (NYME-BPK) are located in Sopron. It has further faculties in Mosonmagyaróvár (Faculty of Agriculural and Food Science, NYME-MÉK), in Győr (Faculty of Apáczai Csere János Teacher Training College, NYME-AK), and in Székesfehérvár (Faculty of Geoinformatics,

NYME-GEO), the last one is located out of the region. Actually, it has further three faculties in Szombathely, because on 1st January 2008 Berzsenyi Dániel College, consisted of three faculties (BDF-BTK, BDF-TMK, BDF-TTK), became a part of the University of West-Hungary, and functions at present as Savaria University Centre (its faculties are currently called Faculty of Humanities, Faculty of Sciences, Faculty of Physical Education, Visual Arts and Music). The fifth largest university of Hungary came into existence with this integration (according to the number of students). Approximately 21,000 students study at the University of West-Hungary.

Figure 1 Higher educational institutions in West-Transdanubia (seats and faculties), 2006.

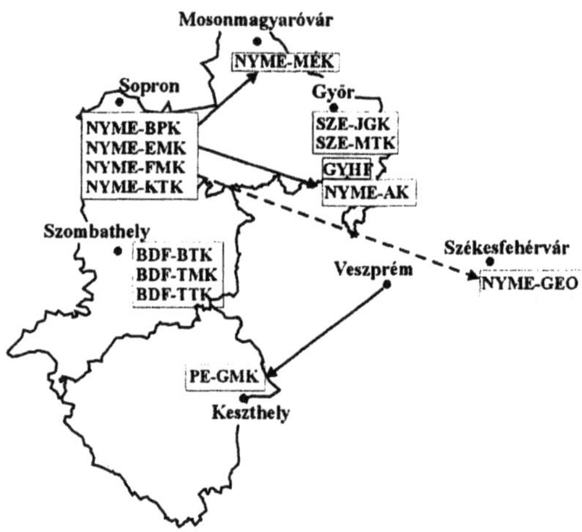

Source: Authors

The other university seated in the region is the Széchenyi István University. It is the successor of the former Széchenyi István College and has been functioning as a university since 2002. It consisted of two faculties in 2006 (Faculty of Engineering Sciences, Faculty of Law and Economics), but the latter one was divided in two parts in 2007 (Kautz Gyula Faculty of Economics and Deák Ferenc Faculty of Law and Political Sciences). Széchenyi István University has approximately 12,000 students and all of its faculties are located in Győr. Both mentioned universities have more doctoral schools. Out of the two universities, the Theological College Győr has its seat in the region as well, and a traditional faculty of the Pannon University (Georgikon Faculty of Agricultural Science, PE-GMK) is also located in West-Transdanubia. Out of the mentioned universities, colleges and faculties, some smaller institutions (e.g. consultation centres) can be found in the region as well (e.g. in Zalaegerszeg, Nagykanizsa).

Table 1 Some characteristics of higher educational institutions seated in West-Transdanubia, 2005/2006

Higher Education Institution	Advanced trade school	College level	University level	Postgr. training	PhD, DLA-	Students total	Number of teachers
	Number of students						
Berzsenyi Dániel College	351	5.972	313	57	0	6.693	265
West-Hungarian University	500	8.168	3.754	1.192	230	13.844	549
Széchenyi István University	218	9.421	2.165	169	100	12.073	337
Theological College Győr	0	253	14	0	0	267	30
TOTAL	1.069	23.814	6.246	1.418	330	32.877	1.181

Source: Higher education statistics, 2005/2006

The higher educational supply of the region is under rearrangement, while institutions try to respond to the changing needs of the region. However, this restructuring process moves slowly, which is clearly indicated by the still existing dominance of teacher training (21%) and management science (28%). At the same time, the proportion of engineering and mathematics (14%) is relatively small, despite the fact that the regional economy needs more engineers (Figure 2).

Figure 2 Higher educational training structure in West Transdanubia, 2003/2004

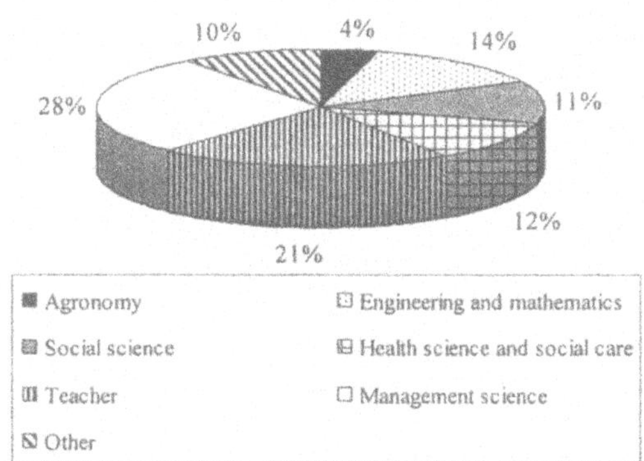

Source: Higher education statistics, 2004/2005

Cross-border Co-operations of West-Transdanubian Higher Educational Institutions

The international contacts of the higher educational institutions may be diverse, which can be categorised by the content, time span, intensity and other character of the co-operation. According to our interviews, the international relations' system of the West-Transdanubian higher educational institutions can be put into the following hierarchical system (Figure 3).

Figure 3 Hierarchy of international relations

Source: Authors

At the top of the pyramid the strategically important co-operations of the institutions are positioned. Typical forms of these are courses that lead to a common degree, and strategic research directions performed together with foreign universities. These types of co-operations require very stable, intense, and well-established institutional relations, and in case of the West-Transdanubian universities and colleges there can be found only a few examples of them.

The overall contracts can be found on a lower level, which are contracts of long-term, general co-operation agreements that are mainly of an educational type but may expand to research co-operation. These framework agreements are generally indefinite, i.e. valid till resolution or withdrawal.

The great majority of higher educational institutions engages in international scholarship programmes (Erasmus, CEEPUS) through which they are members of an international institutional network. Regarding their content, these contacts cover student and teacher exchanges between institutions, both outgoing and incoming.

Universities and colleges – with a foreign partner's approval – may take part in different EU programmes, for example in Phare CBC, Interreg, CADSES, as well as in EU research framework programmes. However, project co-operations often have an ad-hoc character. This means that these relations are generally not durable, and after finishing the project their intensity often declines. Without conscious intensification, these relations do not lead to the evolution of strategic co-operations.

The lowest level of the international contact hierarchy is occupied by non-formalised co-operations, personal vocational contacts, individual actions. Generally, these are the most extensive contacts, since a lot of foreign country relations are carried by the institutions' teachers, who attend different international conferences (committee membership, review, guest instructor, etc.) and international scientific community (foreign country publications, international acknowledged journals, etc.).

The system of international relations in case of a higher educational institution has been forming for decades. It follows from this that traditional universities have more extended and more stable contacts than the younger institutions. Both the age and the type of institutions have an impact on the system of international contacts. Colleges provide mainly educational functions, in their case research co-operations and international contacts receive a much smaller emphasis, than at a traditional university.

Almost all West-Transdanubian universities and colleges have Austrian relations. The partner institutions are mostly located in Vienna, but we explored large number of contacts with other Austrian higher educational centres, for example with Linz and Graz. There are traditional co-operations, which can be originated from the common history of the institutions (e.g. NYME-MÉK – BOKU), while other relations are based on similar institutional profiles, personal contacts (all institutions), common applications and research programmes (e.g. Széchenyi István University – TU Wien), or common educational co-operations (e.g. Széchenyi István University – TU Wien – Technical University Bratislava). The actions are primarily teacher and student exchanges within the frame of the Tempus programme, but there are also direct agreements at institutional level.

In contrast to the existing and explored cross-border contacts, our research stated that the institutions do not take all the advantages of their cross-border situation, for example geographical proximity, similar profiles, easy and quick accessibility or opportunities of common applications. We explored more reasons that impede the cross-border co-operations of West-Transdanubian universities and colleges.

At first, the insufficient language skills of both teachers, researchers and students should be mentioned, because these actors are the participants of educational and research co-operations, teacher and student exchanges as well as different foreign language courses and lectures. In Györ-Moson-Sopron county approximately twenty to twenty-five percent, while in Vas and Zala counties fifteen to twenty percent of the population speaks at least one foreign language, according to the data of the last census in 2001. Although, these proportions around or over the national average of 19.2 percent are quite good in the Hungarian overall context, the language skills of the Hungarian students and population are lagging behind of those of the West-Europeans (Rechnitzer/Smahó 2006). Consequently, Hungarian students are not really interested in courses held in foreign languages, while the lack of these courses being offered at the West-Transdanubian universities encumbers the reception of students arriving from the foreign partner institutions.

Furthermore, cross-border co-operations of West-Transdanubian higher education institutions are hindered by a lack of administrative capacities and financial resources, wage-differentials, and in some cases by the different training structure of the institutions.

Interviews with West-Transdanubian higher educational institutions' leaders show that international research projects are going on at departmental and faculty level. Consequently, international projects and co-operations are also handled at this level, but not at a university level. Therefore, the system of international co-operations within the West-Transdanubian universities and colleges is very fragmented and not embraceable at all, which slows and hinders both the building of strategic contacts and the development of its directions. Austrian and German higher educational institutions develop their international relations much more consciously, based on an internationalization strategy, which is not typical for the West-Transdanubian higher educational institutions at all. The fragmentation of international contacts make it difficult to develop an internationalization strategy at university level concerning future international co-operations.

The Vienna University of Economics and Business Administration (WU) defined more criteria in its internationalization strategy which have to be fulfilled by the potential partner institutions. Among the criteria mentioned are, for example, membership in international networks (PIM, CEMS), the rank of the university or business college; accreditation (EQUIS, AACSB), excellence, elasticity, openness, compliance towards WU; the partner institution's accommodating ability to WU structures; foreign language courses, and German language skills of the partner institute (Sporn 2002). However, Central and Eastern European countries appear as potential co-operation target area of the WU, but the university don't strive to take advantage of geographical proximity. Instead of this, it builds up co-operations with the leading business universities of the neighbouring countries (e.g. Corvinus University, Budapest). This indicates on the one hand that the quality of the partner institution is much more important for the Austrian universities than geographical proximity. On the other hand it proves that advantages of geographical proximity are not utilized adequately by the higher education institutions in the Austrian-Hungarian border region.

Suggestions for Improving Cross-border Co-operations

Most of the international co-operations of West-Transdanubian higher educational institutions evolved during the 1990s, after the opening of the borders. In the second half of the decade, the opportunities as well as financial resources for cross-border co-operation were expanded. The starting of Hungary's EU-accession process opened access to the pre-accession funds, out of which Phare CBC Programme supported especially cross-border co-operations. However, the role of international co-operations has significantly changed from the beginning of the Nineties up until present days: International relations have increasingly become a need instead of an opportunity. This tendency is expected to continue and get stronger in the future: International co-operations will influence and determine the competitiveness of higher educational institutions increasingly, thus they will become one of the keys of their future success. It follows that universities and colleges should focus on the development of new international contacts as well as on the extension and intensification of their existing international relations. Although the intention and the interest in international co-operations exists in the majority of the West-Transdanubian higher educational institutions, universities and colleges do not consider international relations as strategically significant.

From the side of the West-Transdanubian universities, it would be necessary to lay the emphasis on the development of its internationalization strategy and according to this, on a more conscious building of its international contacts. In order to realize this, they should review the already existing but not systematized departmental and personal contacts and research projects, and after that they should define the possible and desired future directions of international contacts.

In order to develop foreign country contacts, it is important to improve the teachers' and students' language skills, and to introduce foreign language training and courses into the training offer of West-Transdanubian universities and colleges. Some of them have already started to implement the mentioned suggestions. They are planning to launch different training courses in German and/or English involving their Austrian partner institutes.

To sum up, it can be said that West-Transdanubian higher educational institutions should develop their internationalization strategy, define their own goals and opportunities and try to fulfil the requirements set up by the potential partner institutions in order to reach long-term success. Finally, we have defined some possible developmental directions of cross-border co-operation as follows:

- Get to know each other properly, introduction, and launch of cross border communication programmes in order to generate and motivate co-operations.
- To create organizational frameworks for the co-operations (e.g. Cross-border Rector's Council, institutional delegates on organizing the contacts, secretariat, etc.).
- To organize a common conference about the situation of our macro region in Europe, and to hold a forum about the possible higher educational co-operations. The frameworks are given within Centrope and Jordes+ programmes, but numerous additional programmes motivate the actors to take advantage of its cross-border situation and accelerate multiregional co-operations.
- Get to know of each other's research capacities and research results in order to be able to plan fruitful future co-operations based on regional capabilities and economic characteristics.
- To carry out a survey on the training supply of different disciplines (at bachelor, master, postgraduate and doctoral level), and to make it available for the students of the cross border region.
- To encourage student mobility through harmonization and mutual acknowledgment of training programmes.
- To publish the list of partner institutions on the universities' websites, and in this way to increase the awareness of the institutions among potential students.

References

Rechnitzer, János/Melinda Smahó (2006), *Regional Characteristics of Human Resources in Hungary during the Transition*, Hungarian Academy of Sciences Centre for Regional Studies, Pécs.

Internet sources:

Sporn, Barbara (2002), *WU-Internationalisierungsstrategie* [http://www.wu-wien.ac.at/portal/international/strategie.pdf].

[www.bdf.hu]

[www.nyme.hu]

[www.sze.hu]

Magnus Grubbe

Non-Governance and the Experience with the "Knowledge Economy" in the Øresund Region[1]

Introduction

The theme of this paper is the integration process of the Øresund Region as a 'knowledge region'. Thus the challenges and initiatives of the integration process that mostly are due to the cross-border nature of the region and national politics will be presented. The paper is divided into two parts. The first part discusses the barriers to the integration at the different political levels and the second is related to the more civic organizational level. Also, the second part is based on interviews with stakeholders representing universities and companies in the region.

The overall image shows a process of integration which is found across many political obstacles and is, for the most part, initiated and furthered by a co-operation between the regional universities. The administrative centre for the organisation of this co-operation is the *Øresund University* (ØU).

The ØU is itself an alliance of twelve universities and institutions for higher education in the overall Øresund Region. Its primary task is to coordinate scientific research and education between the different institutions and universities; but it has also been actively engaged in the dimension of the regional integration regarding the creation of a knowledge-based regional economy. This engagement of the ØU has primarily been through the establishment of the *Øresund Science Region* (ØSR). The ØSR is an overall structure, which binds together a number of different network organisations specific to different business sectors – so called platforms; these network organisations being the actual actors, regarding the concrete, day-to-day integration of the knowledge region.

The Øresund Region is worth studying, because the development of the knowledge-based economy of this region in the last ten to fifteen years reaches beyond the average of the general development in Europe. Thus, the region is an interesting point for basing studies in regional development and knowledge-based economy. However, it has to be taken into consideration that the knowledge-based economy in the regions is by no mean a single or fully unified economy. Consequently we are looking at a process of integration and not a fully integrated region. Thus the cross-border initiatives should not be ascribed too much impact on the development of the knowledge-based economy in the region.

---

1 Since the original presentation in Klagenfurt, some changes have been implemented in this text. These mainly concern the introduction to the second part of the paper concerning the establishment of networks and the transfer of knowledge.

About the Øresund Region

The Øresund Region is a metropolitan region, crossing the national borders of Denmark and Sweden – the name 'Øresund' derives from the strait, or sound, separating the two countries.

The economic and cultural centre of the region is Copenhagen, the capital of Denmark. In comparison with other capitals, Copenhagen primarily stands out due to the fact that the city is located at the very border of Denmark. Besides that it is characteristic for Copenhagen that one third of the total population of Denmark is resident inside the Copenhagen area. On the other side of the strait lies the Skåne Region (Scania) – a region characterised as a peripheral region of Sweden and through history known as having certain structural economic problems; while also being one of the more densely populated parts of Sweden.

Thus, the Øresund Region is characterised by a distinctive population density – twenty-seven percent of the Swedish and the Danish population is resident in it – but also by the crucial fact that it is very well equipped with universities and institutions of higher education. Hence the region encompasses twelve institutions of higher education, with 150.000 students, 14.000 research scientists and 6.500 Ph.D. students, thus providing an essential platform for a knowledge-based economical development.

Managing the Integration Process of the Knowledge Region Øresund

The process of growing into an actual united knowledge-region – understood as a process of articulating and implementing political visions and aims – is conditioned by the fact that the region does not have any joint legislative or administrative authority. Within all political levels the region is split into to two national political systems, which has shown to complicate the integration process and thereby the framework conditions for the integration of a knowledge-based regional economy. Particularly problematic for the Øresund Region are the national levels of the political systems (in Denmark and Sweden).

The National Governments

In general the national governments are – by means of their regional, research and development, economical, and industrial policies etc. – important stakeholders in the development of the regional knowledge-based economy. However, the Øresund Region is characterised by a lack of involvement in the integration process both from the Danish and the Swedish governments. This contradicts the fact that the Øresund Region as a cross-border region requires national policies, which are to be legislated with special regards to this very nature. Nevertheless, the reality is that the national policies within regional planning, scientific research, technology, industry, and economy etc. on neither side of the strait take into account the cross-border nature of the Øresund Region – or at least only with difficulty are these policies combinable with the nature of the region. The national policies on both sides are strongly bound to the national territory. This entails, amongst other things that it is extremely difficult to make the Swedish and Danish public scientific resource funds operate on both sides of the Øresund strait.

Since public funding is crucial to scientific research and development, this is an enormous obstacle for the development of knowledge-based economy in the Øresund Region. Moreover, cross-border projects within research and development are impeded by the different administrative routines and procedures of the national Danish and Swedish research councils (such as *VINNOVA* and *Højteknologifonden*).

On the other hand, it is important to note that the national research councils are aware of the problem and are looking into how to deal with the cross-border nature of the Øresund Region.

Furthermore, it is notable that two-thirds of the R&D-means in Sweden come from private funds. These funds normally do not comply with national borders. However I will – without touching further on it – claim that these private funds contribute only very little to the development of the regional knowledge-based economy.

The Precarious Question of National Region Policy

By some of the stakeholders in ØRS, the lack of involvement from the national political stakeholders is widely perceived as disinterest. However, it should not go unnoticed that the traditions of Danish and Swedish regional policy have an impeding effect on a national and bilateral policy for the Øresund Region. We are dealing with a precarious question of national region policy in Denmark and Sweden.

In Denmark, Copenhagen stands out due to its location on the border between Denmark and Sweden, and because the city contains one third of the total population of Denmark. This creates an economically uneven dynamic in Denmark. Regional policy is therefore essential to maintain fairly equal living circumstances across the country, and it is this imbalance which makes regional policy-making politically precarious. Furthermore, in consistency with regional politics, institutions for higher education and scientific research are somewhat equally dispersed across the country. This approach to regional policy is incompatible with a policy adjusted to cross-border regions such as the Øresund Region, since this approach neglects the provincial regions and may also be seen as failing to serve national interests.

In Sweden, Skåne has historically been among the poorest regions. The economic centre of Sweden is Stockholm and its surrounding regions. Yet the economic development of the Øresund Region entails the possibility that a new economic (and possibly political) centre could emerge. The worry – from the point of view of Sweden – is that around one-third of the Swedish economy is pointed towards Copenhagen instead of Stockholm.

Also, the public support for the development of a national Øresund policy is very low, especially in the northern regions, which are the economically weakest ones in Sweden.

The Sub-national Level and the Øresund Committee

On the regional and local level the political stakeholders have established the 'Øresund Committee' as a political forum for the Øresund Region. But regardless of the mutual organ there have been considerable problems in agreeing on mutual aims. The main hindrance seems to be the lack of a collective involvement in the Øresund integration project. The local authorities are blamed that they are perceived to be culpable of acting in self- as opposed to the interest of the whole Øresund Region and to be active in making themselves visible rather than the Øresund Region. However the co-operation in the Øresund Committee has recently changed; the committee has developed from being a forum whose main task was to agree on, implement and complete isolated joint projects, to become a political organ, in which mutual political aims are agreed upon; an organ, which acts as a unit towards each of the national governments. But it is still too early to study the effect of this new approach.

Given that the politicians and the public authorities (both national, regional and local) have constituted the most problematic part of the integration process of the knowledge region, it is clear that the process has suffered a marked lack of overall political governance.

It is therefore noticeable that the integration process of the knowledge-based economy in the Øresund Region has mainly been, and still is, a bottom-up process that is initiated and conceived by the ØU and ØSR.

The Daily Work with Knowledge Transfer and Innovation in the Øresund Region

The ØSR is the platform for the regional development of the knowledge-economy in the Øresund Region – the ØSR is the overall motor of the integration of the knowledge region, which consists of three strings, equivalent to the so called triple helix model of knowledge-based economy: academia, industry and public authorities. Or more precisely, because of the cross border nature of the Øresund Region a so called "double triple helix network" has developed.

The practical integration, however, takes place via five platforms organised under ØSR. The platforms are specific to different sectors, and each platform facilitates more specialised networks. Though every platform works differently, they are all characterised by the same fact that they built on relatively sector specific networks – embedding scientific researchers, industrial partners and public authorities.

Figure 1 The organisation of the platforms of the Øresund Science Region

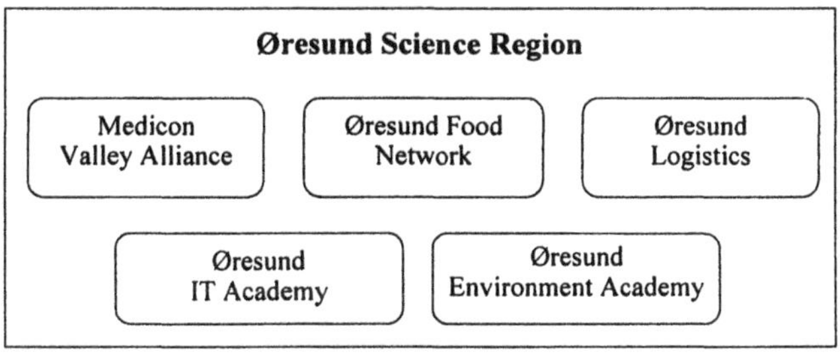

The platforms have their *raison d'être* as actors in the integration of the knowledge-based economy in the Øresund Region. As may be seen above the integration has not occurred yet within the field of research and innovation funding. This makes the co-operation between scientific researchers and companies across the strait unnecessarily difficult.

Only EU funding for regional development and scientific research transcends the national borders. Though the Interreg funds can not be used for scientific research, they are successfully used for financing the researcher and company networks. In addition the research and development funding from the EU frame programme could be used for financing projects across the strait, but it has proven to be extremely difficult to attract such funding to the region.

Networks

The platforms offer a certain institutionalization of the co-operation between scientific researchers and companies, and to some extent also public authorities. This institutionalization takes place via co-operative projects and networks. Thus the secretariats of the different platforms facilitate several projects and networks that are generally aimed at developing specific questions within limited subject areas. These questions often result in formulations of research projects with partners from the universities or the industry from both sides of the strait and end up as applications for research or innovation funding.

Often the networks are established across different sectors. It is an obvious conclusion that the fact that the secretariats of the platforms are located in the same office space supports the co-operation and the sharing of ideas and thereby the development of new cross-sector networks.

The Virtual Food Factory is an example of such a cross-sector network, which is engaged in the process and the production of food and has participants from both the food sector and the IT sector. Another example is the network *Food + Pharma = Unlimited Health*, which is a network of stakeholders from the food sector and the pharmaceutical sector and focuses on the possibilities of using food in disease control.

The facilitating role of the platforms is aimed at initiating, administrating, coordinating with and contributing to the initial capital of new networks. The initiating role of the platforms is often pointed out by participants as being decisive. The platform does not dictate the subjects and focus areas of new networks and projects, but they are able to gather the different stakeholders from the universities, the industry and the public authorities from both Denmark and Sweden around a particular subject of interest. In fact, the assembling of similar networks would also be possible without the platforms, but according to the participants involved, it would be very resource demanding if one would have to find the right partners for similar networks or projects without the platforms.

Once the networks are established they are only rarely able to maintain themselves. External impulses are therefore necessary. Concerning this matter the platforms' secretariats are important through their initiatives and support to keep up the momentum in the networks. The background for this problem of keeping networks vivid and productive is that the participants have to invest time in the networks to uphold and further them, but since the financial resources of the networks in general are quite limited, the involvement and commitment of the participants to the networks are also mostly proportionately limited. Besides that there is sometimes a certain opportunism among the participants and some appear to free-ride. In this regard the platforms play a decisive role as coordinators, organizers and facilitators in relation to holding up the networks and projects.

Over time, however, networks with a sustainable internal dynamic and those which are able to uphold and further themselves – so called 'mature' networks – develop. These 'mature' networks are also characterised by the long-term commitment to establishing and maintaining confident relationships; allowing constructive dialogue and better interchange of knowledge, which in turn – and in the longer term – lead to a sound exchange of knowledge and concrete innovation.

Conclusion

Finally, one can conclude that the integration of the Øresund Region as a Knowledge Region and a regional knowledge-based economy was realized and pushed forward largely by the universities. Also, there has been a marked failure of the political actors, both in Denmark and Sweden, to make national research and innovation funding available throughout the whole Øresund Region which has been a large obstacle for the integration process; and it is clear that the integration will not reach a satisfying stage until this obstacle is removed.

Nevertheless, it is equally clear that the integration process has made significant progress in the right direction. This is mainly due to the concrete achievement of the platforms under ØSR. This highly institutionalized model has proven overall to be a good platform for reciprocal knowledge-transfer and innovation, the quality of which is perhaps evidenced most clearly in the appearance, despite the major obstacles, of these durable 'mature' platforms.

List of Authors

ALFIREVIĆ, Nikša
Faculty of Economics, University of Split, Split/Croatia

BRKIĆ, Nenad
School of Economics and Business, University of Sarajevo, Sarajevo/Bosnia and Herzegovina

ĆULUM, Bojana
University of Rijeka, Faculty of Arts & Sciences, Rijeka/Croatia &
The Association for Civil Society Development SMART, Rijeka/Croatia

ELTANTAWI, Josef
Strategic Development, Kapsch TrafficCom AG, Vienna/Austria

FORČIĆ, Gordana
The Association for Civil Society Development SMART, Rijeka/Croatia

FUDURIĆ, Morana
Faculty of Economics and Business, University of Zagreb, Zagreb/Croatia

GABELICA, Nino
Civil Association Posmrtna Pripomoc, Zagreb/Croatia

GNJIDIĆ, Vladimir
Dukat Dairy Industy Inc., Zagreb/Croatia

GRUBBE, Magnus
Øresund Food Network, Øresund Science Region, Øresund/Denmark

HREPIĆ, Zdeslav
Columbus State University, Columbus(GA)/USA

KUTLEŠA, Miše
Elementary School Brestje, Sesvete/Croatia

LANGER, Josef
Department of Sociology, School of Management and Economics, Alpen-Adria-Universität Klagenfurt, Klagenfurt/Austria

MAKAR, Bojan
Altera, plc, Ludbreg/Croatia

PAVIČIĆ, Jurica
Faculty of Economics and Business, University of Zagreb, Zagreb/Croatia

RECHNITZER, János
Hungarian Academy of Sciences, Centre for Regional Studies, West Hungarian Research Institute, Györ/Hungary

RELJA, Renata
Faculty of Philosophy, University of Split, Split/Croatia

RENDULIĆ, Darko
ALSTOM Hrvatska plc, Karlovac/Croatia

RIGONI, Gabriella
ERDISU Trieste, Trieste/Italy

RUPRECHTER, Manfred
WMV "Wechselwirkung in Marketing und Verkauf", Vienna/Austria

SAGMEISTER, Gunhild
Department of Sociology, School of Management and Economics, Alpen-Adria-Universität Klagenfurt, Klagenfurt/Austria

SALIHOVIĆ, Almir
The Central Bank of Bosnia and Herzegovina, Sarajevo/Bosnia and Herzegovina

SERTIĆ, Vanja
Moving Board plc, Zagreb/Croatia

ŠIMURINA, Jurica
Faculty of Economics and Business, University of Zagreb, Zagreb/Croatia

SMAHÓ, Melinda
Hungarian Academy of Sciences, Centre for Regional Studies, West Hungarian Research Institute, Györ/Hungary

SOPTA, Martina
Faculty of Economics and Business, University of Zagreb, Zagreb/Croatia

STROHMEIER, Gerhard
Department of City, Region and Spatial Development, Faculty of Interdisciplinary Studies, Alpen-Adria-Universität Klagenfurt, Vienna/Austria

VLAŠIĆ, Goran
Faculty of Economics and Business, University of Zagreb, Zagreb/Croatia

Index

www.ingramcontent.com/pod-product-compliance
Ingram Content Group UK Ltd.
Pitfield, Milton Keynes, MK11 3LW, UK
UKHW020121290926
15471UKWH00003B/204

9 783631 585573